BATTLEFIELD TOURISM

THE LEGACY OF THE GREAT WAR

A Series sponsored by the Historial de la Grande Guerre Péronne-Somme

General Editor
JAY WINTER

Previously published titles in the Series

Antoine Prost
IN THE WAKE OF WAR
'Les Anciens Combattants' and French Society

Patrick Fridenson
THE FRENCH HOME FRONT 1914–1918

Stéphane Audoin-Rouzeau
MEN AT WAR 1914–1918

Gerald D. Feldman
ARMY, INDUSTRY, AND LABOR IN GERMANY 1914–1918

Rosa Maria Bracco
MERCHANTS OF HOPE

Adrian Gregory
THE SILENCE OF MEMORY
Armistice Day 1919–1946

Ute Daniel
THE WAR FROM WITHIN
German Working-Class Women in the First World War

Annette Becker
WAR AND FAITH
The Religious Imagination in France, 1914–1930

BATTLEFIELD TOURISM
Pilgrimage and the Commemoration of the Great War in Britain, Australia and Canada, 1919–1939

BY DAVID W. LLOYD

BERG

Oxford • New York

First published in 1998 by
Berg
Editorial offices:
150 Cowley Road, Oxford, OX4 1JJ, UK
70 Washington Square South, New York, NY 10012, USA

Berg is an imprint of Oxford International Publishers Ltd.

Library of Congress Cataloging-in-Publication Data

A catalogue record for this book is available from the Library of Congress.

British Library Cataloguing-in-Publication Data

A catalogue record for this book is available from the British Library.

ISBN 1 85973 174 0 (Cloth)
1 85973 179 1 (Paper)

Typeset by JS Typesetting, Wellingborough, Northants.
Printed in the United Kingdom by WBC Book Manufacturers, Mid-Glamorgan.

Contents

List of Illustrations

List of Abbreviations

AA	Australian Archives
AIF	Australian Imperial Force
ANL	Australian National Library
AWM	Australian War Memorial
BEF	British Expeditionary Force
BESL	British Empire Service League
BL	British Library
IWGC	Imperial War Graves Commission
IWM	Imperial War Museum
NAC	National Archives of Canada
NGC	National Gallery of Canada
PRO	Public Record Office
RSSILA	Returned Sailors' and Soldiers' Imperial League of Australia
YMCA	Young Men's Christian Association

Acknowledgements

It is impossible to mention all of the people who have assisted in the preparation of this book. The following acknowledgement can only indicate the degree of debt.

Essential financial assistance without which the thesis from which this book developed was provided by the grant of the Kater Scholarship, administered by the Cambridge Commonwealth Trust, as well as funding provided by the Cambridge Historical Society, Clare Hall, the Historial de la Grande Guerre, the Smuts Fund, and the Worts Travelling Fund.

I would like to thank the staff of all the organisations, libraries and archives mentioned in the notes and bibliography. For permission to reproduce copyright material held in Archives I am grateful to the Australian War Memorial, the National Library of Australia and the Imperial War Museum.

Thank you to the following who have shared their thoughts on their particular areas of expertise: Stéphane Audoin-Rouzeau, Annette Becker, Robert Dare, Adrian Gregory, Ken Inglis, Catherine Jamet, Bill Nasson, Barry Smith and Maria Tippett. In particular thanks to Jay Winter without whose counsel and advice this book would have been a far poorer work.

Many thanks to my parents, brother, sisters and friends for their support. In particular thanks to my wife Jeanine whose support and encouragement has been constant throughout the germination and completion of the book.

Finally, thank you to David Phelps, Sara Everett and Kathryn Earle for their efforts in editing and producing this book.

Introduction

> For while it is difficult to establish the links between collective and individual experiences, the traumatic effects of this century cannot be understood without reference to their effects on the individual.
>
> – O. Bartov, 'Trauma and Absence: France and Germany, 1914–1945'[1]

This book is an exploration of British and, for the purposes of comparison, Australian and Canadian tourism and pilgrimages to the battlefields, cemeteries and memorials of the Great War in the 1920s and 1930s. Many pilgrimages were public events which were described and analysed in newspapers and magazines. Journalists' stories, together with the guide books travellers carried and the accounts they wrote of their visits or provided for their friends and relatives, all contributed to the collective memory of the war. However, each journey was also an individual experience. The meaning of the visit ultimately depended upon the travellers' memory of wartime experiences, whether these occurred at the front, were experiences of bereavement, or centred on his or her imagined vision of the war. These journeys were not passive activities. Tourists and pilgrims assumed that at particular places and moments it was possible to renew, re-create or capture something of the war and the experiences which defined it.

The impulse to visit places associated with the war was shared by people in many of the ex-combatant nations, not just those considered in this study. Verdun was a major pilgrimage site for the French, while the battlefields of the old Western Front, as well as the battlefield of Tannenberg in the East, drew thousands of German tourists and pilgrims.[2] Many American travellers also

1. O. Bartov, 'Trauma and Absence: France and Germany, 1914–1945', in P. Addison and A. Calder (eds), *Time to Kill: The Soldier's Experience of War in the West 1939–1945* (London, 1997), p. 348.

2. A. Prost, 'Verdun', in P. Nora (ed.), *Les Lieux de Mémoire*, Vol. II *La Nation* (Paris, 1984), p. 125. S. Brandt, 'Le Voyage Aux Champs de Bataille', *Vingtième Siècle Revue d'histoire*, 41 (Janvier-Mars 1994), pp. 21–2. *Tablet*, 164 (Sept. 1934), p. 293.

visited the battlefields in this period.[3] The appeal of these sites to tourists and pilgrims is indicative of the pervasive presence of the war and the sense of loss which it engendered in the fabric of life in many of these countries. Robert Whalen has noted that everyone 'involved in a war is in some way a war victim'.[4] Post-war tourism and pilgrimages reflected the continuing presence of the war in the lives of all its victims.

The approach adopted in this book concentrates on individual responses to and memories of the war. Such an approach has significant implications for our understanding of the cultural history of this period. Cultural history is in a state of flux, with its focus alternating between a series of antinomian concepts such as high or low culture, tradition or modernity, the sacred or the profane, the manipulation of political meaning by the elites or the decoding of mentalities, and masculinity or femininity. While these concepts illuminate different facets of cultural history, they often obscure the richness of cultural experience because the interaction or even elision between the different poles is overlooked.

The debate regarding the role of the war as a cultural divide between tradition and modernity illustrates the limitations of an overemphasis on one of two seemingly antithetical concepts. Many scholars who have studied the works which constituted 'high culture' in this period conclude that the war experience overturned traditional values and culture and led to a modern consciousness. In *The Great War and Modern Memory* Paul Fussell relies upon the novels, memoirs and poetry of a small group of British ex-officers to argue that the experience of war led to the creation of the 'dominant form of modern understanding' which is 'essentially ironic'.[5] Modris Eksteins and Samuel Hynes also contend that the war ushered in a modern consciousness, although they differ over the extent of the change

3. G. K. Piehler, 'The War Dead and the Gold Star: American Commemoration of the First World War', in J. R. Gillis (ed.), *Commemorations: The Politics of National Identity* (Princeton, 1994), pp. 168–85.

4. R. Whalen, *Bitter Wounds: German Victims of the Great War* (Ithaca, 1984), p. 15.

5. P. Fussell, *The Great War and Modern Memory* (London and New York, 1975), p. 35.

and the form it took.[6] While they have drawn on sources other than the small range of British ex-officers selected by Fussell, their emphasis has remained on European intellectuals.

Implicit in the work of Fussell, Eksteins, Hynes and others is the assumption that the opinion of the intellectual elite either anticipates or reflects the impact of the war on society in general. However, as Jay Winter has argued, the confrontation with mass death and bereavement during and after the war transcended distinctions between high and low culture, tradition and modernity.[7] All levels of society had to come to terms with the memory of the war; but in facing this challenge British and European culture proved more resilient than many scholars have assumed. The confrontation with the memory of the war was played out in a variety of contexts, including the process of constructing and unveiling war memorials, ceremonies of remembrance such as Armistice Day, and popular poems and novels.[8] Moving from 'high culture' to a broader study of the culture of the period, historians have concluded that traditional concepts of masculinity and courage continued to dominate the wartime thinking of many groups and that war memorials often reinforced or accentuated the heroic.[9] Other scholars argue that pre-war social values were reaffirmed in the 1920s, particularly in British middlebrow literature, which stressed continuity with the past and the need to safeguard the traditions of nineteenth-century fiction against modernism.[10]

6. M. Eksteins, *Rites of Spring: The Great War and the Birth of the Modern Age* (London, 1989). S. Hynes, *A War Imagined: The First World War and English Culture* (London, 1990), pp. 283, 423–5, 458–9.

7. J. M. Winter, *Sites of Memory, Sites of Mourning: The Great War in European Cultural History* (Cambridge, 1995), pp. 2–5.

8. Winter, *Sites of Memory, Sites of Mourning*. A. Gregory, *The Silence of Memory: Armistice Day 1919–1946* (Oxford and Providence, 1994). R. Bracco, *Merchants of Hope: British Middlebrow Writers and the First World War* (Oxford and Providence, 1993). H. Orel, *Popular Fiction in England 1914–1918* (Hemel Hempstead, 1992).

9. L. Stryker, 'Languages of Sacrifice and Suffering in England in the First World War', Ph.D. thesis, Cambridge University, 1992. G. Mosse, 'National Cemeteries and National Revival: The Cult of the Fallen Soldier in Germany', *Journal of Contemporary History*, 14 (Jan. 1979), pp. 1–20.

10. R. Wall and J. M. Winter (eds), *The Upheaval of War: Family, Work and Welfare in Europe, 1914–1918* (Cambridge, 1988), p. 4. Bracco, *Merchants of Hope*, pp. 12–13.

The dichotomy between tradition and modernity has also influenced writing about battlefield tourism and pilgrimages. Eksteins suggests that the figure of the battlefield tourist is emblematic of modernism.[11] However, Eksteins' study ignores the other travellers to the battlefields who were referred to or described themselves as pilgrims. The language of the sacred and the act of pilgrimage both infused and were in conflict with battlefield tourism. The interaction between the two modes of travel was a product of the concurrent development of a tourism industry and the renewal of the practice of pilgrimage in the years prior to and after the war. It also reflected the continuing influence of wartime imagery and language.

A significant aspect of the debate about the role of the war as a cultural divide is the question of the war's effect on attitudes to death and mourning. Both Jeffery Lerner and Pat Jalland suggest that the war was a major turning-point in the history of death. Lerner contends that despite the 'surge of interest in visiting foreign graves and in erecting war memorials', there was 'no real return to pre-war funeral and mourning customs' because the war identified these practices with a morbid and antiquarian outlook and left people exhausted with death.[12] Jalland argues that despite the obvious need for customary rituals and spiritual consolation 'the Great War accelerated the decline of Victorian mourning customs' and that death became a 'major taboo of the British people'.[13]

By contrast, David Cannadine concludes that 'inter-war Britain was probably more obsessed with death than any other period in modern history'.[14] Other historians also support Cannadine's thesis, arguing that the obsession with death was shared by many

11. M. Eksteins, 'Michelin, Pickfords and the Great War: Tourism on the Western Front 1919–1991', Paper presented at Histoire Culturelle Comparée du Premier Conflit Mondial: La Guerre et La Mémoire de la Guerre, Colloque, Péronne (1992). French translation in J. J. Becker *et al.*, *1914–1918. Guerre et Cultures* (Paris, 1994).

12. J. C. Lerner, 'The Public and Private Management of Death in Britain 1890–1930', Ph.D. thesis, Columbia University, 1981, pp. 1, 103–4, 120–31, 136.

13. P. Jalland, *Death in the Victorian Family* (Oxford, 1996), p. 358.

14. D. Cannadine, 'War and Death, Grief and Mourning in Modern Britain', in J. Whaley (ed.), *Mirrors of Mortality: Studies in the Social History of Death* (London, 1981), pp. 189, 231.

combatant nations.[15] The remarkable popularity of battlefields, cemeteries and memorials for tourists and pilgrims in the inter-war years also challenges the view that many people were exhausted with death or that it had become a taboo. Pilgrimages were among a range of ceremonies and rituals of mourning and commemoration which brought consolation to many people in the aftermath of the war. Implicit in the act of making a pilgrimage was an instinctive spiritualism which expressed itself in the belief that it was possible to get closer to the spirit and even the spirits of the dead by visiting sites associated with the war. The continuing fascination of the war for many people has been obscured by the tendency for scholars to concentrate on the 'war books boom' in the late 1920s and early 1930s. The 'war books boom' is important, but it was just one moment in the process of remembrance of the war which took place throughout the inter-war years.

In response to the crisis created by the strain of the war and the confrontation with mass death communities and individuals drew upon religion and the sacred. Traditional religion offered a language and imagery with which to express the grief of the nation and assisted in the creation of rituals which people were able to draw upon to mourn the dead and come to terms with their grief.[16] Catherine Moriarty stresses the importance of Christian iconography in English war memorials, arguing that in the face of mass death Christian symbolism 'provided an accessible and palliative language' for a nation in mourning.[17] Annette Becker's study of religious faith in France during the Great War and in the 1920s includes pilgrimages to the battlefields as an example of the way in which spirituality merged with the memory of the war in post-war commemoration.[18]

15. B. Hüppauf, 'War and Death: The Experience of the First World War', in M. Crouch and B. Hüppauf (eds), *Essays on Mortality* (Kensington, NSW, 1985), pp. 65–86. Whalen, *Bitter Wounds*, pp. 22–9.

16. A. Wilkinson, *The Church of England and the First World War* (London, 1978), pp. 300–4.

17. C. Moriarty, 'Christian Iconography and First World War Memorials', *Imperial War Museum Review*, 6 (1992), p. 74.

18. A. Becker, *La Guerre et La Foi: De la Mort à la Mémoire* (Paris, 1994), pp. 111–17.

By contrast George Mosse argues that ceremonies of commemoration did not reflect the role of traditional religion, but represented the secular appropriation of the sacred. Drawing mainly upon the example of Germany, he contends that a myth of the war experience was created which re-fashioned the memory of the war into 'a sacred experience which provided the nation with a new depth of religious feeling, putting at its disposal ever-present saints and martyrs, places of worship and a heritage to emulate'. He suggests that to varying degrees this process also occurred in the other combatant nations such as Britain and France.[19] An alternative formulation of the argument that commemoration represents the secular appropriation of the sacred is the suggestion that it became a civil religion. Antoine Prost concludes that in France the ceremonies of remembrance expressed a civil religion, rather than traditional beliefs, because they celebrated the citizens themselves and provided a moral lesson in the obligations which must be fulfilled in order to maintain the Republic.[20] Ken Inglis also uses the expression to describe Anzac Day in Australia and New Zealand, although he cautions against ignoring the role of traditional religion.[21]

Religious imagery, rituals and belief played a significant role in many pilgrims' visits to battlefields, cemeteries and memorials. Religious organisations assisted bereaved relatives to visit war graves, and large pilgrimages often included a religious service. Religious belief offered many pilgrims solace through the knowledge that they would be united with their loved ones in the afterlife. Although the popular sense of the sacred did not always accord with the views of the established Churches, it indicates the importance of religion in the mourning process in Britain. As a result the use of the sacred did not reflect the existence of a cult of the fallen soldier or a civil religion.

19. G. Mosse, *Fallen Soldiers: Reshaping the Memory of the World Wars* (New York, 1990), pp. 6–7.

20. A. Prost, 'Les Monuments Aux Morts, Culte Républicain? Culte Civique? Culte Patriotique?', in P. Nora (ed.), *Les Lieux de Mémoire*, Vol. I *La République* (Paris, 1984), pp. 214–15, 219–22.

21. K. S. Inglis, 'Anzac Day in Australia and New Zealand', Paper presented at Histoire Culturelle Comparée du Premier Conflit Mondial: La Guerre et La Mémoire de la Guerre, Colloque, Péronne (July 1992). French translation in Becker *et al.*, *Guerre et Cultures*. K. S. Inglis, 'War Memorials: Ten Questions for Historians', *Guerres Mondiales et Conflits Contemporains*, 167 (Juillet 1992), p. 16.

In the process of remembering and commemorating the dead and the war the sacred merged and was in tension with the profane. The interrelationship between the sacred and the profane was a key feature of battlefield tourism and pilgrimages. Many travellers felt that in visiting the battlefields or war memorials they were coming to a sacred place; but there was another side to these journeys. Mosse notes that battlefield tourism trivialised the war experience, because travellers stayed in comfortable surroundings and with the passing of time the battlefields were cleaned up and lost their horror. As a consequence the traveller's memory of the war was influenced by the comfortable aura which surrounded the journey.[22] Although Mosse makes an important point, the extent to which battlefield tourism trivialised the war experience should not be exaggerated. The post-war development of a dichotomy between the battlefield tourist and the pilgrim indicates the desire felt by many people that their grief and the achievements of the fallen should not be trivialised.

The dichotomy between the tourist and the pilgrim also drew upon and expressed the continuation of the wartime divide between the front and the home front; between masculinity and femininity. In the development of this dichotomy the individual memories and experiences of ex-servicemen and the bereaved merged with a collective memory of division between civilians and soldiers. Eric Leed emphasises the way in which the experience of combat separated men from the society for which they fought. He argues that one response to this feeling of 'psychic and social estrangement from civilian life was the ritualisation and memorialisation of the war experience in veterans groups'.[23] The theme of separation is also articulated by many historians writing about women's wartime experiences. Sandra Gilbert and James Longenbach both stress the way in which the war empowered women and thus separated them from the men in the front lines.[24]

22. Mosse, *Fallen Soldiers*, pp. 152–6.

23. E. Leed, *No Man's Land: Combat and Identity in the First World War* (Cambridge, 1979), p. 3.

24. S. M. Gilbert, 'Soldier's Heart: Literary Men, Literary Women and the Great War', in M. R. Higonnet *et al.* (eds), *Behind the Lines, Gender and the Two World Wars* (New Haven and London), pp. 197–226. J. Longenbach, 'The Women and Men of 1914', in H. M. Cooper *et al.* (eds), *Arms and the Woman: Gender and Literary Representation* (Chapel Hill and London, 1989), pp. 97–123.

However, the belief that soldiers were alienated from civilian society and its values by the war is not shared by all scholars. The study of trench newspapers suggests that the soldiers retained strong links with their civilian culture.[25] This conclusion has also been affirmed by Charles Kimball's thesis on British ex-servicemen's organisations and by Joanna Bourke in her book on British masculinity.[26] An analysis of tourism and pilgrimages both confirms and challenges the existence of a divide between men and women, between the front and the home front in Britain. It indicates the complex and fluid nature of relations between masculinity and femininity. At one level civilians, including the bereaved, were separated from ex-servicemen because they did not fight in the trenches. This created a tension between them. At the same time many women and men were united in the experience of mass death. While people on the home front did not see their loved ones die, they worried about, prayed for and in many cases mourned them. In the commemoration of the dead the bereaved, particularly women, were joined with ex-servicemen as pilgrims. Together they were aligned against another indeterminate group described as 'tourists'. Although the actions of tourists on the battlefields were frequently criticised in writing about battlefield travel, it is likely that few travellers considered themselves to be tourists.

The degree of unity between men and women differed between Britain, Canada and Australia. Many Australian historians argue that the Australian memory of the war excluded and marginalised women, because the Anzac[27] tradition privileged the achievements of Australian servicemen in the foundation of the nation.[28] They also point to the continuing significance of Anzac Day as a male celebration of the war. This contrasts with

25. J. Fuller, *Troop Morale and Popular Culture in the British and Dominion Armies 1914–1918* (Oxford, 1990), pp. 175–7.

26. C. C. Kimball, 'The Ex-Service Movement in England and Wales, 1916–1930', Ph.D. thesis, Stanford University, 1990. J. Bourke, *Dismembering the Male: Men's Bodies, Britain and the Great War* (London, 1996).

27. The expression 'ANZAC' was initially the acronym for the Australian and New Zealand Army Corps.

28. M. Lake, 'Mission Impossible: How Men Gave Birth to the Australian Nation - Nationalism, Gender and Other Seminal Acts', *Gender & History*, 4 (Autumn, 1992), pp. 305–22. C. Shute, 'Heroines & Heroes: Sexual Mythology in Australia 1914-1918', *Hecate*, 1 (Jan. 1975), pp. 18–20.

Britain and Canada. In Britain bereaved women were an important feature of large battlefield pilgrimages and they dominated newspaper accounts of the pilgrimages to the Cenotaph and the grave of the Unknown Warrior. Similarly, commemoration appears to have particularly focused on the bereaved in Canada, even though Canadian servicemen were frequently described as having achieved Canada's independent nationhood through their wartime endeavours.

The political context of remembrance and its role in the formulation of national identity was also influenced by the interrelationship between individual and collective memory. This interrelationship has not always been addressed by historians. Bob Bushaway argues that the language of sacrifice and the rituals of remembrance were used to purge 'the demons of discontent and disorder' and to deny the mass of British society 'a political critique of the War'.[29] He does not specify which groups were manipulating remembrance, but it is likely that he means the ruling elites. Bushaway's study of the impact of remembrance assumes that it is possible to analyse society as a monolithic entity. His approach leaves little room for individual responses and feelings and he largely ignores their role in attributing meanings to the languages and rituals of remembrance. Consequently, Bushaway misses the impact of popular responses in the transformation of memorials such as the Cenotaph and the grave of the Unknown Warrior into places of pilgrimage, which in turn helped to determine their meanings. The government, newspapers and the elites played a role in this process, but it was in response to events rather than simply the manipulation of them.

While remembrance was inherently conservative, because it offered solace to communities and individuals in the face of mass death, it was also a fluid and textured discourse which encompassed a range of responses and a variety of political positions. This complexity is reflected in the work of Alex King and Adrian Gregory. King isolates two levels of political meaning in commemoration. The first, emphasising the sacred, encompassed a wide consensus that the dead were special and should be honoured, while the second, which concerned the attempt to relate values linked with the dead to contemporary issues, was

29. B. Bushaway, 'Name Upon Name: The Great War and Remembrance', in R. Porter (ed.), *The Myths of the English* (Cambridge, 1992), p. 161.

characterised by differing views and debate.[30] Gregory argues that the conservative tendencies of Armistice Day did not represent the manipulation of remembrance, but expressed a widely felt desire for unity in the aftermath of the war. He traces the changing meaning of the ceremony, from its concentration in the first years after the war upon the sacrifice made by the dead for King and Country, to the belief that the sacrifice was made to ensure that the Great War would be the war to end all wars.[31]

Individual memories and experiences also merged with collective memory in the organisation of and in newspaper accounts describing large public pilgrimages. The organisers of these pilgrimages often believed that they expressed the identity of the nation. The work of J. H. Grainger and Raphael Samuel suggests that in Britain the war led to a retreat to a domestic vision of national identity which celebrated the sedentary habits of the people and their unity rather than patriotism or a sense of a national obligation to the rest of the world.[32] In pilgrimages such as 1928 British Legion pilgrimage this was reflected in a determination that their tone should be understated and dominated by respect for the dead. In Australia and Canada the war was perceived as a rite of passage to nationhood.[33] As a consequence in both Dominions, but particularly in Australia, the qualities of their servicemen, which were believed to have contributed to their military successes, were idealised as the unique qualities of the nation. In Canadian and Australian pilgrimages the articulation of national identity was also infused by issues of imperial identity. In the 1936 Vimy Ridge pilgrimage the desire to assert an international Canadian identity was in tension with this imperial identity. By contrast, Australian pilgrimages were dominated by a more insular concept of national identity. The Anzac tradition

30. A. M. King, 'The Politics of Meaning in the Commemoration of the First World War in Britain, 1914–1939', Ph.D. thesis, University College, London, 1993, pp. 351–2.

31. Gregory, *The Silence of Memory*, pp. 5, 34–41, 118–33, 225–6.

32. J. H. Grainger, *Patriotisms: Britain 1900–1939* (London, 1986), pp. 318–61. R. Samuel, 'Exciting to be English', in R. Samuel (ed.), *Patriotism: The Making and Unmaking of British National Identity*, Vol. I *History and Politics* (London, 1989), pp. xviii–xxviii.

33. P. Berton, *Vimy* (Toronto, 1986), pp. 293–5. N. McLachlan, *Waiting for the Revolution: A History of Australian Nationalism* (Melbourne, 1989), pp. 187–208.

privileged the achievements of Australian ex-servicemen, rather than the collective achievement of the nation. This left greater scope for this tradition to merge with an imperial identity, because there was a largely unacknowledged assumption that when these men excelled they did so while fighting on behalf of the Empire.

The book is divided into five chapters. Chapter 1 is a study of the concurrent development of tourism and the renewal of the practice of pilgrimage in Great Britain in the period 1850–1939, as well as the development of a dichotomy between battlefield tourists and pilgrims in the inter-war years. Chapter 2 is a close analysis of the pilgrimages to the Cenotaph and the grave of the Unknown Warrior. It explores the role of popular agency in the success and significance of these memorials. Chapter 3 charts the changes in the popularity of battlefield travel as well as the variety and changing meanings of the war which travellers perceived in the landscape. Chapter 4 is a study of the private and public roles of battlefield pilgrimages. It concentrates on the experiences of the bereaved and ex-servicemen, the significance of religion for pilgrims, links between the journey and the expression of national identity and the pilgrim's search for a meaning to the war experience. Finally, in Chapter 5 the examples of Australia and Canada are briefly considered in order to explore some of the wider implications of the role of tourism and pilgrimage in the commemoration of the war, in particular the role of the bereaved and ex-servicemen, and the influence of pilgrimages in the expression of national and imperial identity.

1

Tourism and Pilgrimage, 1860–1939

> The French have a better term for what are described in this country as battlefield tours. They call them pilgrimages.
>
> - *The Times*, 7 June 1920

The fifty years before the Great War and the inter-war period were a time of extraordinary change in the practice of travel. It was characterised simultaneously by the evolution of a modern tourist industry and the resurgence of pilgrimages. Battlefields such as Waterloo were among the sites which attracted large numbers of travellers in the years before 1914, although it was rare for these journeys to be described as pilgrimages. During the Great War writers anticipated the post-war popularity of the battlefields for travellers, and often described this journey as a pilgrimage to a sacred place. In the aftermath of the war many people who journeyed to its battlefields, cemeteries and memorials were described as pilgrims. These journeys were one facet of a wider increase in the popularity of pilgrimages in this period. However, the numbers of pilgrims were dwarfed by the burgeoning tourist industry, which included battlefield tours within its itinerary. The dichotomy between the tourist and the pilgrim was an important feature of the ways in which battlefield travel was imagined. This dichotomy was founded upon a perception of the war which sanctified the sacrifice of the fallen and which expressed a belief in the post-war continuation, albeit in a modified form, of the divide between the front and the home front.

Tourism and Pilgrimage, 1860–1914

The story of the evolution and expansion of the travel industry in the nineteenth century is often equated with the growth of a tourist industry.[1] While there is little doubt that the tourist industry was an extremely important development in this period, such an approach omits the simultaneous resurgence of other more traditional forms of travel such as pilgrimages. This obscures the complexity of the nature of travel in this period, because its development is characterised as a linear progression towards a concept of travel as the pursuit of pleasure. Thus Eric Leed describes this process as a change from the ancient to the modern conceptions of travel: 'The ancients valued travel as an explication of human fate and necessity; for moderns it is an expression of freedom and an escape from necessity and purpose. Ancients saw travel as a suffering, even a penance; for moderns, it is a pleasure and a means to pleasure.'[2] Despite the elegant simplicity of this progression, both the modes of travel and the meanings which contemporaries attributed to it were more subtle and involved a number of alternative ways of perceiving the journey. The motives people ascribed to travel, and in particular, travel to the Continent, often included a higher or moral purpose, such as the act of making a pilgrimage. The attribution of a higher purpose to travel also provided a means of distinguishing between different categories of traveller.

The organised practice of travel for leisure or private satisfaction, rather than for business or out of necessity, was not a new development in the nineteenth century, particularly for people from the upper classes.[3] However, in this century a form of mass commercial travel developed which was both quantitatively and qualitatively distinct from anything which had occurred before. The development of the railway and the steamship, as well as the impact of industrialisation and urbanisation, facilitated the creation of a travel industry.[4] Further, the growth of industrial capitalism meant that increasing numbers of people were able to afford to travel, while changes in working conditions, such as the introduction of the bank holiday in 1870,

1. A. J. Burkart and S. Medlik, *Tourism: Past Present and Future* (London, 1974). L. J. Lickorish and A. G. Kershaw, *The Travel Trade* (London, 1958).

2. E. Leed, *The Mind of the Traveller: From Gilgamesh to Global Tourism* (New York, 1991), p. 7.

3. M. Feifer, *Going Places: The Ways of the Tourist from Imperial Rome to the Present Day* (London, 1985), pp. 2, 8.

4. Burkart and Medlik, *Tourism*, pp. 11–19. Lickorish and Kershaw, *The Travel Trade*, pp. 29–31.

provided greater leisure time. Assisted by these developments, seaside resorts became the premier holiday destinations in Great Britain. By 1911 as many as 55 per cent of people in England and Wales took at least one trip to the seaside each year.[5]

In the years prior to 1913 there was also an astonishing growth in the number of people travelling to the Continent. While precise figures for the size of this growth do not exist, an indication of its extent can be gained from the figures for cross-Channel passengers collected by the South Eastern and Chatham Railway.

Table 1. Cross-Channel Passengers 1860–1913

Year	Average number of Passengers embarking and disembarking per year	Percentage increase
1860–9	309,942	
1870–9	387,922	25.2
1880–9	484,940	25.0
1890–9	589,968	21.7
1900–9	913,510	54.8
1910–13	1,205,110	31.9

Source: J. Simmons, 'Railways, Hotels, and Tourism in Great Britain 1839–1914'.[6]

The extent of the change represented by these figures is apparent when they are compared with the 1830s, when the cross-Channel traffic each year was around 100,000 people.[7] The number of people travelling had increased by 300 per cent in 1860, by 500 per cent in 1900 and by 1200 per cent in 1913.

By the outbreak of the Great War travel had become an important commercial activity. Travel agents organised tours for this growing body of travellers. Many of them began by assisting people travelling within Great Britain. For example, Thomas Cook commenced by organising a party to visit a temperance meeting on 5 July 1841. He then arranged tours to Scotland in the 1840s and parties to the Great Exhibition in 1851. His first tour to the Continent, in 1856, was a tour through Belgium and

5. J. Urry, *The Tourist Gaze: Leisure and Travel in Contemporary Societies* (London, 1990), p. 18.

6. J. Simmons, 'Railways, Hotels, and Tourism in Great Britain 1839–1914', *Journal of Contemporary History*, 19 (Apr. 1984), p. 216.

7. Lickorish and Kershaw, *The Travel Trade*, p. 35.

the Rhineland to the Exhibition in Paris. Thomas Cook's annual profit rose from approximately £20,000 a year in the 1880s to around £86,000 per annum in the period from 1900 to 1913.[8] The money generated by the growing industry had significant implications for European economies. A. J. Norval claims that in the period before the Great War Switzerland was visited annually by between 350,000 and 450,000 tourists who spent around 200,000,000 francs a year. In the same period France derived 350,000,000 francs per annum from her tourist trade. The growing importance of tourism for the French economy led to the setting up of the Office National du Tourisme in 1910.[9]

The industrial and technological factors which fostered the development of the fledgling tourist industry also facilitated a resurgence in the practice of undertaking pilgrimages to religious sites. The nineteenth century was a time of religious revival in Western Europe and one of the most remarkable expressions of this was the spate of visions of the Virgin Mary which occurred in the latter half of the century. The most significant of these visions include those at Lourdes, Pontmain and La Salette in France, Knock in Ireland and Pompeii in Italy. The Catholic Church embraced the new technology and possibilities of mass travel to develop the sites of Marian apparitions and to organise mass pilgrimages to them. This is most clearly evident in France, where over three million people participated in pilgrimages to religious sites in 1873. In the years that followed national pilgrimages to Lourdes were organised from Belgium, Poland, Italy, Germany, Spain, Ireland, Portugal and Switzerland.[10] By 1908 at least a million people travelled to Lourdes annually.[11]

The practice of making pilgrimages to religious sites was also revived in Great Britain. The first English pilgrimage to Lourdes took place in 1883.[12] The climate of increasing tolerance for Roman Catholicism in England combined with the example of

8. P. Brendon, *Thomas Cook: 150 Years of Popular Tourism* (London, 1991), pp. 215, 245.

9. A. J. Norval, *The Tourist Industry: A National and International Survey* (London, 1936), pp. 45, 279.

10. D. Blackbourn, *The Marpingen Visions: Rationalism, Religion and the Rise of Modern Germany* (Hammersmith, 1995, originally published 1993), pp. 17, 54–6.

11. P. Assouline, *Lourdes: Histoires D'eau* (Paris, 1980), p. 85.

12. P. Marnham, *Lourdes: A Modern Pilgrimage* (London, 1980), p. 18.

Lourdes to encourage the renewal of domestic Roman Catholic pilgrimage sites, such as Walsingham, which was visited by the first official pilgrims since the Reformation in 1897.[13] The tendency to identify travel with the act of pilgrimage was also promoted by the opening up of the Holy Land to tourists in the nineteenth century. The journey was perceived by many British travellers as an expression of Protestant piety.[14] H. Rider Haggard titled his account of the journey he made to Palestine, under the auspices of Thomas Cook's, *A Winter Pilgrimage*. He wrote that he hoped to be numbered among the pilgrims who have journeyed to the Holy Land since AD 333, and who have written about their experiences. His impressions on first seeing Nazareth reflect the piety with which he made the journey: 'there lay Nazareth, the holy spot, that like thousands of other pilgrims in every generation, for years I had desired to see. How is it possible for even the most cynical and faithless to look upon that place save with a heart of deepest reverence?'[15] Thomas Cook's were heavily involved in organising these tours. In 1891 they published a guidebook to Syria and Palestine and by 1900 they had assisted 12,000 people to visit the Holy Land.[16]

During the period before the Great War there were a number of competing attitudes to travel. At one level travel was linked with leisure. Members of the elites were attracted by the luxury and excitement of the resorts on the Riviera.[17] Similarly members of the middle classes and increasing numbers of people from the working classes relaxed at British seaside resorts.[18] At the same time the justifications for foreign travel, particularly among the middle classes, often stressed the moral or higher purpose of the journey.

13. V. Turner and E. Turner, *Image and Pilgrimage in Christian Culture: Anthropological Perspectives* (Oxford and New York, 1978), p. 175.

14. J. Pemble, *The Mediterranean Passion: Victorians and Edwardians in the South* (Oxford, 1988), pp. 55–63.

15. H. Rider Haggard, *A Winter Pilgrimage: Being an Account of Travels Through Palestine, Italy and the Island of Cyprus, Accomplished in the Year 1900* (London, 1901), pp. 2, 207.

16. J. G. Davies, *Pilgrimage Yesterday and Today. Why? Where? How?* (London, 1988), pp. 148–51.

17. Feifer, *Going Places*, pp. 206–8.

18. J. Walton, *The English Seaside Resort: A Social History 1750–1914* (New York, 1983), pp. 196–8.

John Pemble notes that among the tourists to the Mediterranean in the late nineteenth century travel was seen as something 'suspect and subversive'. Instead of leisure travellers to the Mediterranean emphasised the themes of education, health and pilgrimage. The popularity of the guidebooks issued by publishers such as John Murray attests to the preoccupation of travellers in the pre-war period with the educational role of travel. These books catered to the demand for detailed information regarding the sites to be visited and the artefacts to be studied, so that travellers could learn from their journey.[19] Similarly health combined with pleasure as the motives which were used by those members of the aristocracy and gentry who travelled to the seaside. One scholar notes that with the advent of middle-class visitors in the nineteenth century health became the primary motive used to justify a visit to the seaside.[20] The identification of travel with the theme of pilgrimage in Great Britain was generally limited to places with ties to the Christian religion, such as Catholic shrines or the Holy Land. However, travel might also become a pilgrimage if the place which was visited was perceived as special in some way. Ian Ousby has found that the language of shrines and of pilgrimage was used to describe journeys to places associated with great English writers.[21]

The perception of a higher purpose in travel was also intimately connected with issues of class and status. In the period from 1860 to 1900 the growth in traffic to the Continent resulted from its increasing popularity for the middle classes. Those who could afford to travel generally had an income of £300 to £600 a year.[22] Thomas Cook described them as 'ushers, governesses, practical people from the provinces, and representatives of the better style of the London Mercantile Community'.[23] However, the real explosion in growth took place in the fourteen years before the Great War. In this period members of the lower middle classes first began to travel to the Continent. Holidays in Belgium and Holland were comparatively cheap; a week in Holland cost

19. Pemble, *Mediterranean Passion*, pp. 53–4, 71.

20. Walton, *The English Seaside Resort*, pp. 5–7.

21. I. Ousby, *The Englishman's England: Taste, Travel and the Rise of Tourism* (Cambridge, 1990), pp. 8, 22.

22. Brendon, *Thomas Cook*, p. 85.

23. W. Fraser Rae, *The Business of Travel: A Fifty Years Record of Progress* (London, 1891), pp. 68–9.

four and a half guineas, while a week in Belgium cost three and a half guineas.[24] The Toynbee Workmen's Travelling Club claimed that it was as cheap and easy to spend a week on the Continent as it was to go to Margate.[25]

In the 1870s and 1880s the activities of Anglo-Saxon tourists abroad were a favourite topic for humour in journals such as *Punch*. People who travelled with Thomas Cook's were referred to as '"Cook's Circus," "Cook's Hordes" and "Cook's Vandals"'.[26] The new travellers were ridiculed for their ignorance and vulgarity, a charge which Pemble demonstrates to have been unfounded and which some contemporaries exposed as false.[27] They were even accused of desecrating the tourist attractions by their presence. One writer described a picnic by a Cook's party near the temple of Osiris, claiming this: 'excess of grotesqueness in profanation is more insulting surely than to be sacked by barbarians'.[28] James Buzard argues that in the nineteenth century the 'tourist' was distinguished from the traveller as a response to a perceived rush or deluge of people travelling to the Continent. The language of 'anti-tourism' offered a means for individual travellers to define themselves as different and superior to the other 'tourists' they encountered. Travellers stressed the romantic justifications for travel, emphasising solitude, privacy and a personal semi-private relationship with the scene gazed upon by the individual.[29] This language presaged that which would be used to distinguish between tours and pilgrimages to the battlefields, cemeteries and memorials of the Great War.

Battlefields as Tourist Attractions Prior to the Great War

Battlefields played an important role as attractions in the growing tourist industry. One of the earliest travel agents, Henry Gaze,

24. R. G. Studd, *The Holiday Story* (London, 1950), p. 55.
25. Pemble, *The Mediterranean Passion*, p. 1.
26. Brendon, *Thomas Cook*, p. 89.
27. Pemble, *Mediterranean Passion*, pp. 75–8. Brendon, *Thomas Cook*, pp. 94–7.
28. P. Loti, *Egypt* (New York, 1910), quoted in D. Manley (ed.), *The Nile: A Traveller's Anthology* (London, 1991), p. 156.
29. J. Buzard, *The Beaten Track: European Tourism, Literature and the Ways to 'Culture' 1800–1918* (Oxford, 1993), pp. 5–7, 80–104.

took his first party to visit Brussels and the battlefield of Waterloo in 1854.[30] Similarly the first tour of the Workmen's Travel Club was to Waterloo.[31] Travel to the battlefield of Waterloo was often considered to be educational. The maiden tour organised by the Polytechnic Touring Association in 1886 was for a group of schoolboys with their masters to travel to the battlefield of Waterloo and the Swiss Alps.[32] A thriving industry in the sale of relics and souvenirs developed at the site, which led the 1913 Thomas Cook's guide to warn travellers:

> It is hardly necessary to say that buttons, spurs, helmets or sword-handles can be purchased cheaper in Sheffield or Birmingham, where they are manufactured than on the field of Waterloo; nor must we forget that the battle was fought in the year 1815, and therefore the numerous guides of about fifty years of age who declare they were in the engagement are not to be relied upon implicitly.[33]

Attempts were also made to attract tourists to the battlefields of South Africa following the conclusion of the Anglo-Boer war in 1902. One writer advised potential travellers that the battlefields around Ladysmith and the Tugela were not only the most accessible, but also the most picturesque in South Africa.[34] Similarly a guidebook to the battlefields of South Africa enthused: 'The Tugela River itself has stirring romance, and every kopje and boulder between Colenso and Ladysmith hides a tragedy. The nobleness and grandeur of that tragedy is written in monuments on the hills, where among the thorn bushes and giant aloes, with the placid river flowing beneath, they tell their stories of heroic gallantry to the nation.'[35]

In the nineteenth century there was already uncertainty about the appropriateness of battlefield travel. The closer in time to the fighting that tourists arrived the more disturbing it appeared. The tourists who followed the progress of the Franco-Prussian

30. E. Swinglehurst, *The Romantic Journey: The Story of Thomas Cook and Victorian Travel* (London, 1974), p. 174.

31. J. A. R. Pimlott, *Toynbee Hall: Fifty Years of Social Progress: 1880–1934* (London, 1935), p. 160.

32. E. M. Wood, *The Polytechnic and its Founder Quintin Hogg* (London, 1932), p. 152.

33. Thomas Cook, *Cook's Travellers Handbook – Belgium and the Ardennes* (London, 1913), p. 80.

34. *The Times*, 29 Sept. 1902.

35. J. Singleton, *The Battlefields of Natal Revisited* (Durban, n.d.), p. 2.

war were criticised in a leading article in the *Observer*, which stated: 'It seems to us that nothing can be worse than for tourists to follow the track of armies, gratifying a mere lust for excitement which is not free from cruelty.'[36] Thomas Cook's announced tours of the battlefields of the Anglo-Boer War long before the fighting was finished.[37] This drew unfavourable comment from *Punch*

> . . . In Myriads behold they come
> And almost ere the guns are dumb,
> The picnickers' champagne will pop
> Upon the plains of Spion Kop.
> O flag! O Tourist! Powers twain
> That all the world resists in vain,
> Where 'neath the one the other picks
> the wings and legs of festive chicks,
> And strews the battlefield with bones,
> Newspapers, orange peel, plum stones -
> There is the reign of darkness done,
> And freedom's fight is fought and won.[38]

So many tourists were coming to South Africa that the High Commissioner, Sir Alfred Milner, called on them to stop, as they were interfering with the war effort.[39] These criticisms generally ceased with the conclusion of the fighting.

The growing popularity of battlefields with travellers coincided with changes in attitudes to the dead. These changes were characterised by an increasing sensitivity to the need to remember and commemorate the dead. This in turn attached a greater meaning to war cemeteries; they became sacred places.[40] After the battle of Waterloo in 1815 the individual dead were buried in a mass grave and were largely forgotten. Thomas Laqueur concludes that the image 'one is left with at Waterloo is one not only of anonymity but of complete individual dissolution'.[41] The

36. *Observer*, 31 July 1870.

37. *Cook's Excursionist and Home Foreign Tourist Advertiser*, L (Apr. 1900), p. 3.

38. *Punch or the London Charivari*, 118 (Apr. 1900), p. 279.

39. *The Times*, 16 Apr. 1900.

40. G. Mosse, *Fallen Soldiers: Reshaping the Memory of the World Wars* (New York, 1990), pp. 34–50.

41. T. W. Laqueur, 'Memory and Naming in the Great War', in J. R. Gillis (ed.), *Commemorations: The Politics of National Identity* (Princeton, 1994), p. 151.

situation after the Crimean war bore strong similarities to that after Waterloo. A retired British officer decided on his own initiative to attempt to build walls around the cemeteries and to maintain the graves.[42] Only in the 1880s was a Committee created to investigate the situation, and the graves passed into the care of the Office of Works.[43] When Stephen Graham visited the battlefields of the Crimea in 1911–1912 the number of people visiting the cemeteries had dwindled away.[44]

By contrast, the descriptions of war cemeteries during the American Civil War drew heavily upon the language of the sacred. Lincoln's address before the Union graves in the Arlington cemetery on the battlefield of Gettysburg in November 1863 points towards the battlefield becoming a sacred place. He argued that 'in a larger sense we cannot dedicate, we cannot consecrate, we cannot hallow this ground. The brave men living and dead who struggled here have consecrated it far above our power to add or detract.' Lincoln's speech echoed the rhetoric of journalists, who stressed the sacred nature of the ground to the Union. In the period before 1914 the battlefield was visited by thousands of pilgrims. Theodore Roosevelt was the first President to deliver a Memorial Day address in the cemetery in 1904, and the crowd may have included as many as 25,000 to 30,000 people.[45]

The growing acceptance of the need to commemorate and remember the fallen was evident during the Anglo-Boer war. A society, with royal patronage, was founded to locate and tend the graves of individual soldiers.[46] The Chairman of the Graves Fund stated that the least the Fund could do was 'to ensure that the individual memory of the soldiers who had fallen on the battlefield . . . should be as imperishable as he was sure their fame would be'.[47] However, there was no formal policy to preserve all the graves, and those which were located away from the main

42. H. Bolitho (ed.), 'A Victorian Woman in the Crimea', *English Review*, LIX (Oct. 1934), p. 468.

43. P. Longworth, *The Unending Vigil: A History of the Commonwealth War Graves Commission 1917–1967* (London, 1967), p. 26.

44. S. Graham, *Part of the Wonderful Scene: An Autobiography* (London, 1964), p. 47.

45. J. S. Patterson, 'A Patriotic Landscape: Gettysburg, 1863–1913', *Prospects*, 7 (1982), pp. 322-5.

46. *The Times*, 13 Dec. 1900.

47. *The Times*, 26 June 1901.

centres were rarely maintained.[48] Although it was not comprehensive, the care which was taken of the soldiers' graves in the Anglo-Boer war is indicative of the shift which had occurred in the decades since Waterloo. The Great War greatly accelerated this change, and significantly altered the way in which travel to its battlefields would be imagined and described.

The Impact of the Great War

The growth of a tourist industry in the latter half of the nineteenth century meant that during the Great War many people were conscious that the battlefields would become a focal point for tourists after the war. At the end of 1914 *The War Illustrated* printed photographs of civilians searching for German bullets and other souvenirs in the grass. The caption read: 'Souvenir hunting has become quite an industry where the fire of battle has raged, and it is certain that the traffic in war souvenirs will flourish in the years to come when the battlefields are the haunt of summer tourists.'[49] In March 1915 Thomas Cook's announced in *The Times*, in order to put a stop to stray enquiries, that they would not be organising sightseeing expeditions to the battlefields, at least until the war was over, owing to French opposition.[50]

Writers who visited the battlefields described scenes which they expected would interest the tourists who would flock there after the war, such as an old church with a dud shell lodged in it near the Ypres Salient or a museum, in a barn, of objects found on the battlefield.[51] Similarly servicemen wrote about their dug-outs as future tourist sites, while two of the best known trench newspapers, the *New Church Times* and the *BEF Times*, included advertisements for imaginary charabanc and railway tours of the battlefields.[52] His anticipation that the battlefields would be future

48. Laqueur, 'Memory and Naming in the Great War', p. 152.

49. *The War Illustrated*, 1 (Dec. 1914), p. 431.

50. *The Times*, 31 Mar. 1915.

51. A. Conan Doyle, *A Visit to Three Fronts, Glimpses of the British, Italian and French Lines* (London, 1916), p. 12; E. Gosse, 'The Battlefields of the Ourcq', *Cornhill Magazine*, XLII (Jan. 1917), p. 27.

52. A. P. Herbert, 'The Dug-Out (A Memory of Gallipoli)', in *Half-Hours at Helles* (Oxford, 1916), p. 44. *New Church Times*, 1 (May, 1916), *BEF Times*, 1 (Dec. 1916) in *The Wipers Times: A Complete Facsimile of the Famous World War One Trench Newspaper* (London, 1973), pp. 86, 126.

tourist sites led J. W. Gamble to write that Ypres 'will be flooded with sight-seers and tourists after the War, and they will be amazed by what they see. The ancient ruins of Pompeii and such places will be simply out of it.'[53]

Many wartime descriptions of the battlefields imbued them with the qualities of a sacred place, and future travellers to them became pilgrims. For many ex-servicemen the language of pilgrimage expressed their special relationship with the dead and with the memory of the war. Servicemen in the front lines were surrounded by death. While this could lead to an insensitivity to death, it also produced an awareness that the death of their comrades on the battlefield had made that ground a special place. Servicemen were a common sight in the cemeteries which were being constructed along the battle front.[54] Hugh Pollard described the Ypres salient as 'holy ground' because every acre contained the graves of English, French and Canadian soldiers.[55] Douglas Gillespie wrote to his old Headmaster in Winchester School from the front line, suggesting that the fields of battle are 'sacred in a sense' and expressing his hope that after the war the British and French Governments would combine to make a broad road in no man's land from the Vosges to the sea: 'Then I would like to send every man, woman, and child in Western Europe on pilgrimage along that Via Sacra, so that they might think and learn about what War means from the silent witnesses on either side.'[56]

The language of pilgrimage expressed the belief of some servicemen that their link with the fallen and their memories of the war were special. An officer who fought at the Somme wrote to a friend: 'I went along the "sunken road" all the way to Contalmaison. Talk about sacred ground . . . there's a kind of wrench about seeing the new chaps swagger over it so carelessly, and seeing it gradually merged into the "behind the line" country. I have a feeling it ought to be marked off somehow, a permanent memorial.'[57] Similar sentiments were expressed by A. P. Herbert in his poem 'Beaucourt Revisited':

53. J. W. Gamble, letter 23 Dec. 1915, IWM, P.P. MCR 82.

54. A. W. Hill, 'Our Soldiers' Graves', *Journal of the Royal Horticultural Society*, XLV (Oct. 1919), p. 5.

55. H. B. C. Pollard, *The Story of Ypres* (London, 1917), pp. 62–3.

56. A. D. Gillespie, *Letters From Flanders* (London, 1916, 3rd edn), Appendix.

57. J. Buchan, *Nelson's History of the Great War*, Vol. XVI (London, 1917), p. 55.

> The new troops follow after, and tread the land we won,
> to them 'tis so much hill-side rewrested from the Hun;
> We only walk with reverence this sullen mile of mud;
> The shell-holes hold our history, and half of them our blood.[58]

Popular authors and writers of propaganda drew upon the language of pilgrimage to provide a greater meaning to the loss and bereavement caused by the war. They referred to the journey which the relatives of the dead would make to the graves of their loved ones as a pilgrimage. J. A. Hammerton wrote that after the war many a 'pilgrim of sorrow' would seek the 'consecrated ground' of Plugstreet wood, while another writer expected that Ypres would be visited by 'such troops of pilgrims as have never been seen before – multitudes of them wearing black'.[59] Pilgrims even began to make these journeys in wartime fiction. In *Crucifix Corner: A Story of Everyman's Land*, by the popular writers C. N. and A. M. Williamson, the parents of Jim Beckett, who is believed to have died in the fighting, join with a girl posing as Jim's fiancée and her brother Brian, blinded in the war, on a journey across the Western Front. When Brian first proposes the scheme he says:

> You say your Jim spent some of his happiest days . . . [in France and Belgium], and now he's given his life for the land he loved. Wouldn't you feel as if he went with you, if you made a pilgrimage from town to town he knew in their days of beauty – if you travelled and studied some scheme for helping to make each one beautiful again after the War?[60]

The descriptions of the battlefields as a place of pilgrimage did not just include the journey by bereaved relatives to the graves of the dead. A war correspondent who spent time near the front line claimed that every visit to Ypres 'was for me a pious pilgrimage to the place of sacrifice of the best of England's sons'.[61] The nature of the battlefield itself could make the traveller a pilgrim. Popular writers claimed that the men's sacrifice had

58. A. P. Herbert, 'Beaucourt Revisited', in D. Hibberd and J. Onions (eds), *Poetry of the Great War: An Anthology* (Basingstoke, 1986), p. 73.
59. J. A. Hammerton, *The Wrack of War* (London, 1918), p. 40. Dr Dearmer, 'Ypres', *Cornhill Magazine*, 40 (June 1916), p. 716.
60. C. N. and A. M. Williamson, *Crucifix Corner: A Story of Everyman's Land* (London, 1918), p. 36.
61. G. Valentine Williams, *With Our Army in France and Flanders* (London, 1915), p. 110.

altered the land on which they had shed their blood; they had made it sacred. H. E. Brittain wrote: 'Martyrdom hallows, and wherever a man has laid down his life for the country that he loves or a cause in which he believes, or is willing to do so - for the readiness is all - that spot must be for ever sacred, for it is a true calvary, and there is again repeated the infinite tragedy of the Cross.'[62] The battlefield of Ypres was variously described as one of the 'High Altars' of Sacrifice, 'holy ground, the supreme sacramental place of our nation' and 'the most hallowed spot on earth'.[63]

A number of factors combined to provide the battlefields with the qualities of a sacred place, thus turning a site for tourists into a place of pilgrimage. Firstly, the scale of death and bereavement during the war meant that there was a need for a language to give mass death meaning. The Great War was the bloodiest war ever fought by the people of Great Britain. While the exact number of British casualties will never be known, it has been estimated that there were 722,785 dead and 1,676,037 wounded British servicemen.[64] Such losses were unprecedented, and the people of Britain experienced the trauma this created as individuals, in communities and as a nation. The realities of a modern war fought outside Great Britain meant that there was little opportunity during the war to visit the graves of the dead or see the places where they died. Descriptions of the pilgrimages which people would make after the war looked forward to a time when the war was over and at last they would be able to complete the process of mourning.

Secondly, wartime imagery stressed the spiritual nature of the struggle. During the war soldiers were portrayed as heroes sacrificing themselves for their country; a sacrifice which was likened to that of Jesus Christ.[65] One of the most popular hymns

62. H. E. Brittain, *To Verdun From the Somme: An Anglo-American Glimpse of the Great Advance* (London, 1917), p. xv.

63. J. Oxenham, *High Altars: The Battlefields of France and Flanders as I Saw Them* (London, 1918). W. McNair, *Blood and Iron: Impressions From the Front in France & Flanders* (London, 1916), p. 254. J. Buchan, *Nelson's History of the Great War*, Vol. VII (London, 1915), p. 54.

64. J. M. Winter, *The Great War and the British People* (London, 1986), pp. 70-3.

65. T. Bogacz, '"A Tyranny of Words": Language, Poetry, and Antimodernism in England in the First World War', *Journal of Modern History*, 58 (Sept. 1986), pp. 646-52.

used at services of remembrance, John Arkwright's 'O Valiant Hearts', identified the sacrifice made by servicemen in the war with that of Christ.[66] Christ also joined the men in the trenches in a much-loved wartime poem 'Christ in Flanders', which was one of the most popular and the most anthologised poems of the war.[67] This imagery assisted in elevating travel to battlefields into a similar spiritual experience, particularly because the battlefield experience was equated with the *via dolorosa* of Christ. The distinguished British historian A. F. Pollard stated in a lecture that the 'descent, the humiliation, and the suffering are not good things in themselves, but only as sacrifice. It is the spirit that matters and the purpose that sanctifies the squalor of the *via dolorosa*.'[68] The link between the *via dolorosa* of the passion and the *via sacra* of pilgrimage was an easy one to make. May Sinclair subtitled her poem 'Field Ambulance in Retreat', '*Via Dolorosa, Via Sacra*'.[69]

Finally, the example of Gettysburg and Lincoln's address combined with the present example of France to provide a model for the sanctification of the battlefields and travel to them. When Douglas Gillespie developed his plan for a 'Via Sacra' along the Western Front he was thinking of the example of the Union Cemetery at Arlington.[70] The example of this cemetery also reminded people of Lincoln's legendary Gettysburg address, which had become synonymous with the history of the cemetery. A journalist in the *Morning Post* suggested that America could help in the task of building Gillespie's Via Sacra because 'she has made stately pleasances of meditation in some of the scenes of her Civil War – places still haunted by the words of Lincoln's Gettysburg oration, the noblest of all modern valedictories to the undying dead'.[71]

The example provided by France was even more important. In France the battlefields were closely identified with the

66. L. Adey, *Class and Idol in the English Hymn* (Vancouver, 1988), p. 217.

67. L. Whitnell, 'Christ in Flanders', in C. W. Reilly, *Scars Upon My Heart: Women's Poetry and Verse of the First World War* (London, 1981), p. 127.

68. A. F. Pollard, 'A Parable of the War', cited in S. Wallace, *War and the Image of Germany: British Academics 1914–1918* (Edinburgh, 1988), p. 77.

69. M. Sinclair, 'Field Ambulance in Retreat', in Reilly, *Scars Upon My Heart*, pp. 98–9.

70. Gillespie, *Letters from Flanders*, pp. 233–4.

71. *Morning Post*, 28 Apr. 1916.

sacred.[72] The single road to Verdun was referred to as the *Voie Sacrée* (Sacred Way). The battlefield of Verdun was described similarly as a sacred place by British writers, and an analogy was often drawn between it and Ypres. John Buchan claimed that 'Ypres was to Britain what Verdun was to France – the hallowed soil which called forth the highest virtue of her people'.[73] The guides to the battlefields which were published in Great Britain in late 1917, by the French Michelin company, also encouraged people to see a journey to the battlefields as a pilgrimage:

> such a visit should be a pilgrimage, not merely a journey across the ravaged land. Seeing is not enough, one must understand; a ruin is more moving when one knows what has caused it, a stretch of country which might seem dull and uninteresting to the unenlightened eyes, becomes transformed at the thought of the battles which have raged there.[74]

Tourism and Pilgrimage in the Inter-War Period

In late 1917 John Masefield published *The Old Front Line*, an account of his journey along the remains of the British positions from the first day of the battle of the Somme. In his account Masefield imagined the tourists who would 'walk at ease where brave men once ran and dodged and cursed their luck, when the battle of the Somme was raging'.[75] One reviewer felt that Masefield's book foreshadowed already 'in this Age of Soldiers, the Age of Pilgrims which is to come'. The reviewer was confident that this 'Age' would be characterised by 'such a passion for travel and pilgrimage as was never heard of'.[76] The reviewer correctly anticipated the temperament of people in Great Britain in the 1920s and 1930s. The conclusion of the war in 1918 ushered in a new period of travel. It was the heyday of the seaside

72. S. Audoin-Rouzeau, *Men at War 1914–1918: National Sentiment and Trench Journalism in France*, trans. H. McPhail (Providence and Oxford, 1992), p. 177, quotes from a French trench journal which describes the battlefield as a sacred place.

73. J. Buchan, *Nelson's History of the Great War,* Vol. XVII (London, 1917), p. 107; Vol. XX (London, 1919), pp. 114–15.

74. Michelin & Co., *The Marne Battlefields 1914: An Illustrated History and Guide* (London, 1917), p. 2.

75. J. Masefield, *The Old Front Line: Or the Beginning of the Battle of the Somme* (London, 1917), p. 3.

76. *The Times Literary Supplement*, 833 (Jan. 1918) p. 3.

resort in Britain.[77] The numbers of travellers to the Continent quickly returned to and then exceeded pre-war levels. From 1921 to 1930 the number of people from Great Britain travelling abroad rose from 559,905 to 1,058,936, before falling away with the onset of the Great Depression.[78] Their numbers rose again in the late 1930s, reaching a peak of 1,436,727 in 1937.[79]

The war played a significant role in the nature of travel in the inter-war period. The Workers' Travel Association and the Wayfarers' Travel Agency were set up with the primary purpose of using travel to promote international peace.[80] Over seven million visits were made to the Imperial War Museum in the 1920s and 1930s, and the war memorials which were erected in towns and villages throughout the country were described as tourist attractions.[81] More importantly, travel to the battlefields was a significant feature of post-war tourism. A 1936 study of the tourist industry noted that among the explanations for the post-war rise in tourism was the fact that 'many hundreds of thousands of people, from all parts of the world, rushed to the scene of war during the years immediately following 1918 merely to satisfy a morbid curiosity', in addition to the 'large numbers who had lost relatives in action, and who wished to visit the battlefields to pay their last homage to the departed ones'.[82]

Travel companies seized the opportunities to offer tours to the places which had dominated the newspapers and many people's thoughts and dreams for four years. Thomas Cook's announced two types of tours to the battlefields: the first, costing thirty-five guineas, offered maximum luxury in both the mode of travel and accommodation, while the second was a popular tour costing nine and a half guineas.[83] These tours helped Thomas Cook's to make a profit of £139,268 in 1919, which was just

77. J. Walvin, *Beside the Seaside* (London, 1978), pp. 116–18.

78. F. W. Ogilvie, *The Tourist Movement: An Economic Study* (London, 1933), p. 99.

79. E. Brunner, *Holiday Making and the Holiday Trades* (London, 1945), p. 6.

80. H. Gosling, *Up and Down Stream* (London, 1927), pp. 210–11. *Geoffrey Franklin* (London, 1933), p. 103.

81. IWM, *Annual Reports* (1922–39). J. A. Hammerton (ed.), *Wonderful Britain: Its Highways, Byways and Historic Places*, Vol. III, 22 (London, 1928–9), pp. 1017–36, 1083–1102, 1137–56.

82. Norval, *The Tourist Industry*, p. 48. See Chapter 3 for a detailed discussion of patterns of travel to the battlefields.

83. *Traveller's Gazette* LXIX (Aug. 1919), p. 13.

over the figure for 1913. Although the amount was well below the average annual profit of over £200,000 made in the 1920s it must have helped the firm to recover from the gap in its business due to the war.[84] Thomas Cook's was joined by the other major travel agencies, including Dean and Dawson Ltd, Alpine Sports Ltd, Pickfords Ltd, Polytechnic Touring Association Ltd, Frame's Tours, Lazenby's Tours, Touring Guild, British Touring Club and American Express. Railway companies also organised tours of the battlefields from the major regional centres of Great Britain.[85]

Travel agents were not the only group who were able to take commercial advantage of tourism to the battlefields. At least thirty guidebooks to the battlefields, in English, were produced in the three-year period from 1919 to 1921. A number of other guides were published intermittently throughout the inter-war period. The most prolific producer of battlefield guides was the Michelin Tyre Company. By 1921 Michelin had produced fifteen guidebooks in English. While Michelin gave the funds received from the sale of the guides to the reconstruction of the devastated areas, the potential of the guides as advertising for the company was not lost on the rival tyre company B. F. Goodrich, who also produced a guide to the battlefields, which included eighteen pages of advertisements for their tyres.[86]

Both the Belgian and French Governments also sought to take advantage of the commercial opportunities offered by battlefield tourism to aid in rebuilding their shattered economies. *The Times* announced in February 1919 that the Office Nationale du Tourisme had divided France into areas which could be visited using services under its control, and a scheme was arranged for camp-hotels to be set up in the Arras, Rheims and Verdun regions until proper accommodation could be provided.[87] A supplement to *The Times* in September 1919, sponsored by the Office Nationale du Tourisme, described the potential for touring in France, stressing that a 'visit to France is for ever more a pious visit to the ramparts where the civilisation of the world was defended'.[88] The Belgian Government asked the British Government to specify

84. Brendon, *Thomas Cook*, p. 259.

85. *Railway and Travel Monthly* XX (June 1920), p. 424.

86. B. F. Goodrich Co. Ltd, *Guide to the War Regions of France and Belgium* (London, n.d.), pp. 9–27.

87. *The Times*, 14 Feb. 1919.

88. *The Times*, 6 Sept. 1919.

the areas of the battlefield it wanted to be preserved in their ruined state to act both as a reminder to future generations and to 'attract the foreigner and Belgian tourist to an otherwise bare and poor countryside'.[89]

Religious pilgrimages were also popular in the inter-war years. Annette Becker argues that in France there was a rise in pilgrimages to Roman Catholic shrines such as Lourdes or to local shrines, both during the war and in its aftermath.[90] While it is not certain that the war directly encouraged Roman Catholic pilgrimages in Great Britain, in the years after the war Roman Catholic pilgrimages were renewed with a new fervour. The diocese of Liverpool began organising annual pilgrimages to Lourdes in 1923.[91] In 1928 60,000 people made a pilgrimage to Carfin Grotto in Lanarkshire, to see a replica of the Grotto at Lourdes. The replica included a stone which a party of Scottish pilgrims had brought back from there in 1920.[92] The link between the war and Roman Catholic pilgrimages was much closer in the case of the Roman Catholic ex-serviceman's pilgrimage to Lourdes in September 1934. A party of 500 British ex-servicemen joined with 100,000 ex-servicemen from both the former Allied and Central powers in a pilgrimage to Lourdes to pray for peace.[93]

The success of Lourdes pilgrimages can only have been enhanced by the extraordinary cure of the ex-serviceman John Traynor, who was severely wounded by machine-gun fire at Gallipoli. In 1923 he was discharged from hospital as an incurable case. He decided to join the Liverpool diocese pilgrimage to Lourdes. When he arrived there he suffered from epilepsy and an atrophied arm, his skull had been trepanned and he had partial paralysis in his legs. By the time he left Lourdes the epilepsy had disappeared and he had the full use of his arm and had regained the ability to walk. The news of his miraculous cure preceded him to Liverpool, where the police had to charge an excited

89. IWGC, K. Lyon to the Secretary of the Battle Exploits Committee, 16 July 1920, PRO, WO 32 - 5569.

90. A. Becker, *La Guerre et La Foi: De la Mort à la Mémoire* (Paris, 1994), pp. 62–5, 134–5.

91. A. Dahlberg, 'The Body as a Principle of Holism: Three Pilgrimages to Lourdes', in J. Eade and M. J. Sallnow (eds), *Contesting the Sacred: The Anthropology of Christian Pilgrimage* (London, 1991), p. 36.

92. *Daily Mail*, 1 Oct. 1928.

93. *Pilgrim's Scrip* (Nov. 1934).

crowd at the Railway Station to create a passage for him and his wife to pass.[94]

There was also a renewal of the practice of Anglican pilgrimage in these years. This was essentially an Anglo-Catholic phenomenon, but it is intriguing that it arose after the war.[95] It is possible that the increased exposure to Roman Catholicism in France during the war may have encouraged this development. In 1924 two hundred Anglo-Catholic pilgrims travelled to the Holy Land. While there, a service was conducted among the British graves at the cemetery in Jerusalem.[96] The first Anglican pilgrimage to Walsingham took place in 1923, and cathedrals became an increasingly popular place of pilgrimage in the late 1920s.[97] These culminated in the Great Cathedral Pilgrimage in 1934. Pilgrims paid for tickets and travelled to cathedrals in order to raise money to assist people who had fallen on hard times as a consequence of the economic slump.

Although the Great Cathedral Pilgrimage was motivated by the economic conditions of the early 1930s, there were some ties between it and the war. The stress on unity in the pilgrimage reflects the idea of the united nation, which had been such a potent wartime image.[98] Also, it commenced at Canterbury Cathedral, in a service which coincided with an annual British Legion service to return the flags used on Armistice Day to the care of the Cathedral.[99] In addition, some of the cathedrals the pilgrims visited were linked to other pilgrimages to places associated with the war. The guide to the cathedrals produced for the pilgrims referred to both the Unknown Warrior's grave in Westminster Abbey and the grave of Nurse Edith Cavell in Norwich Cathedral. In describing St Albans Cathedral the guide drew an analogy between the experience of the saint after whom the Cathedral was named and the death of Edith Cavell.[100]

94. R. Cranston, *The Mystery of Lourdes* (London, 1956), pp. 118-23.

95. Davies, *Pilgrimage*, pp. 152-60.

96. S. Dark, *The Anglo-Catholic Pilgrimage: A Diary of the Great Adventure* (London, 1924).

97. Davies, *Pilgrimage*, pp. 156-8.

98. R. Lloyd, *The Church of England in the Twentieth Century*, II (London, 1950), pp. 244-7.

99. *British Legion Journal*, 13 (June 1934), p. 429.

100. F. Irving Taylor, *The Cathedral Pilgrimage* (London, 1934), pp. 154, 232, 181-2.

The links with the war were much closer in the case of the national 'Peace Pilgrimage' which took place from May until 18 June 1926. It was organised by the Women's International League for Peace and Freedom, who were assisted by twenty-eight other women's groups. Thousands of women participated in the pilgrimage, which attempted to force the British Government to sign the Optional Clause of the International Court of Justice, which entailed accepting compulsory jurisdiction in all disputes of a legal nature. The Pilgrimage also called for a World Disarmament Conference. The pilgrims passed through many small towns throughout Great Britain, where meetings were held, and in all but one instance the people voted to support the objects of the pilgrims. The names of the towns which had voted for the proposals were displayed on staffs carried by the pilgrims. The pilgrimage was closely linked with the memory of the war. One banner, carried by a pilgrim, showed a woman gazing at the crosses in a war cemetery, while another showed a boy playing with toy soldiers, and was titled 'The Unknown Warrior'. Many of the women who participated had lost loved ones in the war, while the *Daily Herald* told the story of a man in Hookwood who presented the pilgrims with a bunch of flowers with the inscription: 'May your peace efforts succeed from those bereaved in the War.'[101]

However, the pilgrimages which received the most attention in the British newspapers were those to the battlefields, cemeteries and memorials of the war. In 1928 the *Morning Post* claimed that:

> Since the War there has been a revival of that reverent and adventurous spirit which inspired the Pilgrimages of the Middle Ages. The Ypres Pilgrims have set an example that may well be followed for many generations, and the sons and grandsons of the men who fought in the Great War will likely enough visit on certain dates marked with a white stone, the battlefields where England and the Empire were saved.[102]

Large pilgrimages, such as the British Legion pilgrimage, in which 10,000 pilgrims participated from 4 to 8 August 1928, and the pilgrimages to the Cenotaph and the grave of the Unknown

101. *Daily Herald*, 19, 21 June 1926. *Manchester Guardian*, 15 June 1926.
102. *Morning Post*, 6 Aug. 1928.

Warrior in London in November 1920, were major events which dominated the front pages of both the London and provincial newspapers for days. Even smaller pilgrimages were often the subject of stories in the newspapers. *The Times* printed accounts of pilgrimages organised by charitable organisations such as the St Barnabas Society and ex-servicemen's pilgrimages, as well as detailed accounts of visits to the battlefields.

The language of pilgrimage dominated the way in which battlefield travel was described and imagined. Sites such as Ypres or Newfoundland Park on the Somme, or the war cemeteries and memorials to the missing, were often described as sacred places. One traveller asserted: 'It is hallowed ground, this country of the graves.'[103] The words of John Oxenham greeted visitors to Newfoundland Park: 'Tread Softly here, go reverently and slow'; while a sign was set up in Ypres advising travellers that it was 'Holy Ground' [Figure 1].[104] Such an *ad hoc* response to the

Figure 1. A Notice on the Cloth at Ypres which reads: 'This is Holy Ground. No stone of this fabric may be taken away. It is a heritage for all civilised people. 3 August 1919 Town Mayor', bequeathed by Mr A. T. Sharp, AWM J00629.

103. 'War Graves in Flanders', *Round Table* XVI (Mar. 1926), p. 317.

104. V. C. Hyde, 'The Greatest No More War Advertisement', *British Legion Journal*, 16 (Feb. 1937), pp. 293–4. B. Willson, *From Quebec to Piccadilly and Other Places: Some Anglo-Canadian Memories* (London, 1929), p. 305.

sacred quality of the battlefields was crystallised on the French battlefields. At the Ossuary at Fort Douaumont on the battlefield of Verdun the figure of an angel with her finger to her lips motioned pilgrims to silence. At Notre Dame de Lorette an inscription on the tower of the Ossuary addressed travellers:

> You who pass as pilgrims near their tombs,
> Climbing their Calvary and its bloody roads,
> Hear the clamor of the hecatombs:
> 'People be united, be human.'[105]

Although it is clear that battlefield tours and pilgrimages were an important feature of post-war travel, it is difficult to ascertain who participated in them. When describing large pilgrimages such as the 1928 British Legion pilgrimage journalists often claimed that people from all parts of Great Britain and all walks of life took part.[106] There is no doubt that people from all levels of society were described as and referred to themselves as pilgrims. The visits of poor bereaved relatives to the war cemeteries arranged by organisations such as the Church Army and the Salvation Army were usually called pilgrimages. Equally, when King George V travelled to the cemeteries on the Western Front in 1922, he stressed that 'he should go as a private pilgrim with no trappings of State nor pomp of ceremony'.[107] The British Prime Minister Stanley Baldwin addressed a telegram to the President of France in similar terms, stating that 'still labouring under the loss of a generation of our youth, I felt the need of making this pilgrimage in privacy and meditation' before he visited France.[108]

However, in practice certain groups were most clearly identified with pilgrimages. One of the most important of these was bereaved relatives. Many of them travelled with voluntary organisations, including the Church Army, the Salvation Army and the YMCA. All three organisations had assisted relatives to visit critically injured soldiers during the war; and once it concluded, they transferred their energies to helping the bereaved. Two new benevolent groups, the St Barnabas Society and the War Graves Association, were also set up in the first years after

105. A. Becker, 'From Death to Memory: The National Ossuaries in France after the Great War', *History and Memory* 5 (Fall/Winter 1993), p. 42.

106. *The Times*, 5 Aug. 1928.

107. F. Fox, *The King's Pilgrimage* (London, 1922).

108. *The Times*, 5 June 1928.

the war to assist bereaved relatives to visit war graves. The St Barnabas Society was founded by a New Zealand padre, Reverend H. Mullineux, who had served with the New Zealand forces during the war. During the 1920s the Society took parties of pilgrims to Italy, Greece, Gallipoli and the Holy Land, as well as to the old Western Front. The War Graves Association was a very different organisation. It was founded by Mrs S. A. Smith in Leeds, who had lost her son in the war. At first she attempted to set up an association to return the bodies of the dead to England; but when this failed, she organised a group of subscribers who assisted relatives to visit the war cemeteries. During the inter-war years they organised a pilgrimage every Whitsuntide.[109] The Association was largely limited to Yorkshire and the North of England, and appears to have had strong links with the savings clubs which were set up to save money for holidays.[110]

Ex-servicemen were another group who were closely associated with the practice of battlefield pilgrimages. A number of ex-servicemen's groups, including the Ypres League and the British Legion, organised pilgrimages in this period. The Ypres League was founded by a Canadian, Beckles Willson, who had been a writer of propaganda during the war.[111] In 1919 he campaigned against what he saw as the desecration of Ypres by tourists and the tourist industry.[112] He claimed that he was inspired by the opportunity he saw to draw the men who fought in the defence of Ypres together with bereaved relatives of the men who died there in a common association. The two principal objects of the League were to 'commemorate the Immortal Defence of the Salient, and to keep alive that spirit of fellowship which was so powerful a lever and so beautiful an element in the war'. Pilgrimages of ex-servicemen and bereaved relatives were considered to be an important means of furthering these objects.[113] In the late 1920s and 1930s the British Legion also

109. *The Times*, 10 June 1936; *Yorkshire Post*, 10 June 1936.

110. J. Walvin, *Leisure and Society 1830–1950* (London and New York, 1978), p. 142.

111. A. R. Young, '"We Throw the Torch": Canadian Memorials of the Great War and the Mythology of Heroic Sacrifice', *Journal of Canadian Studies*, 24 (Winter 1989/90), p. 11.

112. Willson, *From Quebec to Piccadilly and Other Places*, p. 305.

113. G. E. De Trafford, 'Lest We Forget', *A Journal of Remembrance*, 1 (Dec. 1931), p. 78.

played an increasingly significant role in the organisation of pilgrimages. The pilgrimage to Belgium and France organised in 1928 was and remains the largest British pilgrimage to the old First World War battlefields. After 1928 pilgrimages were organised at the area, branch and sub-branch levels, and in 1934 the Legion printed a series of brief guides to the battlefields in the *British Legion Journal* to assist ex-servicemen who wished to visit them independently.[114] In the late 1930s the British Legion also began to organise visits to war cemeteries for bereaved relatives, a service in which the Legion would achieve a predominant role after 1945.[115]

Organisations such as the Ypres League and the British Legion only represented a small proportion of the men who served in the war. The membership of the Legion never exceeded 500,000. This has been explained by the Legion's identification with the values of the upper- and middle-class officers who provided its leadership in the 1920s and 1930s.[116] The Ypres League was also a bastion of traditional values. The close link between the League and the upper levels of society was confirmed when the King and the Prince of Wales became the League's Patrons and Sir John French, the Commander of the BEF in the first years of the war, its first President. These organisations were unlikely to have appealed to those working-class ex-servicemen and other ex-servicemen who did not identify with these values. Battalion and other unit associations offered an alternative. In the late 1920s and 1930s many of them also organised pilgrimages to the battlefields. However, all of these organisations shared a common commitment to the active recollection of the war and wartime comradeship. Many ex-servicemen appear to have wished to forget their wartime experiences and to return to their civilian lives in the inter-war years.[117] Consequently, those ex-servicemen who participated in the battlefield tours and pilgrimages organ-

114. 'By Charabanc over the Battlefields', *British Legion Journal* (June–Nov. 1934).

115. *British Legion Journal*, 18 (Sept. 1938), p. 94.

116. G. J. De Groot, *Blighty: British Society in the Era of the Great War* (London and New York, 1996), pp. 268–9. C. C. Kimball, 'The Ex-Service Movement in England and Wales, 1916–1930', Ph.D. thesis, Stanford University, 1990, p. 181.

117. J. Bourke, *Dismembering the Male: Men's Bodies, Britain and the Great War* (London, 1996), p. 155.

ised by the Legion, the Ypres League and other ex-servicemen's groups probably represented the minority who wished to relive their wartime experiences or to renew wartime bonds and comradeship.

A further distinguishing characteristic of battlefield pilgrims and tourists was that they needed both the money and the time to be able to undertake a visit to France or Belgium. The St Barnabas Society calculated that the costs of one of its pilgrimages was at least £4.[118] The costs of a battlefield tour could be greater, because tourists usually stayed in hotels rather than hostels, and had to make their own travel arrangements. One traveller calculated that the costs for two people to visit the battlefields of the Somme for a week would be at least £20.[119] For the majority of people these were significant sums. For most of the inter-war period the average industrial wage for men and boys was only £3 per week.[120] A British Institute of Public Opinion Survey published in 1939 showed that only one-third of workers earning £4 per week or less could afford to go away at all.[121] Also travellers required the time to visit the battlefields. As late as 1937 only four million workers out of a workforce of eighteen and a half million earning £250 per annum or less were entitled to paid holidays.[122] Consequently, those members of the working class who could afford the costs of travel to the battlefields could only visit them during holidays such as Easter, Whitsuntide and the August bank holiday.

In response to the costs of travel to Belgium and France there were repeated requests in the House of Commons for the Government to provide free travel for relatives in the early 1920s and even as late as 1930.[123] The Government determined that it could not afford to pay the costs of assisting poor relatives, which it calculated could be as high as £2,000,000.[124] In the early 1920s

118. *Daily Mail*, 2 June 1924.

119. *Leeds Mercury*, 7 July 1924.

120. J. Stevenson, *British Society 1914–45* (Harmondsworth, 1984), p. 120.

121. Brunner, *Holiday Making and the Holiday Trades*, p. 18.

122. J. A. R. Pimlott, *The Englishman's Holiday: A Social History* (Hassocks, 1976, first published 1947), pp. 214–21.

123. Hansard, 110 HC Deb. 5s. 12 Nov. 1918, p. 2477; 112 HC Deb. 5s. 13 Feb. 1919, p. 272; 134 HC Deb. 5s. 18 Nov. 1920, p. 2107; 164 HC Deb. 5s. 4 June 1923, p. 1770; 242 HC Deb. 5s. 30 July 1930, pp. 533–4.

124. Hansard, 116 HC Deb. 5s. 20 May 1919, p. 178.

a small sum was given to voluntary organisations, such as the YMCA, the Salvation Army, the Church Army and the St Barnabas Society, to facilitate their travel programs, but it was suspended in 1923.[125] While these organisations offered limited financial assistance to poor bereaved relatives, the demand would have outweighed their ability to provide such assistance. Also, bereaved relatives may have been unwilling to go through the process of proving that they needed financial assistance, which could require a statement from their local clergyman and the local pension office in order for them to receive such help.[126] People also banded together in local savings clubs, such as the Hendon Excursion Savings Association, to raise money to help poor pilgrims travel to the battlefields.[127] Despite these efforts it is likely that a significant proportion of battlefield tourists and pilgrims would have come from the upper and middle classes and the better-paid members of the working class.

One consequence of the difficulties of overseas travel was the importance of pilgrimages to places associated with the war in Great Britain. One of the earliest domestic pilgrimages was organised by the Australian Natives Association and the Anglo-Australian Association on 25 April 1918 to the graves of Australian and New Zealand soldiers in England.[128] In November 1923 there was also a pilgrimage involving 30,000 people to the grave of Nurse Edith Cavell in Norwich Cathedral,[129] while the official guidebook to the Scottish National War Memorial in Edinburgh described a pilgrimage around the Memorial.[130] The largest pilgrimages were to the Cenotaph and the grave of the Unknown Warrior in London; these involved over a million pilgrims, and are the subject of Chapter 2.

125. Hansard 164 HC Deb. 5s. 4 June 1923, p. 1770.

126. Church Army, 'Guide for Graves Pilgrims', PRO, WO 32 - 5879.

127. Minutes of Proceedings of the IWGC, 26 Sept. 1934, NAC, RG 38 Vol. 349.

128. *British-Australasian*, XXXVIII (May 1918), p. 3.

129. *Eastern Daily Press*, 13 Nov. 1923.

130. I. Hay, *Their Name Liveth: The Book of the Scottish National War Memorial* (London, 1931).

The Dichotomy between Battlefield Tourism and Pilgrimage

In the descriptions of battlefield tours the language of pilgrimage merged with that of tourism. The travel magazine published by Thomas Cook's claimed that: 'To all thoughtful people Easter will appear an appropriate time for visiting those consecrated fields wherein Freedom endured the agony of her Gethsemane, and but for the sublime heroism of men would have found her Golgotha. The battle areas will therefore be visited by the tourist not as a show but as a shrine.'[131] Similarly, the description of an excursion to the battlefields organised by the Workers' Travel Association in 1928 emphasised the cost of the war and asked potential travellers: '"The Salient" will always be a memory in British history, where, in the mud and dust of Flanders the line was maintained, but at a fearful cost, as is indicated by the long succession of British cemeteries which are seen. Is it not worth while to make a pilgrimage to this spot?'[132] As late as 1936 an article on holidays in Belgium advised that in 'planning a Belgian holiday the Coast should provide the tonic. From a seaside base a pilgrimage should be made to Ypres, and visits paid to Ghent and Bruges.'[133]

However, on the battlefields there was a tension between the sacred and the profane, or what George Mosse has termed the 'trivialisation' of the war experience.[134] The threat posed by the behaviour and the imagined behaviour of tourists was a recurring theme of descriptions of battlefield travel. An attempt was made in the House of Commons to exclude tourists from the battlefields until the relatives of the dead had visited their graves.[135] In December 1919 Rudyard Kipling issued a plea to travellers to show reverence when they were on the battlefields. He called on them to remember that it is 'holy-consecrated in every part by the freely offered lives of men, and for that reason not to be overrun with levity'.[136] In 1925 questions were asked in the House of Commons about the exploitation of British pilgrims by French and Belgian

131. *Traveller's Gazette*, LXX (Mar. 1920), p. 3.
132. Workers' Travel Association Ltd., *1928 Holidays* (n.p., n.d.), p. 18.
133. *Field,* CLXVIII (July 1936), p. 125.
134. Mosse, *Fallen Soldiers*, pp. 152-6.
135. Hansard, 117 HC Deb. 5s. 1 July 1919, p. 751.
136. *The Times,* 5 Dec. 1919.

tourist agencies.[137] Again in 1927 the St Barnabas Society accused an unnamed travel agent of deliberately buying all the available accommodation in Ypres and of preventing real pilgrims from staying in the city.[138]

Unease at the presence of tourists on the battlefields was widely felt, and influenced travel companies and guidebooks. The brochure for Thomas Cook's tour to the Somme quoted Kipling's reminder to tourists that it 'rests with the individual tourist to have respect for the spirit that lies upon all that land of desolation and to walk through it with reverence'.[139] Similarly Muirhead's guide to the battlefields observed that it should be superfluous to remind the visitor 'that the ground he is visiting is holy ground, consecrated by the heroism and the grief of nations'.[140]

One explanation for the growth of this fear of the tourist is the active role of the newspapers in promoting it. Many articles were published about the threat of desecration faced by Ypres. H. J. Greenwall wrote that he had expected that Ypres would be a place where widows and orphans would come on pious pilgrimages. Instead, the pilgrims have come, but they are 'morbid seekers after sensation. Vandals. Ghouls of the battlefield.'[141] His comments led to a flurry of letters to the *Daily Express* deploring the desecration of Ypres.[142] A poem 'trippers in Belgium' accepted that it was right that people should see the scars of the battlefields, but it questioned:

> Yet is it well that high and sacred things,
> The scenes of martyrdom, the hero's grave,
> Should furnish forth a trippers' holiday?[143]

While in 'Sacrilege' another poet asked:

> A show a place for morbid minds!
> Can there be eyes that would not gaze

137. Hansard, 184 HC Deb. 5s. 12 June 1925, p. 2379.

138. St Barnabas Society, *Menin Gate Pilgrimage* (London, *c.*1927), p. 2.

139. Thomas Cook, 'How to See Paris and its Environs and the Battlefields', (*c.*1925), Thomas Cook Archive.

140. F. Muirhead, *Belgium and the Western Front, British and American* (London, 1920), p. lxiv.

141. *Daily Express*, 23 Sept. 1919.

142. *Daily Express*, 24, 25, 29 Sept.; 6, 8 Oct. 1919.

143. *Evening News*, 18 June 1919.

> On Ypres with a thought that finds
> Great holiness among her ways?[144]

The language used to describe the threat posed by the battlefield tourist also drew upon pre-war attacks on tourists, concentrating on their vulgarity and ignorance. Rowland Fielding was disgusted when he conducted an American Army doctor over the old Loos battlefield, because the doctor was entirely absorbed in collecting souvenirs. He wrote to his wife: 'It is horrifying to see this sacred ground desecrated in this way, and still more so to think when the cheap tripper is let loose. With his spit he will saturate the ground that has been soaked with the blood of our soldiers.'[145] P. R. Butler advised pilgrims to seek out the solitude of the Lille Gate in Ypres in order to avoid the 'inanities of trippers', while J. C. Lewis likened Ypres to Wembley, because of the 'unattractive trippers piloting their still more unattractive children around the points of interest'.[146] The emphasis on the vulgarity of trippers was predicated upon the superiority in judgement and taste of the observer.

A similar sense of superiority underlay the portrayal of tourists as ignorant and unthinking. E. F. Williams described the arrival of such a party in Ypres as follows:

> In they come with a rattle and a clatter through the Menin Gate, all packed together in huge char-à-bancs, and after a raucous voiced guide has pointed out the very obvious Cloth Hall ruins, they are whirled away again to one of the show places, perhaps Hill 60, and when they get back home they think they have seen Ypres and the Salient, and perhaps begin to wonder what all the fuss was about.[147]

Another writer told the story of a tourist who asked a war graves gardener what the column of stone was at a crossroads on the old Loos Battlefield. When told that it was the Memorial to the Fifty-fifth West Lancashire Division, he asked: 'But why did they put it here of all places, right off the beaten track?'[148]

144. *Daily Express*, 24 Sept. 1919.

145. R. Fielding, *War Letters to a Wife, France and Flanders 1915–1919* (London, 1929), p. 367.

146. P. R. Butler, 'Twenty-One Years After', *Blackwood's Magazine*, CCXXXVIII (Dec. 1935), p. 838. J. C. Lewis, 'A View of France and Flanders in 1928', *Household Brigade Magazine* (Winter, 1928/9), pp. 18–20.

147. E. F. Williams, 'Ypres Calling', *Ypres Times*, 3 (Apr. 1927), p. 153.

148. 'The Loos Battlefield Revisited', in E. Swinton (ed.), *Twenty Years After: The Battlefields of 1914–18, Then and Now*, Vol. 1 (London, 1936-1937), p. 531.

The dichotomy between the tourist and the pilgrim represented more than a sense of social superiority over the people who joined organised tours. It also expressed the belief that the wartime sacrifice offered by the fallen was sacred and that the nation was obligated to respect that sacrifice. Such a belief privileged the grief of the bereaved and the experiences of ex-servicemen. Pilgrims respected the dead by attempting to understand the deeper meanings underlying these sites. Wilfred Ewart wrote that for the pilgrim it is 'necessary to project oneself onto a particular condition of mind in order to acquire something of the atmosphere and significance of Ypres . . . Unless of course you are a "tourist" who goes to gape at a battlefield (from a charabanc) as he would gape at a Cathedral or a criminal, his soul being packed in behind with the luggage.'[149]

Such a perception of the war was threatened by the commercialisation of the battlefields where these men had died and the graves where they were buried. A poem by a British serviceman, Philip Johnston, in January 1918 satirised the commercial exploitation of the battlefields:

> Ladies and Gentlemen this is High Wood, . . .
> You are requested kindly not to touch
> Or to take away the comp'ny's property
> As souvenirs you'll find we have on sale
> A large variety all guaranteed.
> As I was saying, all is as it was,
> This is an unknown British officer;
> The tunic having lately rotted off,
> Please follow me - this way . . . the *path* sir, *please*,
> The ground which was secured at great expense,
> The company keeps absolutely untouched,
> And in that dug-out (genuine) we provide
> Refreshments at a reasonable rate.
> You are requested not to leave about
> Paper or ginger-beer bottles, or orange peel,
> There are waste-paper baskets at the gate.[150]

One pilgrim refused to use the services of a travel agency because 'the thought of such a thing being turned into a money-making

149. W. Ewart, 'After Four Years: The Old Road to Ypres', *Cornhill Magazine*, XLIX (Dec. 1920), p. 734.
150. *Nation*, XXII (Feb. 1918), p. 618.

business was unendurable to me'.[151] The National Federation of Disabled and Demobilised Soldiers and Sailors even resolved not to organise pilgrimages to the battlefields, because the 'Federation was not out to make money out of those who had died'.[152]

The distinction between the tourist and the pilgrim also drew upon and in some instances reconfirmed the language and emotions underlying the wartime divide between the front and the home front. This divide was a recurring presence in the interwar years, and in particular in the literature of the 'war books boom' in the years 1928 to 1932. In *Good-bye to All That* Robert Graves wrote: 'England looked strange to us returned soldiers. We could not understand the war-madness that ran wild everywhere, looking for a pseudo-military outlet. The civilians talked a foreign language; and it was newspaper language. I found serious conversation with my parents all but impossible.'[153]

Ex-servicemen's groups such as the Comrades of the Great War and the National Federation of Disabled and Demobilised Soldiers and Sailors both identified the tourist with the war profiteer, who had not participated in the sacrifices required to win the war.[154] The divide is also evident in a number of ex-servicemen's accounts of their return to the battlefields. In the novel *We'll Shift Our Ground* an ex-serviceman explained that he gave up being a battlefield guide because he saw a ghost:

> It was my own face in my shaving-mirror, which I suddenly saw like someone else's; and what was the trouble with it, to my notion was that it began to look out of life. As though rattling out my rigmarole to the non-combatants who came to see the crucifix that had been miraculously preserved and the dug-out with the caricature of the Kaiser declaring war, had disqualified me from the old trench companionship, without making me an ordinary being.[155]

H. M. Tomlinson concludes his war novel *All Our Yesterdays* with the return of two ex-servicemen to the battlefields of the Somme. There they see a party of tourists whose visit to the

151. *Country Life*, XLVIII (Sept. 1920), p. 318.

152. *DSS Bulletin*, 2 (June 1920), p. 71.

153. R. Graves, *Goodbye to All That: An Autobiography* (London, 1929), p. 283.

154. *Comrades Journal*, II (June 1920), p. 4. *DSS Bulletin*, 2 (Apr. 1920).

155. E. Blunden and S. Norman, *We'll Shift Our Ground* or *Two on a Tour* (London, 1933), p. 113.

battlefield is a time of fun and frivolity. The behaviour of the tourists shocks one of the veterans, who says to his companion: '"There's High Wood. There's the Butte. And you see what it all means to them. They allowed it to come, and they kept it going, and now the bitter end is a souvenir for them. It is not easy to forgive them."'[156]

The divide between the front and the home front often merged into a divide between men and women. The belief that the wartime experience of men on the battlefields was something which women could not understand was often reflected in popular fiction and the newspapers.[157] It was also evident in descriptions of battlefield travel. In the best-selling author Elinor Glyn's romantic novel *Six Days* the hero, Major David Lamont, escorts his new love Laline Lester over the battlefields in France. The description of their journey assumes that Laline is an outsider to the war experience. When confronted by the cemeteries, shattered trees and ruined villages she admits to David:

> 'Oh! And to think that I laughed and danced through it all - and only played at war work! Of course Of course, we never understood.' 'That's it,' said David and there was a mist in his eyes. 'Dear France.'[158]

There were also instances of ex-servicemen focusing on women to illustrate the gulf created by these men's greater sensitivity to the war experience. Wilfred Ewart wrote that in Lens 'War grinned out of the immediate past and on every side, but this made no difference to the 1920 "flapper" who eyed the young mechanics in blue overalls and "got off" as frequently as in the Bois de Boulogne.'[159] John Gibbons described how his attention was drawn to a young woman who was a member of a party of tourists in Ypres because 'I was wondering why on earth she had to wear rather highly coloured beach-pyjamas to Do Our Heroes' Graves, but I supposed it was the Gay Continent and all that'.[160]

156. H. M. Tomlinson, *All Our Yesterdays* (London, 1930), p. 538.

157. C. M. Tylee, *The Great War and Women's Consciousness: Images of Militarism and Womanhood in Women's Writings, 1914–64* (Houndsmills and London, 1990), p. 184, discusses this theme in women's writing about the war.

158. E. Glyn, *Six Days* (London, 1924), pp. 104–5.

159. W. Ewart, 'Vimy Heights to Auburs Ridge', *Ypres Times*, 1 (July 1922), p. 94.

160. J. Gibbons, *Roll On, Next War! The Common Man's Guide to Army Life* (London, 1935), p. 100.

Although the imagery of a divide between the front and the home front and between men and women underlies the dichotomy between the tourist and the pilgrim, this imagery needs to be read in the context of people's response to mass death and bereavement after the war. A distinction was commonly drawn between women as a symbol of those civilians who did not understand ex-servicemen and their experiences, and women as bereaved mothers and widows. One ex-serviceman described meeting a mother crying before her son's grave and realising 'how terribly the mothers of England must have suffered during the war, not only by day, but in the long reach of the night, when fears and torment of mind prevent sleep'.[161] Through bereavement women shared in the sacrifice which was considered to be a fundamental feature of the war experience, and thus earned the right to be classed as pilgrims. Ian Hay even wrote that the true pilgrims on the St Barnabas pilgrimage to Salonika and Gallipoli were the mothers, wives and sweethearts of the dead, not the ex-servicemen, because it was the women who mourned the dead.[162]

In her novel *Honourable Estate* Vera Brittain contended that the scars of the war were shared by women and that their visits to the graves of the dead were an important means of coming to terms with the war experience. The heroine Ruth falls in love with an American serviceman, Eugene, who dies in 1918 on the Argonne. When she is first told that his grave has been completed at Romagne-sous-Montfaucon she is unable to visit it. She tells her close friend Denis: 'Some day I shall have to go to Romagne; I shan't feel I've really said good-bye to Eugene till I've been there. But it's too soon at present. I'm still not a whole person, and I can't go yet.' Only when she has come to terms with her war experiences and has therefore agreed to marry Denis, can she make a pilgrimage to Eugene's grave. After visiting his grave she dreams of Eugene seeing her off at a railway station in which he smiles and salutes her as she travels away from him to begin the next phase of her life.[163]

161. E. M. Channing-Renton, 'The Somme Battlefields and War Cemeteries, Summer 1926', *Ypres Times*, 3 (Oct. 1927), p. 89.

162. I. Hay, *The Ship of Remembrance* (London, *c.*1926), p. 12.

163. V. Brittain, *Honourable Estate: A Novel of Transition* (London, 1936), pp. 497, 533–4.

Further, the divide existed more as an expression of sentiment than a statement of reality. While it was possible to describe the 'tourist' as a symbol of those who had profited from the war or who were oblivious to the sacrifices offered by the dead, bereaved relatives and ex-servicemen, there were few people in reality who had not been touched by the war. Many would have known friends or relatives who had been killed or injured in the fighting or who were bereaved as a consequence of it. Therefore, it is likely that most travellers would have identified with pilgrims rather than tourists. In *We'll Shift Our Ground*, which was based on Edmund Blunden and Sylvia Norman's experiences when they visited the battlefields in 1932, Duncan, an ex-serviceman, returns to the Western Front to try to come to terms with his war experiences. He discourages Chloe from coming with him, because she cannot understand what he is returning to. Chloe asserts the importance of the war for women as well: '"It was my war too," she answered in the same quiet voice, "although I never came here. All this, in a queer way, is my background; all the emptiness of it."'.[164]

Conclusion

In the period before the Great War and during the inter-war years there was an unprecedented growth in travel. These years are often associated with the development of the tourist industry. While this was a significant feature of the period, there was also a remarkable resurgence in the practice of pilgrimage. The simultaneous growth of both tourism and pilgrimage challenges a linear model of change which charts the replacement of traditional forms of travel by modern ones. During the war many people anticipated that once it ended its battlefields would also become a popular destination for travellers. These future journeys were frequently described as pilgrimages to a sacred place. The use of the language of pilgrimage developed as part of a wartime search for meaning in the face of the enormous casualties of the war. It was also encouraged by the description of the war as a spiritual struggle and by the example provided by America and, more importantly, France. In the years after the war large numbers of travellers visited the battlefields, as well as

164. Blunden and Norman, *We'll Shift Our Ground*, p. 126.

other places linked to the memory of the war. The rhetoric of battlefield travel assumed that the entire nation was participating in these journeys. In practice battlefield pilgrimages were dominated by two groups: ex-servicemen and bereaved relatives. It was also limited to those people, predominantly from the middle and upper classes, who could afford to pay at least £4 per person to join a tour or pilgrimage.

The language of pilgrimage also served to distinguish between different types of traveller. In the period before the Great War the distinction between the tourist and the traveller offered a means for individual travellers to assert their social superiority to other travellers. The post-war dichotomy between the tourist and the pilgrim bore similarities to the distinction between tourists and travellers. However, it also expressed a perception of the war which stressed the sacred qualities of the fallen and the obligation of the nation to remember and respect their sacrifice. Tourists and the commercialism they represented threatened to trivialise this perception of the war. For some ex-servicemen the dichotomy between pilgrims and tourists also expressed a belief that the divide between the front and the home front persisted long after the Armistice of 1918. At the same time as this language served to divide, it could also unite. While the divide between the front and the home front excluded the majority of women, the definition of a 'pilgrim' joined all those civilians who had been bereaved by the war and others who had been touched by it with ex-servicemen.

2

'Just What 'Ave We Won?' Pilgrimages to the Cenotaph and the Grave of the Unknown Warrior

> 'Yer tellin' me this means peace 'as come,' she shrilled, pointing at the Cenotaph. 'Yer wants us all to remember it an' carry on. Well, carry on. The old man an' two boys are, in Flander, an' I'm wiv 'em. I ain't 'ere at al, guv'nor. You think I am. You think you can see me, but I ain't 'ere, mister. I'm over there wiv the old man an' boys. Ain't it my plice? But yer might tell us that 'ave lost somethink, guv'nor - just what 'ave we won?'
>
> - W. R. Bird, 'From the Things That Are to the Things That Were'[1]

The Cenotaph in Whitehall and the grave of the Unknown Warrior in Westminster Abbey were the objectives of the largest pilgrimages in the inter-war years. There were two periods when the numbers of pilgrims were particularly high. The first was the pilgrimage to the temporary Cenotaph during the seven months from 19 July 1919 to January 1920. The second began on 11 November 1920, when the permanent Cenotaph was unveiled and the Unknown Warrior was buried in Westminster Abbey. The pilgrimage lasted for at least twelve months. While the high points of the pilgrimages were in the period 1919–1921, large numbers of people continued to visit both memorials as pilgrims throughout the inter-war years. Pilgrimages also remained an important feature of the ritual of Armistice Day.

The story of the conception and unveiling of the Cenotaph and the grave of the Unknown Warrior has been told many times.[2]

1. W. R. Bird, 'From the Things That Are to the Things That Were', *Veteran*, 11 (Sept. 1934), p. 15.

2. E. Homberger, 'The Story of the Cenotaph', *The Times Literary Supplement*, 896 (Nov. 1976), pp. 1429–30. K. Inglis, 'Entombing Unknown Soldiers: From

Recently scholars have also stressed the importance of the Cenotaph as a focal point for the grief of a nation confronted by mass death.[3] However, less attention has been paid to the significance of these memorials to the people who travelled to them and how their meanings were determined by popular responses to them. Rodney Mace has observed that most capital cities have a place which expresses its social and political aspirations, and argues that Trafalgar Square is that place in London. He shows how the square gained its real significance from its use by ordinary people, even though it and its monuments spoke the language of the Ruling Class.[4] In the 1920s and 1930s the Cenotaph and the grave of the Unknown Warrior temporarily replaced Trafalgar Square as the central place in London.

The public response to the temporary Cenotaph transformed it from a monument to the British victory into a place of pilgrimage. Its transformation merged the public commemoration of the war with the wartime experience of millions of people whose lives were touched by the war. In particular it came to symbolise the desire of many people for a place where they could commune with the spirit and even the spirits of the dead. The burial of the Unknown Warrior and the unveiling of the permanent Cenotaph in November 1920 and the pilgrimage which followed it were more than a funeral ceremony. They altered the symbolic focus of public commemoration of the dead. Attention moved from the individual who was to be buried, in the past either a military hero or royalty, to the common people. They ceased to be onlookers who participated in the funeral of a public figure; instead, they became pilgrims. Although the Unknown Warrior was intended to provide an alternative shrine to the Cenotaph, in practice the two memorials were closely linked. The meanings which the sites held for people were varied and complex. Both expressed an official rhetoric of heroic sacrifice which celebrated the achievements of British soldiers and

---

London and Paris to Baghdad', *History and Memory*, 5 (Fall/Winter 1993), pp. 7-31. E. Lutyens, 'The Story of the Cenotaph', *A Journal of Remembrance*, 1 (Nov. 1931), pp. 5-6.

3. D. Cannadine, 'War and Death, Grief and Mortality in Modern Britain', in J. Whaley (ed.), *Mirrors of Mortality: Studies in the Social History of Death* (London, 1981), pp. 219-26. J. M. Winter, *Sites of Memory, Sites of Mourning: The Great War in European Cultural History* (Cambridge, 1995), pp. 102-5.

4. R. Mace, *Trafalgar Square: Emblem of Empire* (London, 1976), pp. 15, 19.

commemorated their victory. At the same time they were a place to remember and mourn the dead, as well as memorials which symbolised the grief of the nation.

The Temporary Cenotaph

On 19 July 1919 a Victory March by troops from all the Allied countries was held in London on Peace Day to celebrate the signing of the Treaty of Versailles. A temporary Cenotaph was erected to represent the men who had died in the war. The monument was intended to provide a saluting point for the Allied troops and the victorious Allied leaders, Marshal Foch, Field Marshal Haig, Admiral Beatty and General Pershing. It was an austere structure, thirty-three feet high with a sarcophagus on top. There were wreaths on the front and back of the memorial and on top of the sarcophagus. The dates of the war were inscribed on it in Roman letters along with the words: 'The Glorious Dead', and its sides were lined with flags.

The decision to erect a Cenotaph was only made on 1 July 1919 at the instigation of the Prime Minister, David Lloyd George. He had learnt that the French planned to erect a great catafalque or *cénotaphe*, which the Allied troops would salute in honour of the dead during the French peace celebrations on 14 July 1919.[5] The idea was not well received. The King was uncertain.[6] Both Lord Curzon, who was the chairman of the Committee, and Sir Alfred Mond, the First Commissioner of Works and therefore in charge of the erection of the monument, were not in favour of it. Curzon felt the idea 'would be rather foreign to the spirit of our people, however much in harmony it might be with the Latin temperament'. Mond held the same views, stating that a catafalque was a 'purely Catholic idea and might not appeal to the British public generally'.[7] Similar reasons for rejecting the idea were raised at a meeting of the Cabinet on 4 July, together with concerns that 'it might not be easy for the public to assume

5. The Peace Celebrations Committee was aware of the French plan as early as 17 May 1919. Earl of Derby to Lionel Earle, 17 May 1919, PRO Work 21 - 74.

6. Minutes of a Meeting of the War Cabinet held on 4 July 1919, PRO CAB 23 - 11.

7. Peace Celebrations Committee Minutes, 1 July 1919, Curzon Papers, Oriental and India Office Collections, MSS Eur F112/316.

a properly reverential attitude'.[8] Despite this, Lloyd George prevailed, and Sir Edwin Lutyens was asked to design a temporary memorial to the dead. Ironically, the French *Cénotaphe* was not a success, and it was dismantled on 18 July, the day before Peace Day in Britain.[9]

Many people were disappointed by the Peace Day celebrations. The *Catholic Herald* wrote:

> The great peace day has come and gone.
> Some 'maffickers' have 'mafficked'.
> Much silly twaddle has been talked.
> Lloyd George and George V 'took the salute somewhere in London'.
> At Luton, Coventry and many other centres, there were outbreaks and destruction.
> The whole thing seemed unreal and indeed putrid.[10]

A number of people were opposed to the idea of celebrating victory when the pain of wartime bereavement for many remained acute. On Peace Day the *Daily Herald* published a letter from a 'broken-hearted mother' who asked: 'How will the mothers who have lost their boys spend the day while the joy bells are ringing and the people are making merry?' and answered 'Only the heartless can want a peace day.'[11]

The Cenotaph stood out from the other decorations because of its association with the memory of the dead. The high point in many descriptions of the Victory March was the salute given to the dead at the Cenotaph by individual Allied leaders and contingents of troops.[12] One woman who took part in the procession wrote to her mother that the Cenotaph 'was a *beautiful* thing absolutely simple and grand . . . We passed at the salute and in dead silence. It was appallingly choky.'[13] After the march many people chose to remain at the Cenotaph rather than go to Hyde Park for the organised entertainment. Flowers were placed at the base of the monument and men stood bare-headed, while

8. Minutes of a Meeting of the War Cabinet held on 4 July 1919, PRO CAB 23 - 11.

9. E. L. Kahn, *The Neglected Majority "Les Camoufleurs", Art History and World War I* (Lanham, 1984), pp. 151–8.

10. *Catholic Herald*, 26 July 1919.

11. *Daily Herald*, 19 July 1919.

12. E. C. Bentley, *Peace Year in the City: 1918–1919* (n.p., 1920), p. 108.

13. WRNS, 'In the Peace Procession: From a Wren to its Mother', *Englishwoman*, XLVIII (Sept. 1919), p. 204.

the women bowed low to it. In the evening the League of Arts came to the Cenotaph and sang before it. One newspaper noted that there 'is no doubt about the most impressive thing that happened yesterday. It was the salute of our dead at Whitehall. Many who were in no mood for a very exuberant celebration were able to enter into the spirit of this.'[14]

In the weeks after Peace Day increasing numbers of people came to lay wreaths at the Cenotaph in what was described in the *Review of Reviews* as a 'pilgrimage of the poor people'.[15] A correspondent for the *Evening Standard* claimed that in the week up to 1 August 1919 half a million people 'gathered round this Whitehall shrine'.[16] Many of the pilgrims came as mourners. The *Leeds Mercury* on 23 July referred to the hundreds of people who all day long 'gather round it in reverent silence. The fact that most of them wear black tells its own sad story. From a memorial it has become a shrine, its base heaped up with flowers.'[17]

The Cenotaph also captured the imagination of many ex-servicemen. On 23 July the National Federation of Discharged and Demobilised Sailors and Soldiers organised a Memorial Service in Hyde Park. Fifteen thousand ex-servicemen were joined by a huge crowd, composed primarily of bereaved relatives, in a service which was conducted by the Bishop of London. Before the service the men marched to Hyde Park, saluting the Cenotaph, in silence, as they passed by removing their hats. Once they arrived at the park four ex-servicemen approached the platform on which the Bishop stood carrying a miniature Cenotaph, 'surrounded and crowned with simple blooms', which included a card saying: 'We Honour our Dead Comrades.' Once it was deposited before the Bishop the service began.[18]

The overwhelming support for the Cenotaph influenced the Office of Works' decision to leave the temporary structure in Whitehall during the week after Peace Day, so that people coming from outside London could visit it.[19] Although Mond was

14. *Eastern Daily Press*, 21 July 1919.
15. *Review of Reviews*, LX (Aug. 1919), p. 73.
16. *Evening Standard*, 1 Aug. 1919.
17. *Leeds Mercury*, 23 July 1919.
18. *Daily Telegraph*, 28 July 1919.
19. Sir F. Baines to The General Officer Commanding, London District, 21 July 1919, PRO Work 20 - 1/3.

concerned that the temporary Cenotaph was not strong enough to survive more than ten days, Sir Frank Baines wrote a memorandum arguing that it would not be possible to dismantle the Cenotaph after only one week as 'the public are placing more and more wreaths around the base'. Sir Lionel Earle disagreed, because he felt it was 'more than probable that the public would go on placing floral tributes on this monument months hence', and suggested that the Cenotaph be removed after the following Sunday.[20] He later amended the suggested date for removal to after the August Bank Holiday, because the India Office wished to use it for a march by the contingent of Indian troops, who had been unable to arrive in time for the march on Peace Day. The question appears to have been left undecided until late August, when the intransigence of the Treasury determined the matter. They wanted the Cenotaph to remain until there was parliamentary authority for the expenditure on the proposed permanent Cenotaph.[21]

After 19 July there was a growing demand in the London and provincial newspapers for the Cenotaph to be turned into a permanent memorial to the dead. On 21 July *The Times* published a letter under the pseudonym RIP, which argued: 'The Cenotaph in Whitehall is so simple and dignified that it would be a pity to consider it merely an ephemeral erection . . . I suggest that it should be retained either in its present form or is rendered in granite or stone with bronze wreaths to take the place of the evergreens.'[22] A letter in the *Daily Express* called for the Cenotaph to remain as a 'solace to the bereaved, and as a guide and inspiration for future generations', while a visitor to the memorial was reported as saying 'if only they would leave it here for all time . . . there would never be mothers lacking to keep the spot beautiful with fresh flowers'. Another letter argued that it should be made permanent because it had been 'consecrated by the tears of many mothers'.[23]

Twenty-three members of the House of Commons sent a petition to Mond urging him to impress on the Cabinet the

20. Minutes of a Meeting of the War Cabinet, held on 30 July 1919, PRO CAB 23 - 11. Note to Sir Frank Baine's Memorandum by Sir Lionel Earle, 24 July 1919, PRO Work 20 - 1/3.

21. Sir Lionel Earle Minute to Mr Pitcher, 15 Sept. 1919, PRO Work 20 - 139.

22. *The Times*, 23 July 1919. Also see *Birmingham Post*, 23 July 1919.

23. *Daily Express*, 29 July 1919. *Daily Mail*, 23 July 1919.

desirability of re-erecting the Cenotaph on its present site.[24] Mond also appears to have supported it, drafting a letter to Sir George Riddell, a newspaper proprietor and associate of Lloyd George, expressing the hope that he would use his influence to have 'this idea pushed in the press', and that he would mention it to the Prime Minister.[25] As early as 23 July a Memorandum to Cabinet was prepared outlining the reasons for and against retaining the Cenotaph permanently on its present site.[26] On the same day a number of questions were asked in the House of Commons about the erection of a permanent Cenotaph.[27] The Cabinet met on 29 July to consider whether the Cenotaph should be rebuilt as a permanent memorial, but decided to delay their decision. Lloyd George felt there was much to be said for retaining it on its present site, because of its associations with the salute by the troops on Peace Day.[28] The Cabinet considered the proposal again on the following day. This time they decided to replace the temporary Cenotaph with a permanent replica on the same site.[29]

The Cenotaph remained in Whitehall until January 1920. Throughout the period from August to January large numbers of people continued to visit the site each day. In a letter to the *Manchester Guardian* one writer commented: 'I have been recently three months in London, and constantly passed the Cenotaph, and very rarely saw it without a surrounding group of people.'[30] It quickly became established as the central place of remembrance of the dead. School groups were brought there and deputations came 'from provincial centres to place offerings to the memory of local heroes'.[31] The numbers of pilgrims reached a peak during Armistice Day on 11 November 1919 and over the Christmas period.

The pilgrimage on Armistice Day was seen by many of the participants as a means of publicly expressing grief. Nearly all

24. Letter to the First Commissioner, n.d., PRO Work 20 - 139.

25. Sir A. Mond to Sir G. Riddell, 29 July 1919, PRO Work 20 - 139.

26. Sir A. Mond Memorandum to the Cabinet, 23 July 1919, PRO Work 20 - 139.

27. Hansard, 118 HC Deb. 5s, 23 July 1919, 1366.

28. Minutes of a Meeting of the War Cabinet, held on 29 July 1919, PRO CAB 23 - 11.

29. Minutes of the Meeting of the War Cabinet held 30 July 1919, PRO CAB 23 - 11.

30. *Manchester Guardian*, 15 Nov. 1919.

31. *Daily Graphic*, 16 Jan. 1920. *Daily Express*, 8 Jan. 1920.

the men wore black ties and most of the women also chose to wear black. The crowd which congregated at the Cenotaph was larger than the crowd which gathered there on Peace Day.[32] By 11 a.m. the police estimated that there were 6,000 people crowded around the monument.[33] It was only with enormous difficulty that the police were able to clear a space for the carriage of the French President and Lloyd George so that they could lay wreaths at the Cenotaph. The police had completely underestimated the emotional appeal of the memorial. Only seventeen men were on duty at the site, and they were quite unable to control the huge crowd. Over a hundred additional police, including mounted police, had to be called in to clear a space for the march organised by the Comrades of the Great War to the Cenotaph in the afternoon. It was 4 p.m. before the police could open Whitehall to traffic. One of the main reasons why the police were unable to control the people was because those who reached the Cenotaph were unwilling to leave it.[34] The events at the Cenotaph confirmed it as the central place for the memory of the war dead. When the Memorial Services (November 11th) Committee met to plan Armistice Day in 1920 they recalled the events in 1919 and concluded that the 'general public clearly regard Armistice Day as a day upon which they will have an opportunity of paying homage to the glorious dead'.[35]

A large number of pilgrims also came to the Cenotaph at Christmas time. Women and girls wearing black brought wreaths of holly with red berries to lay at the base of the memorial. Companies of Old Comrades met and then marched to the Cenotaph to place wreaths, after which they marched around the memorial. The pilgrimage began a few days before Christmas Day and reached its height on Boxing Day. It was not only a pilgrimage for London residents. Relatives visiting London also brought tributes to place there, and a deputation even came from Dundee.[36]

By January 1920 the temporary Cenotaph was falling apart, but it continued to evoke powerful emotions. When the Office

32. *Evening News*, 11 Nov. 1920.

33. Minute to the Commissioner, 11 Nov. 1919, PRO Mepo 2 - 1957.

34. Report of Chief Inspector E. Brennan, 14 Nov. 1919, PRO Mepo 2 - 1957.

35. The Second Meeting of the Memorial Services (November 11th) Committee held on 21 Oct. 1920, PRO Work 20 - 1/3.

36. *The Times*, 23 Dec. 1919. *Daily Telegraph*, 27 Dec. 1919.

of Works announced its intention to dismantle it, the *Daily Express* angrily attacked it, arguing that no decision was 'so utterly without soul or sentiment or understanding'.[37] It was only when Sir Lionel Earle explained the fragile state of the Cenotaph that the criticism abated. This awareness of the sentiment associated with the Cenotaph influenced the way in which the Office of Works dismantled it. Large hoardings surrounded the site so that the memorial's demolition could not be seen.[38] An official of the Office of Public Works explained that the Cenotaph had been covered to 'spare the feelings of those to whom the structure is especially sacred'. The *Daily Express* concurred with this approach, stating that the memorial should be dismantled with 'reverence', which meant as noiselessly as possible and where practical at night.[39] When the temporary Cenotaph was removed in January few people expected that its permanent replacement would take long to erect. In July 1920 Curzon suggested that the permanent Cenotaph should be unveiled on Armistice Day 1920.[40] The proposal had popular support, but resulted in a ten-month hiatus between the removal of the temporary Cenotaph and the unveiling of its permanent replacement.

The Temporary Cenotaph – Remembrance and the Sacred

Samuel Hynes notes that after the war there was an impulse to 'terminate the war finally and monumentally' and to 'build the war physically into post-war reality'.[41] The Peace Day celebrations were an important part of this process. They were essentially a military celebration in which the majority of the crowd came to celebrate the British victory. The central event was the march of the Allied troops. Each of Great Britain's allies sent a contingent and the latest weapons were on display, such as the tank, anti-aircraft guns and trench mortars. A pavilion was erected near the statue of Queen Victoria facing Buckingham Palace from which the King took the salute of the Allied soldiers. The march

37. *Daily Express*, 14 Jan. 1920.
38. Office of Works Minute, 3 Jan. 1920, PRO Work 20 - 139.
39. *Daily Express*, 20 Jan. 1920.
40. Hansard, 131 HC Deb. 5s, 13 July 1920, p. 2157.
41. S. Hynes, *A War Imagined: The First World War and English Culture* (London, 1990), pp. 269, 279.

enabled the people of London to pay homage to the soldiers, who in turn paid homage to the King. Other decorations included a series of pylons which were inscribed with the names of the major naval engagements and land battles of the war. They turned the Mall into an avenue of triumph. The Cenotaph played a secondary role in the decorations; it was intended to be a temporary place where the achievements of the dead in the war could also be honoured by the salute of the victorious troops.

From the beginning the response of people to the temporary Cenotaph created a meaning for the memorial which was significantly different from its official meaning. It became a place of mourning and pilgrimage. Three factors were particularly significant in the creation of its image as a place of pilgrimage. Firstly, the way in which the events on Peace Day and the weeks which followed it were described in the newspapers. Secondly, the development of war shrines during the war. Finally, the belief, among pilgrims, that the Cenotaph was a place where it was possible to feel closer to the spirits of the dead.

Newspapers played an important role in the development of people's perceptions of and response to the temporary Cenotaph. They claimed to express public opinion. It is difficult to know where to distinguish between the rhetoric of the newspapers and the public's response; however, it seems likely that the images which the newspapers created of the Cenotaph both expressed and influenced perceptions of the monument.

The description of the events on Peace Day suggested that the Cenotaph was more than an ordinary memorial. Correspondents in newspapers throughout Britain commented on the emotion which surrounded the people who watched the march near it. The *Leeds Mercury* stated that there was 'an area of emotional silence' in and around the monument.[42] Many newspapers told the story of a lady who was led out by a young officer to place a wreath at the Cenotaph before the marching soldiers arrived. She 'remained for a few moments with head bowed in sorrow and pride before again disappearing among the people'.[43] The newspapers undoubtedly exaggerated the emotion surrounding the memorial on Peace Day. Some of the reporters wrote their accounts of people's response to the memorial without

42. *Leeds Mercury*, 21 July 1919.
43. *Glasgow Herald*, 21 July 1919.

being present at the site. The account in the *Daily Graphic* referred to the two lines of soldiers dividing as they marched past on either side of the memorial.[44] In fact, while this was supposed to happen, so many people congregated in Whitehall that the crowd prevented the soldiers from dividing to march on either side of the memorial. The large crowd which surged around one side of the Cenotaph probably ensured that in practice there was no area of 'emotional silence' around it.

As early as 20 July the behaviour of people at the Cenotaph was described in the newspapers as a pilgrimage. The *Sunday Times* stated that 'after the procession had passed through Whitehall, thousands of people made a pilgrimage to the cenotaph . . . where they paused a moment and silently saluted'.[45] Another newspaper described how people who were spending the afternoon of 19 July in a tour of inspection soon became involved in a pilgrimage when 'whether of set purpose or by accident, they came to where Sir Edwin Lutyens' wonderful cenotaph stands'.[46] The images used to portray the Cenotaph in the newspapers stressed that it was a national shrine and that even the land on which it stood was sacred. The *Daily Express* wrote that to 'have pulled down the Cenotaph and allowed the traffic to rumble and roar over the spot where loving hands had placed wreaths and cards to those boys who have passed from our ken would have been nothing less than sacrilege'.[47]

However, the images of the Cenotaph as a sacred place were more than just the rhetoric of the newspapers. In a letter to the *Ex-Service Man* one correspondent complained about the practice of selling postcards at the Cenotaph, arguing that it was 'a desecration of a sacred spot'.[48] An unsigned Memorandum from the Office of Works stated that the main argument for retaining the temporary Cenotaph until the permanent memorial was ready to be erected was that 'the ground upon which the Cenotaph has been built has been consecrated, and it would be highly undesirable to let the traffic again move over that portion of the road on which the temporary monument stands'.[49]

44. *Daily Graphic*, 21 July 1919.
45. *Sunday Times*, 20 July 1919.
46. *Observer*, 20 July 1919.
47. *Daily Express*, 1 Aug. 1919.
48. *Ex-Service Man*, 2 (Nov. 1919), p. 5.
49. Memorandum to Mr Russell, 5 Aug. 1919, PRO Work 20 - 139.

The belief that the Cenotaph was a special place was also reflected in the behaviour of people at the memorial. People showed respect by bowing or uncovering their heads when passing it.[50] Many newspapers became active campaigners for the practice of men taking their hats off whenever they passed the monument, and a question was asked in the House of Commons about it.[51] The most obvious manifestation of the deep feelings created by the Cenotaph was the vast number of flowers placed there. So many flowers were being left at the site in 1919 that the Office of Works hired two Custodians to look after the memorial.[52] Pilgrims attached considerable importance to the act of leaving flowers at the Cenotaph. Sir Frank Baines argued that it would be wrong to remove the temporary Cenotaph only a week after Peace Day: 'In view of the fact that the Prime Minister personally gave instructions when he visited the Cenotaph that none of the floral tributes should be removed, I fear there might be an out-cry if the Department started to remove the Memorial and displacing the flowers as a natural consequence on Saturday next.'[53] On 6 January 1920, the *Daily Express* undertook to ensure that flowers were placed on the behalf of all absent relatives at the Cenotaph as 'Comfort and consolation beyond words have been given to stricken hearts by the placing of these flowers "for remembrance".'[54]

The attachment of people to the Cenotaph was also indicated by the popularity of souvenirs of it. The Office of Works often received requests for permission to make and sell miniature copies or photos of the Cenotaph. The justification which was usually given was that the relatives of the fallen required a souvenir which would help to 'perpetuate the memory of a fallen relative'.[55] George Mosse argues that souvenirs of a place, object or memory trivialise it and therefore trivialise the experience of war they reflect. This is because trivia retain 'pleasant or, at least, thrilling memories'.[56] Mosse has a point. However, in the case of the Cenotaph pilgrims came because they associated it with

50. *Morning Post*, 23 July 1919.
51. *Daily Graphic*, 16 Aug. 1919. Hansard, 120 HC Deb. 5s, 29 Oct. 1919, p. 657.
52. *Daily Express*, 31 Dec. 1919.
53. Sir Frank Baines Memorandum, 23 July 1919, PRO Work 20 - 226.
54. *Daily Express*, 6 Jan. 1920.
55. R. D. Roe to Sir A. Mond, 20 Aug. 1919, PRO Work 20 - 205.
56. G. Mosse, *Fallen Soldiers: Reshaping the Memory of the World Wars* (New York, 1990), p. 126.

the memory of their dead. It therefore seems likely that many attached to a souvenir of the Cenotaph similar feelings of grief and reverence for the dead.

Most people in Great Britain could not visit the graves of the fallen on the battlefields, and the Cenotaph provided a place where they could express their love and devotion for them. It was a shrine: a place sacred to the memory of the dead. The practice of erecting shrines for the dead was an important feature of wartime commemoration which expressed the desire for a place where the dead could be mourned. Alan Wilkinson has described how during the war small shrines decorated with flowers and photos of the Royal Family were erected in the back streets of the East End. They were inscribed with the names of those who had joined up and intercessions were made at them. Similarly, many villages had a cross on the village green inscribed with the names of dead soldiers, and it was also the practice to leave flowers at these sites.[57] Although they were initially the product of the wartime evangelism of the Church of England, the shrines also attracted a high level of public interest and involvement.[58]

The parallel is even closer between the Cenotaph and the temporary war shrine constructed in Hyde Park on the fourth anniversary of the outbreak of war. It was erected to provide a place for people to leave their offerings of flowers, which were to symbolise the Empire's tribute to the graves of the dead. On the first day thousands of Londoners, many of them in mourning dress, came to it, and at least 70,000 floral bunches were left there.[59] It was originally planned to keep the shrine up for two days. The success of the shrine led to plans to erect a permanent shrine, and, ironically, Lutyens was commissioned by Mond to design it. However, it was never erected, because the success of the Cenotaph made it irrelevant.[60] The temporary shrine remained in Hyde Park until October 1919.[61]

57. A. Wilkinson, *The Church of England and the First World War* (London, 1978), pp. 67, 170.

58. A. M. King, 'The Politics of Meaning in the Commemoration of the First World War in Britain, 1914-1939', Ph.D. thesis, University College, London, 1993, pp. 75-7.

59. *Daily Express*, 5 Aug. 1918.

60. C. Hussey, *The Life of Sir Edwin Lutyens* (London, 1950), pp. 386-7.

61. Mrs A. Whitford to the Office of Public Works, 28 Oct. 1919, PRO Work 16 - 26(8).

Alex King correctly notes that the practice of erecting shrines enabled people to respond quickly to the Cenotaph, because they had become accustomed to placing flowers at memorials during the war. King therefore questions the argument of Allan Greenberg that the Cenotaph was the 'focus for the outpouring of four years of pent-up sorrow which had been waiting for victory'.[62] However, this obscures what was significant about the Cenotaph. The shrines were only intended to be temporary monuments, which would provide solace and comfort while the men were away at the front, but which would be removed after the war. The pilgrimages to the Cenotaph brought wartime commemoration into the post-war world. People remained closely linked with their wartime feelings of loss and bereavement. By coming to the Cenotaph pilgrims affirmed their continuing tie with that experience.

The people who visited the Cenotaph also drew upon a widely held belief that the spirit or even spirits of the war dead had not been extinguished by the war or by the Armistice. The Cenotaph provided the focal point for the widespread belief or wish to believe in the continuing presence of the dead. This was evident in the descriptions of the pilgrimage to the Cenotaph on Armistice Day 1919. One columnist commented that during the two-minute silence the Cenotaph 'was no longer a cenotaph, an empty tomb. You could vow the deep flowers took the shapes of the dead they covered; and the sweet, heavy scents spread from a flowered battlefield.'[63] This feeling on Armistice Day in 1919 was more than just the expression of journalistic licence. William Grant, who was present at the Cenotaph, wrote to his family: 'Imagine as I imagined that as I was standing there a Great Phantom army moved by that stone. Swiftly, Silently and singing as they went a song of triumph or Victory which to me seems to hand down to the coming Generations a great message.'[64] When there was a threat to move the Cenotaph, one of the arguments for keeping it on the original site was the presence of the dead. The *Daily Express* made this association, arguing 'there it is the

62. King, 'The Politics of Meaning', p. 202. A. Greenberg, 'Lutyens' Cenotaph', *Journal of the Society of Architectural Historians*, XLVIII (Mar. 1989), p. 11.

63. *Daily Mail*, 12 Nov. 1919.

64. Letter of William Grant to his Family, 12 Nov. 1919, in the possession of his great nephew, Revd Colin Holden. Photocopy courtesy of Prof. Ken Inglis.

"empty tomb" round which hover the spirits of those who died for us . . . there let it stay'.[65]

It is difficult to know whether many people believed that they were in the presence of the spirits of the dead. It does seem clear, however, that the Cenotaph expressed a wish to believe that the dead had not ceased to exist. The *Daily Express* told the story of a grizzled sergeant who came with a small girl to lay a wreath for his son. The sergeant said it is 'comforting to know that we all may go there for a quiet five minutes with our lost boys, so that there is one hallowed spot in the great London town which is an everlasting link with the glorious dead'.[66] Granville Cooke wrote a poem titled 'Cry Not Farewell' which captured the desire to be certain that the dead have not ceased to exist. The penultimate stanza of the poem sums up its message:

> God gave not life that life should pass away,
> Nor love to fade and perish in a day.
> Life is eternal. Love shall e'er remain,
> And we, in his good time, shall meet again.[67]

Significantly, copies of the poem were placed at either end of the Cenotaph for mourners to read.

The Unknown Warrior

On 19 October 1920 the Memorial Services (November 11th) Committee, agreed to bury an Unknown Warrior in Westminster Abbey as part of the same ceremony as the unveiling of the Cenotaph on 11 November 1920. The idea of burying an unnamed British hero beneath the Cenotaph was first raised in the *Daily Express* on 16 September 1919. The proposal was justified on the basis that 'the dust of just one soldier, unknown and undistinguished would lend it a sacredness worthy of so great a monument'. The newspaper claimed the idea had the support of the Lord Mayor of London as well as of a 'prominent official of the Peace Celebrations Committee'. The idea had arisen in response to a rumour that the French planned to bury an unknown *poilu* in the Pantheon in Paris. Around the same time a

65. *Daily Express*, 7 Aug. 1919.
66. *Daily Express*, 1 Aug. 1919.
67. G. Cooke, 'Cry Not Farewell', *Comrades Journal*, II (Jan. 1920), p. 9.

letter to the *Daily Express* suggested burying an unknown soldier in St Paul's Cathedral.[68]

The Comrades of the Great War actively promoted the plan. They argued that there was a need for a place sacred to the memory of the unknown soldier 'so that gratitude for all his sacrifice signifies may be kept green forever, and that when generations come to pass the shrine every head should be bared and every heart humbled at remembrance of his greatness as a man and a comrade, the silent symbol of 700,000 who gladly died that Great Britain might live'.[69] In October 1919 the proposal was raised, on behalf of the Comrades, in the House of Commons by Colonel Ashley. The Government did not support it. Andrew Bonar Law justified the Government's decision on the basis that the idea was 'carried out in a more impressive way by the decision . . . to reproduce in a permanent form the Cenotaph in Whitehall'.[70]

Despite this setback, in November 1919 the Comrades approached the Government directly with a proposal that the body of an unknown soldier should be buried under the Cenotaph. The Government followed the Office of Works recommendation not to pursue the idea, because apart from the problems of converting the actual site into a tomb it would not be 'consonant with the symbolic character of the monument'.[71] The *Glasgow Herald* agreed with the Government's decision, commenting that the 'Cenotaph needs nothing to sanctify it. It has become a national shrine, one of the Empire's hallowed places. No man or woman passes it to-day, even when the traffic surges at its height, without an instinctive glance and a holy thought.'[72]

In October 1920 the idea of returning the body of an unknown soldier to England was successfully proposed by the Reverend David Railton. Its success encouraged a wave of similar burials of unknown soldiers among the other combatant nations.[73] In response to Railton's proposal the Dean of Westminster suggested that the body be interred in Westminster Abbey. When the plan was presented to the King he expressed doubts about

68. *Daily Express*, 16, 23 Sept. 1919.
69. *Comrades Journal*, II, (Nov. 1919), p. 2.
70. Hansard, 120 HC Deb. 5s, 29 Oct. 1920, p. 657.
71. Office of Public Works Note, n.d., PRO Work 20 - 139.
72. *Glasgow Herald*, 13 Nov. 1920.
73. Inglis, 'Entombing Unknown Soldiers', pp. 7–10.

it stating that 'a funeral now might be regarded as belated, and almost, as it were, reopen the war wound which time is gradually healing'.[74] The King recommended that the Dean should ask the advice of the Prime Minister.[75] Lloyd George was in favour of the suggestion. The Dean had also gained the support of Field Marshal Sir Henry Wilson who suggested that the soldier should be called an 'Unknown British Warrior' so that it would also encompass the Navy and the Air Force.[76] According to the account in Wilson's diary, when the proposal was raised in Cabinet the majority opposed the suggestion, but he was able to gain their support by explaining that 'no words could tell how proud we officers and men could be to have one of our simple soldiers buried in Westminster Abbey'.[77]

November 1920 to November 1921 – The Great Pilgrimage

The great pilgrimage of people to the permanent Cenotaph and Westminster Abbey began with the pilgrimage of the body of the Unknown Warrior to London [Figure 2]. The Government deliberately created an aura of mystery around the Unknown Warrior, so that it was possible for all the relatives of the missing to believe that this was the body of their son, husband, brother or lover. General MacDonagh, who was entrusted with the arrangements for disinterring the body and transporting it to England, stated that he had ensured that the burial place of the body was completely unknown because of 'the sacredness of his mission and the mysticism which will for all time surround the burial place'.[78] There are a number of different versions of what happened. It has been suggested that the body was selected from among 4, 6 or 8 bodies.[79] There are also different accounts

74. H. Nicolson, *King George the Fifth: His Life and Reign* (London 1952), p. 343.

75. Lord Stamfordham to Dean Ryle, 7 Oct. 1920, Westminster Abbey Library.

76. Henry Wilson to Dean Ryle, 4 Oct. 1920, Westminster Abbey Library.

77. C. E. Callwell, *Field Marshal Sir Henry Wilson, His Life and Diaries*, Vol. 2 (London, 1927), p. 266.

78. *Western Mail*, 12 Nov. 1920.

79. M. Moynihan (ed.), *God on Our Side: The British Padre's in World War One* (London, 1983), p. 78, puts the number at 4. R. Blythe, *The Age of Illusion: England in the Twenties and Thirties 1919–1940* (London, 1963), p. 8, suggests that 6 bodies were selected, while *The Imperial War Museum Information Sheet*, No. 25, puts the number as high as 8.

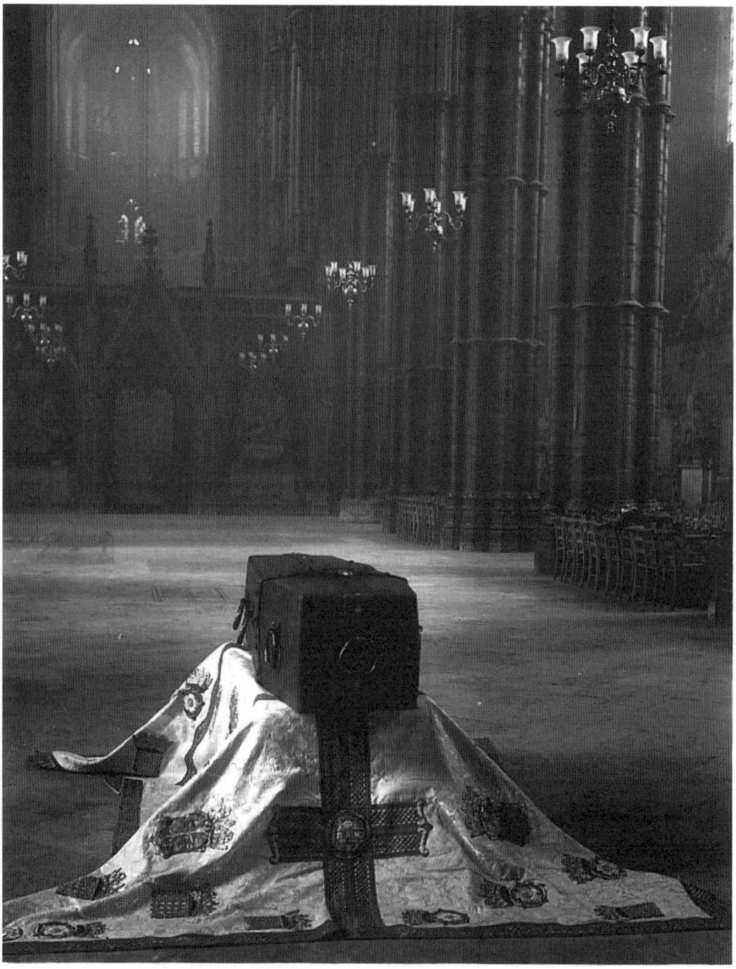

Figure 2. The Coffin of the Unknown Warrior in Westminster Abby, IWM Q31514.

of how the selection was made. It has been argued that the selection was made by a blindfold officer who chose one of the coffins in a chapel in St Pol, or that the selection was made by an officer from a number of bodies placed on stretchers and that the body was then transferred to a coffin.[80]

80. Blythe, *The Age of Illusion*, p. 8. Moynihan (ed.), *God on Our Side*, p. 78.

The confusion about the selection of the body means that it is worth reconsidering what did take place in France. The most reliable account of the exhumation of the body is that of the officer in charge of its selection, Brigadier-General L. J. Wyatt, because it is the only account written by someone who participated in the selection process.[81] He gave instructions that one body should be brought in from each of the four main battle areas, the Aisne, the Somme, Ypres and Arras, on the night of 7 November. It seems likely that the body was selected from among the bodies of soldiers who had died early in the war. The Committee which met to organise the ceremony had to decide whether to bury the bones of the Unknown Warrior or to cremate the body first. They decided that it would be better to bury the bones, as people would identify more closely with the body. The Abbey authorities agreed to this on condition that the body chosen was a 1914 body. There is no indication that the Committee altered this decision.[82] The four bodies were each covered with the Union Jack and placed on stretchers in the chapel of St Pol. Wyatt stated that he then selected one of the bodies, which was placed in a coffin; and the remaining three bodies were buried in the St Pol cemetery. A letter by one of the men responsible for the burial states that in fact the bodies were taken back to the devastated area and left, because it was felt that it would look too suspicious if three bodies were suddenly to appear in St Pol cemetery.[83]

On the morning of 7 November a service was celebrated in the presence of the body by Church of England, Roman Catholic and Nonconformist chaplains. In the afternoon the body was taken to Boulogne under escort. There it was placed in a coffin made of English oak, and a crusader-style sword was attached to the outside of the coffin. The coffin was placed in the Chapelle Ardente in Boulogne Castle, where it was guarded by a detachment of French infantry. On 9 November the body was escorted by the French to Boulogne Quay. At the Quay the body was saluted by Marshal Foch, who had decided on his own initiative

81. *Daily Telegraph*, 11 Nov. 1939.

82. Secretary's Notes of the Meeting of the Memorial Services (November 11th) Committee, held on 19 Oct. 1920, PRO Work 20 - 1/3.

83. Sir Cecil Smith to the Dean of Westminster, 30 July 1978, The Unknown Warrior File, Westminster Abbey Library.

to join the French soldiers sent to pay homage to the body. After a short ceremony pallbearers selected from amongst British and Dominion NCOs placed the coffin on the destroyer *Verdun*, which had been selected to honour the French nation. An honour guard remained around the body as the destroyer crossed the channel.[84]

When the body arrived at Dover on 10 November, a Field Marshal's nineteen-gun salute was given. An honour guard met the body and carried it to the railway carriage which would take it to London. At this point the pilgrimage by the body of an Unknown British Warrior became a national pilgrimage. It was a pilgrimage which was jealously guarded from other countries. The Memorial Services (November 11th) Committee stated that it was 'desirable that the Unveiling and Burial ceremonies be regarded as "domestic" functions in which only the peoples of the British Empire should participate'.[85] A French honour guard which accompanied the body to Dover was only allowed to do so on the condition that they did not accompany the body from Dover to London.[86]

When the body of the Unknown Warrior began its journey from Dover to London there were extraordinary scenes. Crowds of people, many of whom were women, gathered at the stations through which the body passed or on roads running parallel with the railway tracks. At some stations groups stood at the platform to pay homage to the body. Ex-servicemen bearing a Union Jack surmounted by a wreath of bay leaves filled the platform at Faversham. A detachment of Boy Scouts played the Last Post as the body passed. At Gillingham a group of Blue Jackets formed an honour guard. The Royal Warwickshire Regiment paid the body a military tribute at Chatham.[87] While the body was in South Eastern Station, the crowd broke down and scaled the barriers. A number of them swarmed on to the platform, and some even climbed on to the train.[88] When the Unknown Warrior was in Victoria Station an immense crowd gathered, many of whom

84. Arrangements for the Collection of the Unknown Warrior, n.d., PRO WO 32 - 3000.

85. Revised Recommendations of the Memorial Services (November 11th) Committee to Cabinet, 2 Nov. 1920, PRO Work 20 - 1/3.

86. The Foreign Office to Lord Derby, 4 Nov. 1920, PRO WO 32 - 3000.

87. *Leeds Mercury*, 11 Nov. 1920.

88. *Daily Graphic*, 11 Nov. 1920.

were women in black. According to one correspondent, homeward-bound travellers using Victoria Station spoke in lowered tones.[89]

On the morning of 11 November the body of the Unknown Warrior was placed on a gun limber pulled by six black horses, which would carry it from Victoria Station to the Cenotaph. A Union Jack was placed over the coffin and a trench helmet, belt and bayonet were laid on it. The ceremony was cleverly crafted to ensure that people could identify the Unknown Warrior with the men who fought in the war. For instance, the trench helmet symbolised the average British infantryman. A military procession followed the gun limber. There were over a thousand representatives of the three branches of the armed forces. The procession included the Guards band and the pipers of the Scots Guards, as well as representatives of the mercantile marine. Behind the troops marched four hundred representatives of the ex-servicemen's organisations. The twelve pallbearers comprised the most distinguished military leaders, including Haig, Beatty and French, as well as three Admirals, two Field Marshals, three generals and Air-Marshal Trenchard. As the funeral procession moved off, a Field Marshal's nineteen-gun salute was fired.

Many of the people who lined the route of the Unknown Warrior had been waiting for a glimpse of the body through the night or from very early in the morning. As the procession left Victoria Station the pilgrims who had maintained a night vigil over the body marched behind the procession. Soon the numbers of people became too great and they were forced to halt, as the procession continued along streets lined with people in mourning. The bands accompanying the body played a funeral march. When the sound of the approaching music was heard, the crowd fell silent and waited for the body to pass.

The King joined the ceremony at the Cenotaph. The body arrived at the Cenotaph at 10.45 a.m. Three minutes 'intense silence' passed before the ceremony commenced with the hymn 'O God Our Help in Ages Past'. The hymn released the emotion which many people were attempting to suppress, and a number broke down and wept. The Archbishop of Canterbury then said the Lord's Prayer. At this point Big Ben sounded 11.00 a.m. and the King unveiled the Cenotaph. At the end of the chimes there

89. *Leeds Mercury*, 11 Nov. 1920.

was two minutes' silence. Again the emotion was too much for many people. One correspondent remembered that there were two women who shrieked hysterically during the silence.[90] People throughout the city were at an emotional fever pitch. Away from the events in Whitehall a mob invaded the offices of the *Workers' Dreadnought*, a socialist newspaper, when voices were heard during the two minutes' silence.[91]

After the unveiling, the King placed a wreath at the Cenotaph and the procession moved to Westminster Abbey, where the burial service was held. At the same time as the service in Westminster Abbey a Roman Catholic Mass for the dead was conducted at Westminster Cathedral. Many of the women in the Abbey began to cry during the service and a number fainted. The accounts of people who were present for the service suggest the cathartic effect it had. One woman wrote:

> If tears came to me during the service as they came to many, they were mingled with gladness, for in that beautiful building and that music that thrilled my soul I felt very near to my lost boys . . . It was with a full heart that I left the Abbey to join the queue of women waiting to place their wreaths on the Cenotaph.[92]

For others the emotions which the ceremony evoked were difficult to confront. One reporter claimed that after the ceremony at the Cenotaph the man next to him said 'Thank God that this can never happen again' and concluded that it was not 'in the human faculty either to endure or to wish to endure such a strain as was put upon it to-day'.[93] For at least one man, who committed suicide, the ceremony was too much. The coroner concluded that the scenes at the Cenotaph had preyed too much on his mind.[94]

The organisers of the ceremony planned for a pilgrimage lasting three days, after which the grave of the Unknown Warrior would be closed.[95] They were taken completely by surprise by the response of the people, not only in London, but throughout Great Britain. A measure of this extraordinary response is

90. *Cambridge Daily News*, 12 Nov. 1920.
91. *Daily Mail*, 12 Nov. 1920.
92. *Daily Mail*, 12 Nov. 1920.
93. *Leeds Mercury*, 12 Nov. 1920.
94. *Daily Express*, 16 Nov. 1920.
95. Sir A. Mond to the Commissioner of Police of the Metropolis, 29 Oct. 1920, PRO Work 20 - 1/3. *The Times*, 15 Nov. 1920.

revealed by contrasting it with Trafalgar Day, which took place three weeks before 11 November. On that day a reporter found that there was a 'noticeable absence of private contributions' among the wreaths placed at Nelson's Column. He felt this was probably due to the expense of flowers and 'the general unrest and upheaval in which we are living'.[96]

Once the ceremony at the Cenotaph was completed the pilgrimage past the memorial began [Figure 3]. The first pilgrims were two legless soldiers on tricycles. They were followed by hundreds of police, who brought wreaths to place at the base of the memorial. Then came lorries full of badly wounded men. When they had passed the thousands of people who had lined the streets began to queue to pass the Cenotaph. Most of them had brought wreaths or bunches of flowers to place at the base of the memorial. The number of pilgrims was far greater than the police had anticipated, which resulted in delays of up to four hours to pass the Cenotaph. In the afternoon the Abbey was also opened to pilgrims. At least 40,000 people passed through the Abbey before the doors were closed at 11 p.m., an hour later than the scheduled closure time. Thousands more passed the Cenotaph. There were still long queues at midnight, and people continued to visit the site through the night.[97]

Thousands of pilgrims visited the Cenotaph and the Abbey on Friday 10 November and throughout the weekend. So many people were waiting outside the Abbey by 7.30 a.m. on Friday that the doors were opened more than three hours early. As many as 200,000 people passed through the Abbey that day. Many other people chose not to join the pilgrimage, but walked quickly along the pavement and saluted the Cenotaph from a distance. At midnight hundreds of pilgrims still waited to pass the Cenotaph.[98] On Saturday pilgrims from outside London began to arrive in large numbers. According to the *Daily Mail*, many thousands of people, who came to London to support their local football teams, came to the Cenotaph, among whom the men from Blackburn, Blackpool and Sheffield were most noticeable. By the time the Abbey was due to open at midday on Sunday, an estimated 60,000 pilgrims were waiting to see the Unknown Warrior.[99]

96. *Cambridge Daily News*, 22 Oct. 1920.
97. *Eastern Daily Press*, 12 Nov. 1920. *Daily Express*, 12 Nov. 1920.
98. *Daily Mail*, 13 Nov. 1920. *Evening Standard*, 13 Nov. 1920.
99. *Daily Mail*, 15 Nov. 1920.

Figure 3. Scenes at the Cenotaph just after the Unveiling Ceremony. IWM Q31494.

The pilgrimage involved people from all levels of society. While women tended to make up a large percentage of the pilgrims during the week, whole families came to the Cenotaph and the

Abbey at the weekend.[100] The *Daily Express* told the story of two wounded soldiers who walked sixty miles to lay wreaths at the Cenotaph; they had both lost brothers in the war.[101] There were pilgrims from Ireland, Scotland and Wales, and from the Outer Hebrides and the Shetland Islands. Many remote towns sent a representative with the tribute of more than one family. There was a small garden of flowers planted in a box from a parish in Nottinghamshire which bore more than sixty names of the fallen.[102] People of all beliefs became pilgrims. Roman Catholics genuflected at the Cenotaph, while 'Moslems made that solemn bow with their three-motioned invocation to the head, eyes and heart'.[103] One newspaper described how a woman dressed in black knelt before the Cenotaph and raised her child clad in white to it before leaving.[104] It was not just a pilgrimage of individuals. Wreaths were placed at the Cenotaph by regiments of the Army and from a number of large firms in honour of their employees.

On Monday 15 November the traffic was again allowed into Whitehall, but this did not halt the pilgrimage. When omnibuses passed the Cenotaph, the drivers would salute it by slowing and dropping their right hands to their sides, while passengers stood and removed their hats. The officials at the Abbey announced that they would give up any preconceived ideas as to when the grave of the Unknown Warrior should be filled in.[105] The number of pilgrims increased on Wednesday 17 November because it was believed that the grave would be closed in the evening; however, so many people were waiting to visit the grave that the Dean postponed filling it in until the next day. Up to the time the grave was closed an estimated 1,250,000 people visited the Abbey. This was determined by counting the number of people passing a certain point for a set number of minutes and then averaging it. This number was then multiplied by the number of minutes the Abbey was open.[106] This method gave a reasonably accurate estimate of the numbers at the Abbey. How-

100. *Leeds Mercury*, 15 Nov. 1920.
101. *Daily Express*, 13 Nov. 1920.
102. *Daily Mail*, 13 Nov. 1920.
103. *Daily Express*, 16 Nov. 1920.
104. *Daily Express*, 13 Nov. 1920.
105. *Evening Standard*, 15 Nov. 1920.
106. *Lancashire Daily Post*, 19 Nov. 1920.

ever, the final number of pilgrims would have been much greater, because, on most days, more pilgrims visited the Cenotaph than the Abbey.

Also the pilgrimage continued after 18 November. Although the Abbey was closed on 19 November, pilgrims continued to visit the Cenotaph. According to some accounts more pilgrims visited the memorials on the weekend of 20–21 November than at any time during the week.[107] The Salvation Army held a service at the Cenotaph on Sunday afternoon, after which hundreds of wreaths and bunches of flowers were laid there. The pilgrimage continued on the weekend of 28–29 November. On Saturday the Royal Horse Artillery Old Comrades Association held a service and then marched to the Cenotaph, where they placed tributes at its base. Other regiments visited the Cenotaph at the same time. During the afternoon civil organisations, such as the Boy Scouts, Girl Guides and church parties, figured prominently among the pilgrims.[108] By the end of November over 100,000 flowers and wreaths had been left at the Cenotaph. They formed three huge banks of flowers around the memorial.[109]

Arguably the pilgrimage to the Cenotaph and the grave of the Unknown Warrior which began on Armistice Day 1920 lasted for twelve months. The *Westminster Abbey Guide* of 1924 claimed that the space enclosing the grave remained filled with flowers and other tributes throughout this period.[110] The pilgrimage also continued to the Cenotaph. In July the *Glasgow Herald* claimed: 'Daily there is an endless pilgrimage to the shrine, for there are still those who in the wreck and turmoil and anxieties of to-day remember that we have dedicated our endeavours through the years of peace to those who made the peace possible.'[111] According to the Clerk of Works in St James's Palace, between three and four hundred wreaths and other tributes were being placed around the Cenotaph every week. The cards showed that pilgrims were coming from all over the United Kingdom, Ireland and the Dominions.[112] The

107. *Illustrated London News*, 157 (Nov. 1927), p. 894.
108. *Sunday Times*, 28 Nov. 1920.
109. *Illustrated London News*, 157 (Nov. 1920), p. 894.
110. *Westminster Abbey Guide* (London, 1924), p. 3, Westminster Abbey Library.
111. *Glasgow Herald*, 16 July 1921.
112. *The Times*, 24 Aug. 1921.

continuing appeal of the Cenotaph was noted in May 1921 by the First Commissioner of Works, who said that it 'possesses a continuing vitality, and is in effect a centre of pilgrimage and emotion'.[113]

Not only individual pilgrims visited these sites during the year, but also many groups. In January the members of the Bradford City and Coventry City football clubs placed wreaths at the Cenotaph.[114] The Welsh Rugby team and later the Irish Rugby team held wreath-laying ceremonies at the Cenotaph prior to their games against the English team.[115] When the St Hilda Colliery Band organised a wreath-laying ceremony at the Cenotaph, twenty other bands offered to take part. On 7 February a huge crowd gathered to watch the five hundred bandsmen march past the Cenotaph two abreast. The bands from London reflected the widespread appeal of the Cenotaph among working-class people.[116]

This period of pilgrimage culminated in the week of Armistice Day 1921. *The Times* commented: 'There are pilgrims at the Cenotaph on every day of the year, but Armistice Day with all it means and inspires seems to be the beginning of a week of remembrance in which all who can pile fresh flowers at the base of the memorial to the Glorious Dead.'[117] From early in the morning of 11 November people made a pilgrimage to the Cenotaph and the grave. The pilgrimage was not as large as in 1920, but it was still greater than expected. Throughout the day the line of pilgrims was practically unbroken.[118] When the official ceremony at the Cenotaph concluded and the troops at the Cenotaph marched away 'the crowd broke through the Police and surged around the Cenotaph in a seething mass'.[119] The feeling which motivated this behaviour indicates the powerful emotion the Cenotaph could still evoke.

113. Memorandum by the First Commissioner of Works on Battlefield Memorials, 11 May 1921, PRO WO 32 - 3135.

114. *The Times*, 3 Jan. 1921.

115. *The Times*, 17 Jan., 12 Feb. 1921.

116. *The Times*, 7 Feb. 1921.

117. *The Times*, 14 Nov. 1920.

118. *Eastern Daily Press*, 12 Nov. 1920.

119. Rough Notes prepared for the Organiser of the 1922 Cenotaph Ceremony, 1922, PRO HO 45 - 11557.

November 1920 – From Public to Private Mourning

The initial plans for the ceremonies on Armistice Day 1920 did not emphasise the need for a ceremony of mourning which would respond to the private emotions of the nation. The planners of the ceremony envisaged a funeral in the tradition of those given to military heroes such as Nelson and Wellington or the funerals of Queen Victoria or King Edward VII. These public ceremonies presaged the spectacle of the burial of the Unknown Warrior and the huge crowds who watched the funeral procession of the body. However, there was a distance between the private experience of the crowds who watched the public funerals in the period before 1914 and the public ceremony itself. The crowds at those earlier funerals were there as onlookers, not as active participants.

When Nelson's body was returned to England, it first lay in state in Greenwich, where 30,000 people filed past the coffin. It was then taken to London in a barge as part of a procession of black-draped boats between banks lined with people. In London his body was carried to St Paul's as part of a large procession involving royalty, nobles, ministers, Admirals, Generals, 48 sailors from the *Victory* and 10,000 other sailors, watched by huge crowds who bared their heads as the body passed.[120] The funeral of the Duke of Wellington in 1852 was considered 'the apotheosis of all Victorian funerals'. The body was brought to London and 200,000 people filed past it while it lay in state in the Great Hall in Chelsea. The funeral procession was even more lavish than that of Nelson. The carriage which drew his body to St Paul's was 21 feet long by 12 feet wide and weighed 18 tons. Again vast crowds of people gathered to watch the ceremony. They wept as the carriage passed, and the sight of thousands of hats being raised was described by one eyewitness as 'the sudden rising from the ground and settling again of a huge flock of birds'.[121]

In the decade prior to the outbreak of the Great War large crowds also gathered to watch the funerals of Queen Victoria and Edward VII. When Queen Victoria's body was brought from Plymouth to Victoria Station in a special train, people who had

120. T. Pocock, *Horatio Nelson* (London, 1987), pp. 339–40.

121. J. S. Curl, *The Victorian Celebration of Death* (Newton Abbott, 1972), pp. 3–4. E. Longford, *Wellington: Pillar of State* (London, 1972), pp. 403–4.

congregated in the fields knelt. The body was carried in a grand procession on a gun carriage from Victoria Station to Paddington through huge crowds of onlookers. Spectators were struck by the silence of the onlookers as her body passed.[122] The level of public interest in the funeral of Edward VII, in 1910, probably exceeded that in the funeral of Victoria. Edward's body lay in state in Westminster Hall for three days, and 250,000 people filed past it. Again a vast multitude gathered to watch the funeral procession which carried his body to the interment ceremony, and the 'hushed sorrow of the silent multitudes' was stressed.[123]

The ceremonies in 1920 which unveiled the Cenotaph and buried the Unknown Warrior changed the nature of public ceremony. The public ceremony merged with the private experience of a nation of mourners. The focus of the ceremonies was not simply the body of an unknown soldier or the memorial to 'The Glorious Dead', but every individual who had lost a loved one in the war. It brought the experience of ex-servicemen and bereaved relatives together within the public domain. This change arose from the popular response to the proposed plans for the unveiling and the burial.

When the Cabinet decided to erect a permanent Cenotaph they were influenced by its association with the victory parade on 19 July.[124] Mond, who was responsible for the construction of the Cenotaph, denied that it was 'primarily instituted as a place to lay flowers, which seems to be commonly assumed' arguing that its retention was really a commemoration of Peace Day and the British victory in the war.[125] He was determined that the Cenotaph should 'exalt the dignity of sacrifice without the tears'.[126] Thus the initial plan for unveiling the Cenotaph, which was revealed on 12 October, 1920, excluded the relatives of the dead from the ceremony. Similarly the key theme of the plans for the burial of the Unknown Warrior was the provision of a military tribute to the 'fighting forces'. Although it was accepted that any additional space should go to 'selected widows and

122. S. Weintraub, *Victoria: Biography of a Queen* (London, 1987), pp. 636–40.
123. S. Lee, *King Edward VII: A Biography*, Vol. II *The Reign* (London, 1927), pp. 720–2.
124. Minutes of a Meeting of the War Cabinet, held on 30 July 1919, PRO CAB 23 - 11.
125. Sir A. Mond to David Lloyd George, 22 Dec. 1919, PRO Work 20 - 139.
126. H. Bolitho, *Alfred Mond: First Lord Melchett* (London, 1933), p. 204.

mothers, especially of the humbler ranks', most of the available space was already allocated to 1,000 men from the fighting and auxiliary services.[127] It was a tribute to the Military as an institution, not to those who fought; therefore ex-servicemen were largely excluded.

The first amendment to the original plans was the involvement of representatives of the ex-servicemen's organisations. Donald Simpson, who was writing on behalf of the Joint Committee of the United Organisations of Ex-Servicemen, which loosely combined the four major ex-servicemen's organisations, requested that 400–500 ex-servicemen be allowed to form a procession behind the party with the Unknown Warrior.[128] He argued that if this were allowed, the great mass of ex-servicemen would feel that they had been 'properly recognised'. The Government was warned that if the procession were prevented from taking place, it was more than likely that 'unrest among ex-servicemen would seize the opportunity to show its hand'.[129] The Federation of Discharged and Disabled Sailors and Soldiers threatened to organise their own procession to the Cenotaph, as they had found it impossible to find out details of the arrangements for Armistice Day.[130] These threats were effective, and around 400 ex-servicemen followed the body of the Unknown Warrior from Victoria Station to the Cenotaph.

It was widely believed that priority should be given to bereaved relatives in addition to ex-servicemen. This reflected a change in the nature of remembrance, which was the legacy of the popular response to the temporary Cenotaph. The organisers of Peace Day in 1919 were initially reluctant to reserve spaces for widows and mothers, because they believed that the bulk of war widows had remarried.[131] The concession was only granted

127. Secretary's Notes of the Meeting of the Memorial Services (November 11th) Committee, held on 19 Oct. 1920, PRO Work 20 - 1/3.

128. These were the Officers Association, the Comrades of the Great War, the National Federation of Discharged and Demobilised Sailors and Soldiers, and the National Association of Discharged Sailors and Soldiers.

129. Donald Simpson to Sir Douglas Haig, 27 Oct. 1920 (Haig forwarded the letter to the Secretary of the War Office), PRO Work 20 - 1/3.

130. Minutes of the Meeting of the Cenotaph Sub-Committee, held 30 Oct. 1920, PRO Work 20 - 1/3.

131. Memorandum - Peace Celebrations Committee, 25 June 1919, PRO Work 21 - 74.

by the Peace Celebration Committee when the Queen's representative wrote to the Committee expressing the Queen's hope that 'the poor women will not be forgotten'.[132] The thousands of pilgrims in mourning, who came to the Cenotaph on Armistice Day 1919, created an unforgettable impression. It seems likely that this impression fostered the belief expressed in the newspapers that the relatives of the bereaved had to be given priority in the 1920 unveiling and burial ceremonies.

The *Daily Graphic* led the demand for the relatives of the dead to be present at the ceremonies at the Cenotaph and in Westminster Abbey. When the first plan for the unveiling of the Cenotaph was released, it attacked the plan, referring to it as the 'Cenotaph Blunder'.[133] It accused Mond of planning to limit the unveiling to a select party of invited guests and an army of Whitehall officials who had stayed snugly behind their desks while the 'manhood of the nation was fighting and bleeding and dying for British honour and British freedom'.[134] Many other newspapers supported the calls for women to be given priority in the ceremonies.[135]

The belief that the ceremonies on Armistice Day should be for the mothers of the bereaved was shared by many people. Lionel Earle recalled that the Office of Works was 'besieged by hundreds of irate and almost hysterical females'.[136] There was considerable public interest in the selection of the people who would be accommodated in Westminster Abbey and in front of the Cenotaph. Letters were received by most of the popular London newspapers making suggestions about who should go. While a few letters suggested that ex-servicemen, particularly wounded men, should have priority, the majority supported the claim of bereaved women to precedence. One letter even suggested that the relatives of the missing should apply for and wear a small badge.[137]

As a result of the level of public interest, questions were asked in the House of Commons about provision for the bereaved at

132. H. Verney to Sir Lionel Earle, 8 July 1919, PRO Work 21 - 74.
133. *Daily Graphic*, 13 Oct. 1920.
134. *Daily Graphic*, 15 Oct. 1920.
135. *Sunday Express*, 30 Oct. 1920. Also see *Pall Mall Gazette*, 11 Nov. 1920.
136. L. Earle, *Turn Over the Page* (London, 1935), p. 133.
137. *Evening News*, 25–28 Oct. 1920. *Daily Graphic*, 1–2 Nov. 1920.

the ceremonies.[138] The Cenotaph Sub-Committee recorded in the minutes of their meeting on 30 October 'that exclusive priority should be given to the bereaved, social claims of every description being discouraged'.[139] This priority could even exclude ex-servicemen. The Office of Public Works prepared a letter to the British Red Cross inquiring if they felt it was practicable for a limited number of wounded men to be stationed on lorries on Constitution Hill. The writer stressed that 'the desire of the Cabinet is that the greatest possible amount of space should be available for the relatives of those who have fallen in the War'.[140] On 1 November, Lloyd George suggested that if the members of the House of Commons desired it the Government could make arrangements for the relatives of the bereaved to have the places reserved for members of Parliament.[141] When the House of Commons agreed, Curzon was also able to get the agreement of the House of Lords.[142] The only exception was made for 200 places in Westminster Abbey, which were reserved for Members of Parliament and Peers who had lost a son or brother in the war.[143]

The change in the priority of the organisers altered the nature of the ceremonies on 11 November. In place of the 1,000 members of the armed forces who were to make up the congregation in the Abbey over 1,000 places were given to the relatives of the dead. The army was represented by 100 men who had been awarded the Victoria Cross. They provided an honour guard for the Unknown Warrior, lining the gangway between the screen and the grave. The space in front of the Cenotaph was also given to bereaved relatives, who were allocated places by ballot. The Office of Works eventually received 15,000 applications for the 5,410 places it had to allocate.[144] Most of the applications were from people in or near London, which was probably due to the costs of travel to and accommodation in London.[145] In addition,

138. Hansard 131 HC Deb. 5s, 26 Oct. 1920, p. 1587.

139. Cenotaph Sub-Committee, Minutes of a Meeting held on 30 Oct. 1920, PRO Work 20 - 1/3.

140. Unsigned Letter to Sir Arthur Stanley, British Red Cross Society, 1 Nov. 1920, PRO Work 20 - 1/3.

141. Hansard, 134 HC Deb. 5s, 1 Nov. 1920, p. 47.

142. Hansard, 42 HL Deb. 5s, 2 Nov. 1920, pp. 125–6.

143. Hansard, 134 HC Deb. 5s, 4 Nov. 1920, p. 567.

144. E. Bright to the Secretary of the War Cabinet, Curzon Papers, MSS Eur F 112/318.

145. *Daily Graphic*, 3 Nov. 1920.

it would have taken time for people to find out about the ballot and to respond. As the ballot closed on 4 November, this only gave people a week in which to apply.

As a funeral ceremony the pilgrimage to the Cenotaph and the grave of the Unknown Warrior responded to the needs of people after the war. The ceremony emphasised the loss suffered by the relatives of the dead and not the Allied victory. A columnist in the *Nation* wrote that the 'week in London has been one of mourning; and for the first time in history, I suppose the memory of a great war has been kept with a very slight infusion of militarism'.[146] The idea of sacrifice increasingly included not only the sacrifice of the men who died, but also the loss felt by women. One writer claimed that she had chosen not to go to the ceremony in 1920 because she had not lost a husband or son in the war, and she felt she 'had no right to usurp the space belonging to the bereaved'.[147] The *Daily Graphic* published 'A Mother's Tribute' which sums up the most extreme form of this attitude:

> Stick to your guns, Mr Editor,
> Stick to them hard and fast;
> Fight for the women who suffered,
> And held on till the last . . ..
>
> Held on till their Country forgot them –
> The Mothers of sons brave and true.
> And now for ever will suffer,
> For me, for their country, for you.[148]

The figure of the Unknown Warrior also captured the desire of people for a ceremony which would finally bury the dead. This need was particularly felt by the relatives of the missing. In a sense the burial of the Unknown Warrior represented the funeral the bodies of the missing had never received. When the Unknown Warrior was buried in Westminster Abbey many of the newspapers printed stories about women who were coming to the Abbey because they were confident that their son or husband was buried there.[149] The *Manchester Guardian* noted that most of the flowers placed at the grave were addressed to

146. *Nation*, XXVIII (Nov. 1920), p. 271.
147. *Lady*, 18 Nov. 1920.
148. *Daily Graphic*, 8 Nov. 1920.
149. *Evening News*, 12 Nov. 1920.

brothers, sons or husbands, and only a few to the Unknown Warrior.[150] It seems likely that many of these were for the missing. One pilgrim from the north of Scotland even visited the grave in 1921 because a clairvoyant had advised her that her son's bones were interred there.[151]

The Unknown Warrior had a wider appeal than just to the relatives of the missing. H. V. Morton wrote that no matter how many mothers believe that the Unknown Warrior is theirs, 'they are all right; they are all of them right - for he is every mother's son who did not come home from France'.[152] The burial of the Unknown Warrior symbolised the contribution of all unknown soldiers. It enabled the nation to bury symbolically in England all those ordinary soldiers who had died. The *Morning Post* stressed the need for a ceremony which would achieve this:

> It is the trait of the English people to wish to see their dead back to earth - a trait which shows in the pathetic sacrifices that the Burial Clubs in poor quarters can tell of. Many hundreds of thousands have been deprived of that solace during the Great War; and as many of them as could come to join in this procession as to the funeral procession of *their* dead, which indeed it was.[153]

Finally the pilgrimage to the Cenotaph and the grave of the Unknown Warrior brought Great Britain together as a nation of mourners. The ceremony expressed the yearning for unity which marked the first years after the war, as the King and religious, military and political leaders joined with ex-servicemen, bereaved relatives and a multitude of onlookers in mourning an unknown British soldier.[154] In the newspaper accounts the sense of community of the people on the pilgrimage was stressed. One writer compared the scene at the Cenotaph to the days during the war when 'we were all one big happy family'. She claimed that at the Cenotaph people 'took turn about with strangers at camp stools and when a passer-by dropped a ticket to a privileged place eager hands restored it to her'.[155] The sense of community

150. *Manchester Guardian*, 19 Nov. 1920.
151. *Glasgow Herald*, 14 Nov. 1921.
152. H. V. Morton, *The Spell of London* (London, 1926), pp. 17-18.
153. *Morning Post*, 12 Nov. 1920.
154. K. Morgan, *Consensus and Disunity, The Lloyd George Coalition Government 1918-1922* (Oxford, 1979), p. 190.
155. *Evening News*, 11 Nov. 1920.

was extended to all people in the United Kingdom. The *Daily Mail* wrote:

> Sad-faced mothers from every part of the Kingdom laid flowers at the Cenotaph. From Yorkshire and Lancashire, from Devon and Lincoln, from homes on the moors, from cottages in Hampshire, from trim little houses in seaport towns, and from the two million houses of London they came to pay homage to the memory of all who died in the War.[156]

The clearest expression of this unity was the references by journalists to the equality of the pilgrims, with many accounts stressing that class differences had no meaning for them.[157]

Thomas Laqueur has queried 'how profoundly the burial of the unknown warrior elided class and political divisions and how cynical the government was in regarding the ceremony as an occasion for mending the social fabric'.[158] There is little doubt that the newspapers seized the opportunity to assert the unity of the nation. Further, it is likely that the Government appreciated the opportunities which the final format of the ceremonies provided to portray the nation as a cohesive unit. However, much of the form and meaning of the ceremonies derived from government responses to popular pressure rather than overt government planning and management. The rhetoric of the day should not be confused with reality; but two years after the Armistice many people shared common feelings of grief and respect for the dead. The need for a ceremony of mourning which was articulated in the newspapers and reflected in the actions of thousands of people at the Cenotaph and the grave transcended, if only partially and for a moment, other political and social divisions.

The Continuing Pilgrimage – 1921–1950

The Cenotaph and the grave of the Unknown Warrior remained sacred places for years after the initial emotion of the pilgrimages in 1919 and 1920 had died away. In 1928 the Cenotaph was still

156. *Daily Mail*, 13 Nov. 1920.
157. *Daily Telegraph*, 12 Nov. 1920.
158. T. W. Laqueur, 'Memory and Naming in the Great War', in J. R. Gillis (ed.), *Commemorations: The Politics of National Identity* (Princeton, 1994), p. 157.

referred to as 'the only monument in London which passers-by naturally and of their own accord salute.'[159] According to the Dean of Westminster thousands of people still visited the Unknown Warrior during the year in 1930, in addition to the thousands who came on Armistice Day.[160] Even in 1939 flowers and tributes were left at the Cenotaph throughout the year.[161]

One of the most popular plays of 1922, Bruce Bairnsfather's 'Old Bill MP', drew much of its emotional force from the image of the Cenotaph which provided the climax of the play. The character of Old Bill, and England itself, is beset by the twin obstacles of 'Bolshevik gold and German cunning', but Old Bill is able to overcome these by appearing on the village green in his old war kit, and speaking to the villagers. As he confronts them a vision of the Cenotaph appears and the villagers kneel before it. Inspired Old Bill travels to Parliament to become an MP, has an interview with the spirit of the Unknown Warrior in Westminster Abbey, and England is saved.[162] Bairnsfather wrote that the idea for the play had occurred to him when he had been thinking about the disappointing conditions in the post-war world. As he was thinking, he wondered was 'not the lack of adequate memory the cause of a lot of unrest?' Having determined its theme, he needed a high spot which would 'illuminate the main theme of the play', which led him to introduce the vision of the Cenotaph.[163]

As a mystical figure, the Unknown Warrior ranked just behind Jesus Christ in the 1920s. The play 'The Eternal Flame' by C. Watson Mill was beset by controversy in 1928 because the figure of the Unknown Warrior appeared on stage.[164] The author realised that the Censor would object to Jesus Christ as a central character in the play, and therefore chose the Unknown Warrior as 'the most sublime and lovable character apart from Christ'.[165]

159. C. S. Cooper, *The Outdoor Monuments of London: Statues, Memorial Buildings, Tablets and War Memorials* (London, 1928), p. 20.

160. *The Times*, 27 Oct. 1930.

161. Minute, by Superintendent of Canon Row Station, Division 'A', Mar. 1939, PRO Mepo 2 - 3144.

162. B. Bairnsfather, 'Old Bill M.P.', BL Manuscripts, LCP 1922/10.

163. B. Bairnsfather, *Wide Canvas: An Autobiography* (London, 1939), p. 133–4, 143.

164. C. Watson Mill, 'The Eternal Flame', BL Manuscripts, LCP 1928/43.

165. *Daily Sketch*, 4 Oct. 1928.

The opposition to the play was championed by the *Sunday Dispatch*, which argued that the 'introduction of a figure that has become one of the most sacred of national symbols will appear as an intolerable error in taste and sentiment'. The play was also criticised by representatives of the British Legion, the BESL, Arthur Conan Doyle, Sir Ian Hamilton and G. K. Chesterton. Other famous figures rallied to the defence of the play, including George Bernard Shaw, who stated that he 'would like to write a play and in the last act make all these Unknown Warriors rise up, and, while taking their supper, say what they think about the war'.[166]

The pilgrimages to the Cenotaph and to the grave of the Unknown Warrior remained significant features in the ritual of Armistice Day up to 1939. As the war receded from immediate memory, the pilgrims ceased to wear mourning, but they continued to bring floral tributes to place at the Cenotaph in memory of the dead.[167] Visitors developed their own ritual at the grave of the Unknown Warrior. Despite the efforts of the Abbey authorities to prevent pilgrims from leaving flowers at the grave, it became a tradition for them to place single poppies there.

In 1924 the anniversary of the declaration of war inspired a pilgrimage lasting at least three days. On 3 August men and women were seen 'approaching the monument reverently, and occasionally laying flowers at the base' throughout the day. On 4 August crowds of pilgrims moved from the Cenotaph to the Unknown Warrior and then to Downing Street, where the decision to declare war had been made. *The Times* emphasised that this was a genuine pilgrimage, because 'these were not simply sightseeing crowds visiting London's historic places in the tourist spirit. The majority of them had made a little pilgrimage to the places which embody the nation's tribute to those who lost their lives in the War.'[168]

The pilgrimage on Armistice Day was assimilated into the social life of people. Many of those who came to participate in the service at the Cenotaph on Armistice Day stayed to watch the pilgrimage which followed it. Often the pilgrims came as part of a large group to pay tribute to the dead. On 14 November

166. *Sunday Dispatch*, 30 Sept. 1928.

167. *The Times*, 12 Nov. 1923; this was the first year in which the absence of people in mourning began to be remarked upon.

168. *The Times*, 4–5 Aug. 1924.

1926 a number of groups made pilgrimages to the Cenotaph. The groups included 2,500 London Rover Scouts, 3,500 members of the Royal Antediluvian Order of Buffaloes, contingents of the Salvation Army and a number of regimental Old Comrades Associations.[169] Similarly, on 13 November 1927 a large number of organised pilgrimages representing parishes, regiments and different institutions came to the Cenotaph. Most of these processions marched behind bands and a number of them were accompanied by surpliced clergy. Some of them brought hand carts laden with wreaths to place at the Cenotaph. The organisations included 2,000 members of the Royal Antediluvian Order of Buffaloes, the Salvation Army, the British Fascists and the Legion of Frontiersmen.[170]

The pilgrimage to the Cenotaph and the grave of the Unknown Warrior was more than just an adjunct to the ritual of Armistice Day. The pilgrimage generally continued for a period of a week around 11 November. In 1925 the pilgrims began coming to the Cenotaph and grave on the weekend before 11 November, and the *Manchester Guardian* suggested that that year's pilgrimage would last over a week.[171] There were occasions in the 1920s when pilgrimages occurred at times other than Armistice Day. At least until 1924 there was a regular pilgrimage to the Cenotaph at Christmas time. The Christmas pilgrimage developed its own traditions. For instance, holly wreaths were laid at the Cenotaph at this time.[172]

The pilgrimages continued until 1939. In 1936 *The Times* claimed that the appeal of the pilgrimage to the Cenotaph 'has lost nothing in impressiveness with the passing of time. The simple monument that has such grandeur of inspiration drew to itself as vast a throng as in any of the years that have passed.'[173] However, the role of the Cenotaph changed as the Great War became a historical event rather than a present memory. The Cenotaph was becoming increasingly identified with its ceremonial role rather than as a place of pilgrimage. Thus, a Mass-Observation survey found that by the late 1930s many people

169. *The Times*, 15 Nov. 1926.
170. *The Times*, 14 Nov. 1927.
171. *The Times*, 9 Nov. 1925. *Manchester Guardian*, 12 Nov. 1925.
172. *The Times*, 29 Dec. 1924; a photo entitled 'A Christmas Pilgrimage' shows the base of the Cenotaph covered in Holly Wreaths.
173. *The Times*, 12 Nov. 1936.

only removed their hats when they passed the Cenotaph in the weeks surrounding Armistice Day.[174]

In the short term the Second World War temporarily disrupted this trend. From 1939 to 1945 there was no Armistice Day ceremony at the Cenotaph. However, in 1943 and 1944 'an informal pilgrimage to the Cenotaph' involving thousands of pilgrims took place on 11 November.[175] According to *The Times* the 'Civilian pilgrimage' to the Cenotaph on 10 November 1946 lasted many hours.[176] Despite the renewal of pilgrimages towards the end of and in the immediate aftermath of the Second World War, the war seems to have destroyed the privileged place of the Cenotaph in people's emotions. In 1925 H. V. Morton wrote that at the Cenotaph six 'years have made no difference . . . I think that I like it best just standing here in a grey morning with its feet in flowers and ordinary folk going by, remembering.'[177] He returned to the monument in 1950 and found that 'few nowadays pause to examine the Cenotaph, that memorial to battles long ago'.[178]

Comparing the Cenotaph and the Unknown Warrior

Ken Inglis argues that an important motivation for the proposal to bury an Unknown Warrior in November 1920 was an attempt by the Church of England to create a rival shrine to the Cenotaph.[179] Stephen Graham recollected a conversation with Lutyens about the response to the Cenotaph which confirms Inglis's surmise. Lutyens said: 'There was some horror in Church circles. *What!* a pagan monument in the midst of Whitehall! That is why we have a rival shrine in the Abbey, the Unknown Warrior, but even an unknown soldier might not have been a Christian, the more unknown the less sure you could be.'[180]

The belief that the Cenotaph was a sacred place challenged the role of the established Church in helping mourners to come

174. T. Harrison and C. Madge, *Britain by Mass-Observation* (London, 1986, first published 1939), p. 209.

175. *The Times*, 12 Nov. 1943; 13 Nov. 1944.

176. *The Times*, 11 Nov. 1946.

177. H. V. Morton, *The Heart of London* (London, 1925), p. 26.

178. H. V. Morton, *In Search of London* (London, 1951), p. 204.

179. Inglis, 'Entombing Unknown Soldiers', p. 10.

180. S. Graham, *Part of the Wonderful Scene: An Autobiography* (London, 1964), p. 218.

to terms with bereavement. This challenge was accentuated by the fact that the Cenotaph was non-denominational. There was considerable debate about the need for it to include a Christian inscription. Repeated questions were asked in the House of Commons in late July and early August 1919.[181] The issue was also debated in the newspapers and the *Sunday Herald* held a competition to find the best inscription.[182] The Archbishop of Canterbury also sent suggestions for inscriptions to the Office of Works through the Bishop of Winchester.[183] In a memorandum to the War Cabinet Mond conceded that there was considerable support for placing a Christian inscription on the memorial. He sent a large list of the inscriptions which the Office of Works had received to the Cabinet for consideration.[184] Following the response of people to the memorial on Armistice Day 1919 the leading article of the *Church Times* launched a scathing attack on what it called 'cenotapholatry', warning: 'Sentiment is rapidly hardening into a formal cult, to which conformity seems now to be required by public opinion from Kings and Presidents, Princes and Prime Ministers of State.'[185]

If the desire of the Church to create a rival shrine to the Cenotaph was an important motive behind its support for the Unknown Warrior, it was not successful in the 1920s. While the burial of the Unknown Warrior was a powerful event in November 1920, it did not detract from the position of the Cenotaph as the popular focus of the memory of the dead. This is clearly illustrated by the failure of the proposal that the Armistice Day ceremony on 11 November 1923 should be held in Westminster Abbey rather than at the Cenotaph, because it was a Sunday. In October of that year the Cabinet resolved not to hold a ceremony at the Cenotaph, at the suggestion of the Archbishop of Canterbury.[186] There was widespread public opposition to the change. The opposition dwelt upon the sacred nature of the Cenotaph.

181. Hansard, 118 HC Deb. 5s, 29 July 1919, p. 1948; 30 July 1919, p. 2112; 119 HC Deb. 5s, 4 Aug. 1919, 41; 13 Aug. 1919, pp. 1289–90.

182. *Sunday Herald*, 27 July 1919.

183. Bishop of Winchester to Sir A. Mond, 19 Sept. 1919, PRO Work 20 - 139.

184. Sir A. Mond, Memorandum to the War Cabinet, 15 Oct. 1919, PRO Work 20 - 139.

185. *Church Times*, 21 Nov. 1919.

186. Conclusions of a Meeting of the Cabinet held on 15 Oct. 1923, PRO CAB 23 - 46, 48(23).

The *Daily Chronicle* wrote: 'There is no more fitting spot at which to hold such a service, for the Cenotaph, empty tomb as it is in fact, has become a shrine at which the whole Empire tenders its tributes to the heroes whose blood has cemented the imperishable fabric of national unity.'[187] A letter to the editor of the newspaper stated that the Government could go to the Abbey if it wanted, but we, 'the people want the Cenotaph which to us is far more sacred than any Church'.[188] The Cabinet was forced to back down and hold a service at the Cenotaph.[189] According to *The Times* they realised that if no official service was going to be held, people would organise an impromptu service.[190]

In practice, however, the two memorials were linked by their unveiling and burial ceremonies on Armistice Day 1920. But in the early 1920s joint references to them often reflected the greater popularity of the Cenotaph. For example, the leading article of the *Manchester Guardian* asserted that 'the general public, I think, are more devoted to the Cenotaph than to the Unknown Warrior's grave'.[191] When the Cenotaph and the Unknown Warrior are viewed together as memorials they represent the contradictions inherent in the British response to the war.

The memorials drew upon and affirmed the high diction of heroic sacrifice. The Cenotaph referred to the dead as 'The Glorious Dead'. Naming the body which was buried in Westminster Abbey the 'Unknown *Warrior*' also invoked the heroic tradition. This image was reinforced by the decision to bury a crusader-style sword with the body. The Unknown Warrior was described as a 'successor to Aeneas and Arthur' and as the 'Unknown Arthur'.[192] The grave was also compared with the medieval shrine to Edward the Confessor in Westminster Abbey. One account stated that 'Yesterday's pilgrims passed the King's shrine [Edward the Confessor's] by, for they had come to do honour to another lowlier grave, yet there was that in the bearing of the quiet reverent crowds which made one think of those

187. *Daily Chronicle*, 19 Oct. 1923.
188. *Daily Chronicle*, 22 Oct. 1923.
189. Conclusions of a Meeting of the Cabinet held on 22 Oct. 1923, PRO CAB 23 - 46, 49(23).
190. *The Times*, 23 Oct. 1923.
191. *Manchester Guardian*, 14 Nov. 1921.
192. *Outlook*, XLVI (Nov. 1920), p. 478. *Birmingham Post*, 12 Nov. 1920.

old-time Abbey pilgrimages.'[193] The order of Crusaders, which was founded in 1921, acknowledged the Unknown Warrior as the 'Principal Knight and Supreme Head of the order'.[194]

However, owing to their associations with people in mourning, these memorials also evoked the human cost of the war and the pain people felt at that cost. This found expression in the response of pilgrims to the Cenotaph. It became a sacred place because it was associated with the memory and even the spirits of the dead. The need for a means of coming to terms with the dead transformed the burial of the Unknown Warrior and the unveiling of the permanent Cenotaph into a national ceremony of mourning. The priority of the ceremony changed from a tribute to the Army and the British victory, to a tribute from the relatives of the bereaved and ex-servicemen to the dead. Thus the Cenotaph and the Unknown Warrior both acknowledged the victory won by the sacrifice of the nation and the cost that victory had exacted.

While the Unknown Warrior particularly emphasised the tradition of heroic sacrifice, the Cenotaph symbolised all those who had died in the war. In a letter to *The Times* a correspondent argued that the Cenotaph made him think of the lives of the young men who died in the war.[195] Another writer agreed with the correspondent, but felt that the Cenotaph also brought to mind those 'countless myriads of the living who, day after day, in their quiet patience waited in their turn to pass and, in passing, to pay their tribute in memento and prayer'.[196] Some people saw it as a memorial to anyone who had died, not just the war dead. Wreaths were left at the memorial to commemorate not only the war dead but also the dead children and relatives of ex-servicemen.[197]

The Cenotaph could refer to the dead without invoking images of the Allied victory. Thus it appealed to people who did not accept the traditions which that victory affirmed. The practice of leaving political wreaths at the Cenotaph illustrates this widespread appeal. In the afternoon of 11 November 1921 there was

193. *Sphere*, LXXXIII, (Nov. 1920), p. 186.
194. *The Times*, 29 Nov. 1923.
195. *The Times*, 21 June 1923.
196. *The Times*, 25 June 1923.
197. Hansard, 157 HC Deb. 5s, 26 July 1922, p. 460.

a march by at least 5,000 unemployed persons to the Cenotaph in what was called a 'pilgrimage of the unemployed'.[198] The marchers sang music hall songs until they turned into Whitehall, when according to one account a 'strange hush' broke over them. The band broke into a hymn tune and the pace of the unemployed slackened to a slow march. Some of the wreaths they bore were censored by the police because they might be offensive to some mourners. These included inscriptions such as 'To the dead victims of Capitalism from the living victims of Capitalism'.[199] Political wreaths continued to be left at the Cenotaph in the early 1920s.[200]

The Cenotaph was able to appeal so widely because it relied for its interpretation upon the meanings which people brought to it.[201] The column of stone stood for the 'Glorious Dead'; and apart from commemorating the dead it did not explicitly propound an interpretation of the war. Therefore when the meaning of the war was questioned this generally did not cast doubt upon the memorial. In 1930 Laurence Housman wrote that if the stones of the Cenotaph had a voice for the dead they would both cry out for 'a thousand lives laid down, with the hope held, or with the hope lost, that war might be no more' and that 'war itself is a fine thing and worth while'.[202] Irene Rathbone concluded her pacifist novel *They Call It Peace* at the Cenotaph, where two very different women make a pilgrimage in 1934. Nellie always joins the pilgrimage to lay flowers at the Cenotaph on Armistice Day. She lays wreaths for her husband Alf and her brother Ed (who fought in the war, but died later; however, she felt that 'it was really, when you looked at it all round as though poor Ed *had* died in the war'). Nellie finds herself 'comforted, softly uplifted' by her visit to 'The Glorious Dead'. This contrasts with the response of Lorna. It has been years since she has made a visit to the Cenotaph with flowers, and she is certain that this will be her last. Standing in the queue she can make out shapes in the mist above the Cenotaph and hears voices which recall

198. W. Hannington, *Unemployed Struggles 1919–1936: My Life and Struggles Amongst the Unemployed* (East Ardsley, 1973, facsimile of 1936 publication), p. 77, puts the numbers of unemployed as high as 25,000.

199. *Eastern Daily Press*, 12 Nov. 1921.

200. Hansard, 157 HC Deb. 5s, 26 July 1922, p. 460.

201. Winter, *Sites of Memory*, pp. 103–4.

202. L. Housman, *War Letters of Fallen Englishmen* (London, 1930), p. 5.

the horrors of the war. The wreath she leaves at the Cenotaph reads:

IN MEMORY
OF THOSE
WHO DIED IN VAIN.[203]

Conclusion

The pilgrimages to the Cenotaph and the grave of the Unknown Warrior were among the most extraordinary events in Britain in the inter-war years. The development of the temporary Cenotaph into a sacred place reveals the anguish felt by many people confronted by their feelings of loss. The temporary Cenotaph brought the wartime practice of erecting war shrines, as a focal point for the memory of the dead, into post-war commemoration. In the process it became one of the 'most potent symbols of the inter-war years'.[204] The ceremonies for the unveiling of the permanent Cenotaph and the burial of the Unknown Warrior in November 1920 were transformed by popular response from a public funeral, where the people participated as onlookers, into a ceremony of mourning, where they became pilgrims. This brought the private experience of bereaved relatives and ex-servicemen into the ceremony. It expressed the belief that the relatives of the dead, especially women, had made a significant sacrifice during the war.

Both the Cenotaph and grave of the Unknown Warrior remained sacred places throughout the 1920s. Albeit briefly, they replaced Trafalgar Square, for many people, as the symbolic heart of London. The Unknown Warrior was intended to replace the Cenotaph, but instead became closely linked with it. Together the memorials reflect the complexity and ambiguity of the British response to the Great War. The memorials spoke the language of 'high diction', which maintained continuity with the traditions of heroic sacrifice; but they also spoke the language of bereavement. The pilgrimages to these sites made it impossible to bring the war experience to a close in the early 1920s. They presaged the nature of post-war remembrance. To remember did not just

203. I. Rathbone, *They Call It Peace* (London, 1936), pp. 612–17.
204. Homberger, 'The Story of the Cenotaph', p. 1429.

mean a call for people to remember a distant experience; it was a commitment to renew the experience itself. That experience was multifaceted; but loss was at its core.

3

'Murder on Show'? Travel to the Battlefields of the Great War

> The War may have been 'legalised murder' as it was now called. But Post-War is murder on show, with a small price for admission to defray expenses.
>
> – R. H. Mottram, *The Spanish Farm Trilogy*[1]

The war transformed the landscape of the places over which it was fought and provided a new range of sites for travellers to visit. The traveller to Northern France, Belgium, Northern Italy, Northern Greece, Egypt, Palestine, Iraq or Turkey could choose to visit the new battlefields, war memorials, cemeteries or museums. Although there was a constant flow of tourists and pilgrims to these places during the inter-war years, the nature of tourism and pilgrimage was not fixed. The number of visitors to the battlefields fluctuated, and the landscape which they found varied between different battlefields and, particularly on the Western Front, changed in the course of the 1920s and 1930s. Although the Western Front attracted the vast majority of travellers, it is worth briefly considering the battlefields from the other theatres of the British war effort, as they indicate the diversity of responses to and images of the war which these places could evoke.

Travel to the 'Eastern' Battlefields

Travel to the battlefields in Northern Italy, Northern Greece, Gallipoli and the Holy Land was intermittent. This was partly the result of the expense and difficulty of reaching places such as Turkey, Egypt and Palestine. A report prepared by Thomas Cook's for the Australian and British Governments on travel to

1. R. H. Mottram, *The Spanish Farm Trilogy* (London, 1927), p. 792.

the Eastern theatre of operations advised that travellers would need to journey independently, because it was not possible to organise special parties, similar to those conducted to the Western Front by the YMCA or Salvation Army. The report also recommended that travellers be warned about the probability of 'uncongenial surroundings' and 'adverse conditions'.[2] As a result few travellers journeyed to the battlefields in Iraq and Palestine. When a group of military officers visited them in the early 1920s they found the bones of the dead still lying on the ground.[3] Robert Byron had a similar experience when he visited the old British trenches at Gaza in 1929.[4]

Also, the battlefields, memorials and cemeteries in many of these places failed to capture the imagination of the wealthy tourists who could afford to visit them. A good example of this were the battlefields of Northern Italy. Despite an attempt by Thomas Cook's to organise tours of these battlefields by stressing their interest not only 'because of the marks and scars of war, but for the natural beauty of the setting', as well as a pilgrimage by the King and Queen to the war cemeteries, regular tours of the Italian battlefields never became popular.[5] When Vera Brittain wanted to visit the grave of her brother Edward on the Asiago Plateau she found that Thomas Cook's had no scheme in place to escort people to the war cemeteries there.[6]

Thus many of the battlefields in Northern Italy and the Near East were only visited by those bereaved relatives seeking the grave or a sign of a missing loved one.[7] So few people from Great Britain were expected to visit them that the war cemeteries and memorials both commemorated the dead and stood as symbols of Britain's presence in these regions. The Foreign Office urged that the memorial to the missing on Lake Doiran in the Balkans

2. M. G. Shepherd (Official Secretary, Australia House, London) to the Secretary of the Prime Minister's Department, Melbourne, 11 Nov. 1921, AA A1608/1 - F27/1/7 part 1.

3. *The Times*, 12 Dec. 1923.

4. P. Fussell, *Abroad: British Literary Travelling between the Wars* (Oxford, 1980), p. 14.

5. *Traveller's Gazette*, LXX (Sept. 1920), p. 10. *The Times*, 14 May 1923.

6. V. Brittain, *Testament of Youth: An Autobiographical Study of the Years 1900–1925* (London, 1933), p. 522.

7. The St Barnabas Society (*Croydon Pilgrimage, The Second Scottish Pilgrimage, Italian Pilgrimage, The Smaller Pilgrimages* (London, *c.*1925), p. 26) organised a pilgrimage of bereaved relatives to Italy in 1925.

should be unveiled as quickly as possible, as it would reassert the British presence at a time when the Italians and French were active in the area.[8] Fabian Ware argued that 'constant loving care of war graves' displayed to the peoples of the East the 'strength and grandeur of the British Empire'.[9] Lord Plumer even suggested that the people of the Holy Land would see the cemeteries and 'acknowledge that a nation which has made such sacrifices for another country has the prescriptive right to control the destinies of that country so that those sacrifices shall not be in vain'.[10]

Considering the difficulties of travel to the battlefields in the East two places drew a surprising number of travellers: Jerusalem and Gallipoli. In the case of Jerusalem the number of visitors would have been increased by the popularity of the city for travellers to the Holy Land. At the same time both Gallipoli and Jerusalem captured the romance of the war, and this seems to have encouraged a greater interest in the battlefields, cemeteries and memorials in these places. In 1930 over 1,000 people visited the war cemetery in Jerusalem during the four months from January to April.[11] Also, a regular practice developed among parties of pilgrims of visiting the cemetery in Jerusalem in November for Armistice Day.[12] In the early 1920s Turkey was difficult to reach as a result of political conditions. Despite an attempt to make Anzac Cove into a site for visitors, the crisis over Chanak in 1922–3 discouraged potential travellers.[13] Once this crisis was resolved, and despite initial difficulties with the Turkish authorities, at least seven organised pilgrimages were made to Gallipoli in the 1920s and 1930s. The first was in 1925 when the *SS Otranto* landed passengers at Helles.[14] Two pilgrimages were organised by the St Barnabas Society in 1926 and 1928, two were organised by ex-servicemen in 1934 and 1936, and the remaining two pilgrimages involved pilgrims from outside Great Britain, an Australian pilgrimage in 1929 and a French

8. William Tyrrell to Fabian Ware, 27 Jan. 1926, PRO FO 371 - 11346.
9. F. Ware, 'The Price of Peace', *Listener*, II (Nov. 1929), p. 637.
10. *War Graves of the Empire* (London, 1928), p. 47.
11. Minutes of Proceedings of the IWGC, 28 July 1930, p. 12, NAC, RG 38, Vol. 351.
12. L. Katin, 'The Flowering Graves of Palestine', *British Legion Journal*, 13 (Dec. 1933), p. 210.
13. C. E. W. Bean, *Gallipoli Mission* (Canberra, 1948), p. 334.
14. Foreign Office Memorandum, 30 Oct. 1926, PRO FO 371 - 11557.

pilgrimage in 1930. Also in the late 1920s and early 1930s cruise ships from Great Britain, America, France and Germany regularly called at Helles to allow passengers to visit the battlefields of Gallipoli.[15]

The goal for travellers to Jerusalem was the war cemetery on Mount Scopus. The cemetery invited comparisons between the sacrifice made by the soldiers and that of Jesus Christ, a key theme in wartime culture and in post-war commemoration. The IWGC made an exception to their general practice of erecting a cross which was less conspicuous than the Cross of Sacrifice in cemeteries in the East because if 'there was one cemetery where above all the Cross of Sacrifice should stand open to the eyes of all it was the cemetery on the Mount of Olives'.[16] Trevor Allen found that, while the pilgrims on the 1927 St Barnabas pilgrimage to the Near East were in Jerusalem, the war cemetery was 'seldom out of our vision or thought; it lends immediate significance to our visits to the Church of the Holy Sepulchre, the Via Dolorosa, the Mount of Olives and the Garden of Gethsemane'.[17] Following a visit to the cemetery William Ellis wrote that the dead 'on the Hill of Sacrifice, symbolise the best for which the world war was fought, as if seeking a fellowship with that other Young Man who had laid down His life for man's redemption'.[18]

Gallipoli also attracted extraordinary interest. It was the only battlefield outside the old Western Front about which a guide-book was written, and many accounts were published about pilgrimages to Gallipoli. For instance, four books were written about the 1926 St Barnabas pilgrimage.[19] Interest in Gallipoli was not only high in Australia and New Zealand, where many people considered the battle to be their nation's baptism of fire, but also in Britain.[20] Geoffrey Moorhouse has described the signifi-

15. IWGC, *Annual Report* (1930/31), p. 33.

16. F. C. Sillar, 'Stones of Remembrance', *Empire Review*, XLVIII (Dec. 1928), p. 400.

17. T. Allen, *The Tracks They Trod: Salonika and the Balkans, Gallipoli, Egypt and Palestine Revisited* (London, 1932), p. 163.

18. W. T. Ellis, *Bible Lands To-day* (New York and London, 1927), p. 182.

19. St Barnabas Society, *Gallipoli and Salonika* (London, *c.*1926). Allen, *The Tracks They Trod*. I. Hay, *The Ship of Remembrance* (London, *c.*1926). J. Holmes, *A Pilgrimage to Gallipoli* (London, *c.*1926).

20. For a discussion of the significance of Gallipoli in Australia and New Zealand see K. S. Inglis, 'Anzac Day in Australia and New Zealand', Paper presented at Histoire Culturelle Comparée du Premier Conflit Mondial: La Guerre

cance of Gallipoli in the memory of the war experience in the English town of Bury; but its appeal was more widespread.[21] An important reason for this appeal was that Gallipoli retained an aura of romance. Thomas Cook's guide to the battlefield described the expedition to Gallipoli as 'a glorious adventure, a failure perhaps, but none the less an adventure the fame of which shall not be dimmed by age, nor overshadowed by any other deed in history'.[22] The largest pilgrimage of ex-servicemen to Gallipoli, in the 1930s, was known as the 'Pilgrimage of Chivalry'. Such a title would have been unthinkable for a pilgrimage to the battlefields of the old Western Front in the 1930s. The location of the peninsula, with the proximity of Troy, and the involvement of the poet Rupert Brooke with the expedition also encouraged this image of Gallipoli.[23]

The appeal of the Gallipoli battlefields was enhanced by the contrast between them and the Western Front. John North visited Gallipoli because he believed it had an 'inward and spiritual meaning', a feeling which was missing in France, where he found 'no magic in the soil'.[24] In part this was the result of the promotion of the view that, had Gallipoli succeeded, the tragedy of the Western Front might have been avoided. Both Sir Ian Hamilton, the Commander of the Dardanelles Expedition, and Winston Churchill, one of its chief supporters, actively promoted this view.[25] However, few British travellers could forget that the expedition had been a failure which ended in defeat. For many officers the journey provided an opportunity to exorcise the spectre of defeat, and a common theme in writing about the peninsula is the claim that the task was impossible and that for the men to have landed at all was an extraordinary achievement. Field Marshal Birdwood, the Commander of the Anzac forces on the peninsula, marvelled at how completely the Turkish forces

---

et La Mémoire de la Guerre, Colloque, Péronne (July 1992). French translation in J. J. Becker *et al.*, *Guerre et Cultures* (Paris, 1994).

21. G. Moorhouse, *Hell's Foundations: A Town, its Myths and Gallipoli* (London, 1992).

22. Thomas Cook, *The Traveller's Handbook for Constantinople, Gallipoli and Asia Minor* (London, 1923), p. 105.

23. Brooke died before the expedition reached the Dardanelles and was buried on the island of Skyros.

24. J. North, *Gallipoli: The Fading Vision* (London, 1966, first published 1936), pp. 15-16.

on the heights commanded the Allied positions, and asserted his belief that 'had the positions of the Turks and ourselves been reversed, we should never have allowed an enemy to remain on the shore below us'.[26]

Finally Gallipoli, unlike the battlefields of the Western Front, was not reconstructed after the war because there were no villages to rebuild. A number of visitors found that the war seemed much closer to them while they were at Gallipoli. W. T. Forshaw claimed that when he stood in his old trench at Gallipoli the silence seemed 'just a temporary lull'.[27] The untouched landscape enabled many travellers to feel closer to the dead. Pilgrims who visited Gallipoli in 1926 described a sense of unease as they explored the ravines: something seemed to be pulling them back.[28] In 1935 Thornton Cook wrote: 'Now scrambling up the hills and through the ravines more than one of us felt a sure conviction that the great company of the fallen were giving us welcome; they were rallying to meet us in spirit, glad that we remembered, and had come.'[29]

Travel to the Western Front

The Western Front was the premier tourist attraction for British battlefield tourists and pilgrims because it was close to Great Britain, it was the decisive theatre of operations, the majority of the British dead were buried there and it was closely identified with the nature of the war. British travellers concentrated on the areas in which the majority of British troops were engaged; what one guidebook described as 'that swathe of battlefield which is sacred to our own troops'.[30] This meant that travellers

25. I. Hamilton, 'Foreword', in W. E. Stanton Hope, *Gallipoli Revisited: An Account of the Duchess of Richmond Pilgrimage Cruise* (London, *c.*1934), p. 5. W. S. Churchill, *The World Crisis 1911–1918*, abridged edition (London, 1931), pp. 533–4.

26. W. Birdwood, *Khaki and Gown: An Autobiography* (London, 1941), p. 421. Also see A. Hunter-Weston, 'War and Peace at the Dardanelles: An Impression', *Army Quarterly*, III (Oct. 1921), pp. 71–2.

27. W. T. Forshaw, 'A Battlefield Unchanged', *British Legion Journal*, 10 (Aug. 1930), p. 34.

28. Allen, *The Tracks They Trod*, p. 72.

29. E. Thornton Cook, 'Gallipoli: Twenty Years After', *Cornhill Magazine*, 151 (Mar. 1935), p. 260.

30. A. T. Fleming, *How to See the Battlefields* (London, 1919), p. 2.

were primarily concerned with Belgian and French Flanders and the region of Picardy in France. These regions encompassed the fighting in the Ypres Salient, the battles around Loos, the Somme battlefields, the fighting around Arras and Vimy Ridge, and Cambrai. The number of travellers who visited the Western Front fluctuated during the inter-war years. At the same time both the landscape and the imagined landscape of the battlefields also altered. These changes influenced and reflected a variety of attitudes to the war.

The Changing Pattern of Travel

The IWGC kept a rough total of the number of signatures in the visitors' books at its war memorials and cemeteries in Belgium and France in the period 1926 to 1939. Unfortunately the visitors' books themselves have not survived, as the comments left by travellers would have provided an invaluable source for the feelings of travellers on visiting the cemeteries and memorials. The figures are extremely unreliable, because many visitors chose not to sign the books, others would have signed at more than one cemetery or memorial, guided tours often took tourists to the commercial battlefield sites rather than to the cemeteries and the memorials and, finally, people from many different countries visited the cemeteries and memorials and signed the visitors' books.[31] However, they do provide an indication of trends in the appeal of the battlefields to people in the late 1920s and the 1930s. The quantities of signatures collected suggest that in the years of the 'war books boom', from 1927 to 1932, and in the late 1930s the numbers of travellers to the battlefields were particularly high. The period before 1926 is less certain. Contemporaries considered that there was a boom in travel to and interest in the battlefields in the first years after the war. Figures for the number of visits made to the IWM confirm this pattern of interest in places associated with the war, which is characterised by three periods - 1919–1923, 1927–1932 and 1936–1939 - when the interest was particularly high.

In their social history of the inter-war years Robert Graves and Alan Hodge recalled that in: 'August [1919] came the great holiday scramble. Thousands of people set off for the sea on their

31. Minutes of proceedings of the IWGC, 9 Sept. 1931, p. 6, NAC RG 38 Vol. 349.

first holiday for five years . . . But bereaved wives and parents who could afford to do so went on personally conducted tours to the "Devastated Regions" and ate picnics in the trenches with old ammunition boxes as makeshift tables.'[32] The first parties of relatives faced, not only the desolation of the battlefields, which were a veritable desert, but also the depredations of gangs of deserters, who attempted to prey on isolated groups whom they caught in the vast wilderness of the Western Front. Enid Bagnold wrote that immediately after the war a 'certain lawlessness was abroad in the lonelier areas of the battlefields. Odds and ends of all the armies, deserters, well hidden during many months lived under the earth in holes and cellars and used strange means to gain a living.'[33] Many bereaved relatives travelled with the Church Army, Salvation Army, and YMCA. The Church Army conducted 5,000 relatives of the dead to France and Belgium from November 1919 to June 1920.[34] During the years 1920–23 the Salvation Army escorted 18,507 people to the battlefields, while 60,000 people were assisted by the YMCA in the period up to 1923.[35]

Other people travelled to satisfy their curiosity about the places which had been fought over during the war. In 1919 as many as 75 per cent of the inquiries made about holidays in France concerned arrangements for visiting the battlefields and war graves. Similarly in 1920 Thomas Cook's commented that there had never been such a demand for tickets to the Continent at Easter. They suggested that this was partly due to the inflated state of wages and partly due to the desire of people to visit the battlefields.[36] Many holiday-makers at the Belgian coastal resorts, such as Ostend, also took advantage of the day-tours which were offered to the battlefields of the Ypres Salient.[37] By 1924 as many as one million holiday-makers stayed in Ostend alone, and these would have significantly increased the number of tourists to the battlefields.[38]

32. R. Graves and A. Hodge, *The Long Weekend: A Social History of Great Britain 1918–1939* (London, 1940), p. 34.

33. E. Bagnold, *The Happy Foreigner* (London, 1920), p. 239.

34. Church Army, *Annual Report*, (1919/20), p. 31.

35. *Yorkshire Herald*, 2 June 1924. *Red Triangle*, VII (Aug. 1923), p. 188.

36. *The Times*, 30 Mar. 1920.

37. E. F. Williams, 'Ypres Calling', *Ypres Times*, 3 (Apr. 1927), p. 153.

38. Ward Lock & Co. Ltd., *Handbook to Belgium and the Battlefields*, 8th edn (London, 1924), p. 77.

The large variety of guidebooks to the battlefields produced in the early 1920s also point to their appeal. Michelin published 850,000 copies of guidebooks in the seven months up to January 1920, which exceeded the publishing records of such best-selling war novels as Henri Barbusse's *Under Fire*.[39] In the period up to January 1922 the Michelin Company sold 1,432,000 guides in France, England and America.[40] While Michelin were the most prolific in the number of titles produced as well as sales, they were by no means the only publishers of battlefield guides in this period. The books endeavoured to aid travellers and to enable people who could not afford to visit these places to see what they were like, which was particularly important in respect of battlefields as far away as Gallipoli.[41]

The figures for the number of visits made by people to the IWM in the Crystal Palace in the period from November 1920 to 1923 also illustrate that in the immediate aftermath of the war people wanted to know what the war had been like. In the period up to 1923 over three million people visited the IWM.[42] These numbers would have been inflated by the attraction of the Crystal Palace itself; but it is likely that the majority of people came to the IWM to try to understand the war. For instance, ex-servicemen brought their relatives to it in order to show them the places where they had fought.[43] When the popular response to the Cenotaph and the Unknown Warrior in the period up to November 1921 is also taken into account, it suggests that in the immediate aftermath of the war people did not seek to or were unable to forget. Obsession with the war was the rule.

The intensity of this obsession could not be maintained, and in the mid-1920s interest in the battlefields waned. Gardeners at the war cemeteries in France and Belgium noted the decline in the number of visitors to the cemeteries. The caretaker at the Ulster Memorial, near Thiepval, is reported to have stated that from 1922 to 1924 an average of 300 people visited the Memorial every week, but by 1928 only about 150 arrived in a

39. *L'Illustration*, 4011 (Jan. 1920).

40. 'Ce que Michelin a fait pour le Tourisme', Michelin Archive, Clermont-Ferrand, France.

41. T. J. Pemberton, *Gallipoli Today* (London, 1926).

42. IWM, *Annual Reports* (1921–1923).

43. IWM, *Annual Report* (1921/2).

week.[44] At Beaucourt, according to one attendant, months could pass between the arrivals of visitors to some of the cemeteries. Only eight people visited the main cemetery in 1928 up to the arrival of the British Legion pilgrims in August.[45] The Ypres League was affected by the decline in interest in travelling to the battlefields. In 1922 they organised a pilgrimage for 2,000 ex-servicemen and bereaved relatives to Ypres, but in 1923 the League was forced to announce that it was not possible to organise a tour on the scale of the previous year.[46] Instead, two parties of thirty members and sixty members respectively were planned. The proposed tour at Whitsun in 1924 had to be cancelled, as only one or two people expressed an interest in going; and in 1925 the secretary again noted that there was insufficient demand for a large pilgrimage.[47]

The decline in the popularity of travel to the battlefields reflected a wider fall in interest in the war. The attendance figures for the IWM were affected by its move to the Western Galleries in South Kensington. However, even allowing for the impact of this move, the number of people coming to the IWM dropped to its lowest point for the inter-war period. In the year 1922/3 over 900,000 visits were made to it; by contrast, in the first full year after the IWM reopened, from April 1925 to March 1926, only 224,683 visits were made.[48] This pattern is also consistent with the publishing figures for middlebrow novels about the war. There was a spate of publications in 1919, which sharply decreased in the period before the beginning of the 'war books boom' in the late 1920s.[49]

The decline in interest in travel to places associated with the war should not be exaggerated: the IWGC reported that the numbers of people visiting the graves were actually increasing.[50] The contradiction between the experiences of the gardeners and

44. L. J. D. Gavin and J. Harter (eds), *The Story of an Epic Pilgrimage: A Souvenir of the Battlefield Pilgrimage* (n.p., 1928), p. 98.

45. *Evening News*, 7 Aug. 1928.

46. *Ypres Times*, Special Pilgrimage Number, 1 (Aug. 1923). *Ypres Times*, 1 (July 1923), p. 241.

47. *Ypres Times*, 2 (July 1924), p. 85; 2 (Apr. 1925), p. 163.

48. IWM, *Annual Reports* (1922/3, 1925/6).

49. R. Bracco, *Merchants of Hope: British Middlebrow Writers and the First World War* (Oxford and Providence, 1993), p. 14.

50. IWGC, *Annual Report* (1925/6), p. 3.

the Ypres League and the opinion of the IWGC is surprising. Perhaps it is the result of a relative decline in the level of interest in the war compared with the obsession which characterised the early 1920s. While parties of bereaved relatives continued to visit war cemeteries and the St Barnabas Society organised a number of large pilgrimages in this period, the numbers of tourists may have declined as alternative destinations such as the South of France became more appealing.

One reason why the battlefields may have been less attractive to tourists was the growth of the feeling that the scenes of destruction were no longer as inherently interesting as they had been in the first years after the war. They may have even repelled some travellers. A travel book extolling the appeal of Belgium published in 1923 claimed:

> the idea that Belgium was utterly devastated during the late war has become so prevalent as to deter many people from visiting a delightful little country.
>
> Belgium undoubtedly suffered terribly in the conflict, and Flanders was reduced to a shambles. It is a mistake, however, to imagine that the whole country was desolated. Much of the historical and the more beautiful part is unscathed; and much even of the scattered area is already rebuilt.[51]

The second post-war edition of Muirhead's guide to Belgium asserted that the country was 'more than the cock-pit of Europe', which was a significant change in tone from the first edition, which had claimed that the war had changed the nature of travel in Belgium and Northern France.[52]

Many people no longer wanted to be reminded of the pain the war had unleashed. A reaction against the war prompted Philip Gibbs to write in 1923 that the 'very name of the last war sickens many minds who cannot bear the reminder of its blood and sacrifice, and who see nothing but mockery in its results'.[53] One traveller who visited the battlefields in 1925 confessed that he 'rather shrank from coming' because he 'expected something gloomy and funereal'.[54] Charitable organisations were forced to

51. A. J. Brown, *A Joyous Entry into Brighter Belgium* (London, 1923), p. 9.

52. F. Muirhead, *Belgium* (London, 1924), p. lxvii. Contrast F. Muirhead, *Belgium and the Western Front: British and American* (London, 1920), p. v.

53. P. Gibbs, 'The Cemeteries in the Salient', *Ypres Times*, 1 (Apr. 1923), p. 198.

54. 'War Graves in Flanders', *Round Table*, XVI (Mar. 1926), p. 310.

reassure people that they were not needlessly prolonging the grief of the bereaved. The St Barnabas Society emphasised that their pilgrimages 'do not reopen old wounds: they set hearts that have been too long aching at last to rest, they complete an act of Faith, they very definitely leave in the minds of the Pilgrims a sense of peace and of joy that will last until their lives' end'.[55]

By the 1930s the uncertainty about the place of battlefield travel was even more pronounced. Some guidebooks questioned whether the battlefields were an appropriate place to be visited on a holiday. Sidney Clark's budget guide to France doubted whether its readers really liked battlefields. Clark qualified his assertion, noting 'I do not mean by this to minimize the immense significance of these sacred places, but somehow they do not quite fit into the brief cheerful holiday which is ours in France. They stir such profound emotions that we cannot very well pack them in with cathedrals, châteaux, and bright cafés.'[56] Similarly E. M. Newman decided that for the average reader the former front only retained a 'historic interest', and he chose not to comment on it, but instead to 'merely suggest what may be included in a visit to the former theatre of war'.[57]

The year 1926/7 seems to have been a low point in the interest of people in travelling to the battlefields. Despite this, 1927 was the beginning of a remarkable resurgence in world-wide public interest in the war which is most commonly identified with the 'war books boom'. This was the period in which such works as Erich Maria Remarque's *All Quiet on the Western Front*, Robert Grave's *Goodbye to All That* and R. C. Sherriff's play *Journey's End* were published or staged for the first time. John Onions has analysed the chronology of the war books boom. It began in 1927, when eight war novels were published, and reached its height in 1930, with the publication of at least thirty-six war novels. Thereafter the interest in fiction about the war fell away, and only thirteen war novels were published in 1932.[58] The numbers of signatures in the visitors' books at the war cemeteries

55. St Barnabas Society, *Ypres/The Somme* (London, *c.*1923), p. 2.
56. S. A. Clark, *France on £10* (London, 1934), p. 154.
57. E. M. Newman, *Seeing France* (New York and London, 1930), p. vi.
58. J. Onions, *English Fiction and Drama of the Great War, 1918–39* (Basingstoke, 1990), pp. 49–51.

and memorials follow a similar pattern. In 1926/7, the year in which the lowest number of signatures was recorded, there were 67,787 signatures.[59] The number rose in the years before the Depression, peaking in 1931, when 104,000 signatures were made in the four months from May to August. This was an increase of 13 per cent over the same four months in 1930 and of 25 per cent over the same period in 1928.[60] While the new fascination with the war was dominated by an interest in war books, it was not limited to war novels, plays and memoirs. Other events helped to promote the interest in the war which fuelled the 'war books boom'.

One of the most important events, particularly in encouraging travel to the battlefields, was the decision by the American Legion to hold its annual conference in Paris from 19 to 24 September 1927. The American Legion sent at least 20,000 representatives who toured the French Battlefields. Perhaps more importantly, the French Government took the chains away from the Arc de Triomphe for the first time since the victory parade in 1919, and the American Legion conducted a parade down the Champs Elysées. The chains were placed there after the defeat in 1870, and their presence became a powerful symbol in France of their victory over the Germans. The American Legion tour was an unprecedented event, which was reported in newspapers throughout the world. In many countries journalists instigated a growing demand for ex-servicemen to travel to the battlefields, if only to show that the Americans were not the only ones who had won the war! There were calls in Great Britain for a national pilgrimage.[61] The American Legion visit inspired plans for a Canadian pilgrimage, which culminated in the Vimy Ridge pilgrimage in 1936, as well as numerous unsuccessful attempts to organise a national Australian pilgrimage.[62] The American Legion visit may have even played a role in the revival of pilgrimages by French ex-servicemen to Verdun noted by Antoine Prost.[63] The international body of ex-servicemen, *La Fédération Interalliée des Anciens Combattants*, had no doubt that the 1927 American

59. IWGC, *Annual Report* (1926/7), p. 33.
60. *The Times*, 6 Oct. 1931.
61. Discussed in Chapter 4.
62. See Chapter 5.
63. A. Prost, 'Verdun', in P. Nora (ed.), *Les Lieux de Mémoire*, Vol. II *La Nation* (Paris, 1984), p. 111.

Legion visit had begun the resurgence of pilgrimages, which involved ex-servicemen from many different countries.[64]

Public interest in pilgrimages was also reawakened by the opening of the Menin Gate on 27 July 1927, particularly as the ceremony was broadcast on radio by the BBC. An ex-serviceman who was a member of the fourth Battalion of the Duke of Wellington's Regiment wrote: 'The opening of the Menin Gate recreated in the minds of many old 4th's scenes of former days. The Menin Road and its tragedies - what a tale the stones could tell. A great many "Dukes" would have liked to go, but, lacking a leader, no concerted action was taken.'[65] The Menin Gate both provided a goal for pilgrimages and gave them a wider significance. It was the most significant English war memorial on the old Western Front, and in the minds of many English people it was 'the supreme monument of the dead'.[66] Until it was opened in 1927 there was no single destination to which all English pilgrimages could be directed, in order to pay homage to the dead. Also, the unveiling of new memorials to the missing, such as those at the Menin Gate in 1927, Thiepval and Arras in 1932 and the Vimy Ridge in 1936, encouraged pilgrims who had yet to visit the battlefields to do so, particularly if they knew one of the 'missing' commemorated on the memorial.[67]

Also, interest in battlefield travel was encouraged by the public discussion of the need to teach a new generation about the war. In 1928 the leading article in the *Evening Standard* stated that: 'we are approaching a critical period in the matter of war memories', as there was a generation growing up who had no memory of the war, and it was necessary to ensure that 'what we have learnt shall be passed on to the coming generations that our spiritual heritage from the War is not lost'.[68] The Chairman of the British Legion Pilgrimage Committee stated that an object of the pilgrimage they were organising in 1928 was 'to keep before the rising generation the great effort made by the British Empire and to remind them of the tragedy of War'.[69]

64. FIDAC, British Legion Monthly and Special Circulars, 1931.
65. *Iron Duke*, III (Oct. 1927), p. 157.
66. *Radio Times*, 3 Aug. 1928.
67. Church Army, *Annual Report* (1928/9), p. 40.
68. *Evening Standard*, 2 Aug. 1928.
69. *British Legion Journal* (Sept. 1928), p. 64.

Another feature of this period was an increased participation by ex-servicemen in the process of remembering and commemorating the war, which further contributed to the interest in it and the number of travellers to the battlefields. The story of the Old Comrades Association of the thirteenth battalion of the Rifle Brigade was typical. It was founded in 1928, and in 1929 the members conducted their first tour of the battlefields, in which eighteen members and their wives took part. The Association took parties to the battlefields in each year up to 1939, with as many as sixty-five people taking part in 1933 and ninety-two people joining the two parties to the battlefields in 1938.[70] This pattern was repeated in the history of the British Legion's involvement in battlefield tours. The Legion organised its first pilgrimage in 1927. This was a failure, but in 1928 the Legion organised the largest pilgrimage by British ex-servicemen, when 10,000 pilgrims travelled to the Western Front. Although the British Legion was unable to organise a national pilgrimage after 1928, many branches and sub-branches of the Legion continued to organise battlefield tours and pilgrimages in 1929 and throughout the remainder of the inter-war years.

The numbers of signatures in the visitors' books at the IWGC cemeteries and memorials dropped in 1932 to 99,000 owing to the Depression, when the pound was devalued against the franc. More importantly, it became a patriotic duty not to travel abroad. The Chancellor of the Exchequer appealed to the patriotism of British citizens to resist the temptation to travel overseas and thereby to prevent money going out of the country.[71] When the economic situation stabilised the numbers of people visiting the war cemeteries and memorials rose once again. From 1933 onwards the numbers of signatures remained well above 100,000, peaking in the year 1938/9, when there were 157,583 signatures.[72]

One of the startling features of the IWGC figures is the consistently high number of signatures during the 1930s, compared with the mid-1920s. Although the Depression casts its shadow over the late 1920s and the 1930s, in many regions of Great

70. *Rifle Brigade Chronicle* (1929–39).

71. H. S. Lunn, *Nearing Harbour: The Log of Sir Henry S. Lunn* (London, 1934), p. 312.

72. IWGC, *Annual Reports* (1932–9).

Britain and among some groups standards of living continued to rise, particularly after 1933.[73] At the same time the battlefields became more accessible. Whereas it cost £4.5s. to join the 1928 British Legion pilgrimage, in the 1930s a tour might only cost £2. This may have extended the option of visiting the battlefields to people who previously could not have afforded it. The Workers' Travel Association commenced organising tours of the battlefields in 1928, and so many people took these tours in 1929 that a special Easter Weekend trip was introduced in 1930.[74] Provincial newspapers also conducted tours to the battlefields in this period. In 1936 the *Leeds Mercury* organised two tours to Belgium; one was to the Ypres Salient, while the second avoided the war and travelled to Blankenberge. The first tour was the more popular.[75]

At the same time an increasing number of young people travelled to the battlefields. At Easter 1933 800 British schoolchildren visited the Menin Gate, while parties of boys from the major public schools were conducted over the battlefields by organisations such as the Ypres League.[76] In 1937 the IWGC received fifty to sixty letters each week from people interested in the cemeteries in France and Belgium. The majority of these were from the sons and daughters of those who fell, rather than the parents and widows of the dead, as in former years.[77] However, the demand amongst bereaved relatives to see the war cemeteries did not entirely abate. Even in 1939 the Church Army and the Salvation Army continued to conduct parties of relatives to the graves.[78]

The number of visitors to the battlefields peaked in the twelve months immediately prior to the outbreak of the Second World War. Samuel Hynes notes that the literary generation in the 1930s was obsessed both with the Great War and the prospect of another world war.[79] This also may have encouraged large

73. A. Thorpe, *Britain in the 1930s* (Oxford, 1992), pp. 93, 102.
74. *Travel Log*, new series, 14 (Mar. 1930), p. 10.
75. *Leeds Mercury*, 3 June 1936.
76. Minutes of Proceedings of the IWGC, 10 May 1933, p. 5, NAC RG 38 Vol. 349.
77. Minutes of Proceedings of the IWGC, 14 July 1937, p. 4, NAC RG 38 Vol. 349.
78. *War Cry*, 16 (Jan. 1937), p. 6. Church Army, *Annual Report* (1938/9), p. 42.
79. S. Hynes, *The Auden Generation: Literature and Politics in England in the 1930s* (London, 1976), pp. 38–42.

numbers of people from Great Britain to visit the battlefields, particularly as the international atmosphere became increasingly tense in the late 1930s. At the height of the crisis over the Sudetenland, in 1938, 112,000 people, of whom 60,000 were from Great Britain, visited the cemeteries and memorials of the Western Front in the three months from June to August.[80] The number of visits made to the IWM followed a similar pattern, with a sharp jump in the number of visits in 1938. During the year from April 1937 to March 1938, 294,301 visits were made to the IWM; but in the year from April 1938 to March 1939 the number of visits increased to 457,252.[81]

A few people travelled to battlefields, cemeteries and memorials in search of the military lessons of the Great War. The Annual Report of the IWM noted that a large number of people were visiting it to prepare for the war they believed was coming.[82] An account of a tour to the battlefields in 1939 similarly suggested to other servicemen that one reason for visiting the battlefields was to prepare for a possible European war.[83] Many others felt a sense of foreboding, and may have hoped that somehow their visit might stave off the coming tragedy. It was an impulse shared by the people who knelt on benches placed around the grave of the Unknown Warrior to pray for peace at the height of the Munich crisis in 1938 and who continued to return to the benches in 1939.[84] Despite these hopes and prayers Great Britain was caught up in a second world war; but the legacy of this remarkable period of travel remained.

The Changing Landscape of Travel

The landscape of the Western Front dominated the thoughts and memories of the servicemen who took part in the maelstrom of the fighting there and the imagination of people on the home front. Cecil Day Lewis spent the summer of 1919–20 reliving the war through the pages of an illustrated magazine. Later he recalled that already 'the famous battlefields with their splintered

80. Minutes of Proceedings of the IWGC, 14 Sept. 1938, p. 3, NAC, RG 38, Vol. 351.

81. IWM, *Annual Reports* (1937–1939).

82. IWM, *Annual Report* (1938/9).

83. R. K. Exham, 'A Battlefield Tour', *Iron Duke*, XV (Feb. 1939), p. 51.

84. *The Times*, 25 Feb. 1939.

trees, gashed trenches, careening artillery limbers, seemed as remote yet as familiar as the moon whose face their shell-pocked terrain so much resembled . . . the terrible names - Ypres, Loos, Hill 60, Passchendaele, the Somme - sounded in my ears like Troy, Ilion, Scamander, legendary and timeless'.[85] When Christopher Sidgwick visited Ypres in 1935 he found that the battlefields were 'at once as familiar and mythical as one's own mental picture of a fairy-tale'.[86] The landscape which drew travellers to the battlefields was largely an imaginary one. It was not the sites themselves which attracted travellers, but their associations. They were the places where loved ones or fellow countrymen had fought. In fact many of the places had little intrinsic appeal. As one traveller noted one 'bit of devastation is much the same as another'.[87]

Throughout the inter-war years guidebooks emphasised that travel to the battlefields involved more than sightseeing. In 1920 T. A. Lowe assured travellers that

> touring the battlefields is a different thing altogether to touring for the purpose of sight seeing, in fact I can safely say that the mere sight-seer will probably be disappointed with the devastated zones of France and Belgium. But combined with 'atmosphere' and imagination they will draw the tourists like magnets and he will probably return to them again and again.[88]

Bernard Newman made a similar claim in 1936:

> There is very little that could be described as 'scenery,' but in atmosphere and historic associations the district challenges comparison with any. It provides a succession of thrills to anyone who has an ounce of imagination. It will inculcate a store of memories which will abide long after the more transient charms of natural scenic beauty have passed from the mind.[89]

Thus tourism was not simply about the sights one could see, but about recapturing the meaning of the war. Similarly, bereaved relatives and ex-servicemen made pilgrimages to a place and an

85. C. Day Lewis, *The Buried Day* (London, 1960), pp. 84–5.
86. C. Sidgwick, *The Feast of the Locusts: Being a Soldier's Retrospect in Time of War, of a Europe Known in Peace* (London, n.d.), p. 191.
87. A. R. Allerton, 'Hesdin', *Artists' Rifles Journal*, IV (Summer, 1921), p. 81.
88. T. A. Lowe, *The Western Battlefields: A Guide to the British Line, Short Account of the Fighting, the Trenches and Positions* (London, 1920), p. 9.
89. B. Newman, *Cycling in France (Northern)* (London, 1936), p. 88.

experience which existed in the mind of the pilgrim and for which the sites visited provided the focal point. These pilgrimages will be discussed in Chapter 4.

Tourists were often drawn to places not because there was something in particular they wished to see, but because the names of the places resonated with meaning. The Southern Railway guide to the battlefields observed that the 'whole district around Albert abounds with names well known to the British public, along the valley of the Ancre to the North and north-east is Aveluy and Aveluy Wood, and a little further on the famous heights of Thiepval'.[90] Newman advised cyclists who travelled across the battlefields to detour through the lanes around Albert, because here 'are villages whose names will live for ever in British history: Fricourt, Mametz, Pozières, Thiepval, Flers, Guedecourt'. He warned travellers: 'I repeat, there is no scenery here - just pleasant rolling downland dotted with brand-new red-brick villages. But if you do not thrill to their memories and atmosphere, then your imagination is indeed dull.'[91]

Organised tours escorted travellers to all the places whose names had featured in the newspaper headlines during the war. It was an extraordinarily intense introduction. A traveller with the Dean and Dawson four-day tour saw on just one of the days: the German Deutschland battery, Nieuport, the Yser Canal, Ramscapelle, Pervyse, Dixmude, the Houthulst forest, Westroosbeke, Poelcapelle, St Julian, Gravenstaffel, Passchendaele Ridge, Zonnebeke, Polygon Wood, Potsdam Redoubt, Frezenburg Ridge, Westhoek Ridge, Clapham Junction, the Menin road, Inverness Copse, Stirling Castle, Sanctuary Wood, Hill 62, Burr Crossroads, Hellfire Corner and Ypres![92] It was enough to see the imagined place, rather than the place itself. Beckles Willson found that many travellers confused 'the eminence on the other side of the railway ("The Dump") with the immortal Hill 60', because Hill 60 had been undermined by the fighting during the war.[93]

The landscape of the Western Front and the imagined landscape of sites that attracted travellers altered over the years. At

90. Southern Railway, *The Battlefields and War Graves of France and Flanders and How to Visit Them* (n.p., 1924) p. 7.

91. Newman, *Cycling in France*, p. 98.

92. *World Travel Gazette*, XVI (July–Sept. 1923), p. 25.

93. B. Willson, *Ypres: The Holy Ground of British Arms* (Bruges, 1920), p. 60.

first the scenes of death and destruction which could be found on the battlefields were the centre of attraction for many travellers. These scenes provided both excitement and horror, together with a reminder of the suffering of France and the infamy of Germany. Reconstruction removed much of the devastation and most of the wartime aspect of the battlefields. The objective of travel shifted to the few remaining battlefield sites and to the cemeteries and memorials built by the Allies. The imagined landscape was increasingly perceived within the context of the wider meaning of the war for travellers. This meaning fluctuated between an appreciation of the heroism of and the sacrifice made by the men and concern that the horrors of war needed to be remembered and avoided. The dichotomy between these two approaches led to a debate over the meaning of the landscape. Did it sanitise or even glorify war, or was it a lesson in peace?

The first travellers to the Western Front after the war were confronted by a landscape which denied order and even civilisation. William Johnson, whose unit arrived in France immediately after the Armistice, wrote upon seeing the battlefield for the first time: 'we could barely conceive how thoroughly the agents of death levelled the ground . . . leaving nothing emerging more than a foot or two above the surface except for a few former tree trunks bowled over sideways and shattered and splintered until they mimicked ghoulish stalagmites'.[94] In addition to the devastation the battlefield was a vast cemetery, as many soldiers had been buried where they fell, and it took time for these bodies to be located and the cemeteries to be constructed. A Belgian guidebook described West Flanders as 'nothing but a deserted sea, under whose waves corpses are sleeping'.[95]

The devastation summed up the meaning of the battlefield for many visitors. A traveller in Belgium in 1919 noticed several sightseers armed with cameras 'groping about amongst the trenches and debris and snapping photos of any typical bits of ruins to be seen'.[96] Guidebooks directed travellers to the sites of the most impressive ruined buildings and towns. Somerville Story

94. W. W. Johnson, *Dove of Noah*, Part One, *Flight*, p. 34, IWM, P.P. MCR 47.
95. P. Prist, *Ypres* (Bruxelles, n.d.), p. 30.
96. D. Gilmore, 'Belgium in 1919', *Cyclists Touring Club Gazette*, XXXIX (Feb. 1919), p. 21.

advised tourists to the Ypres Salient that they should see 'the so-called "tank cemetery" and view the sites of woods, chateaux, villages and even a cemetery of which no vestiges exist, all blown away by shell fire!'[97] The Michelin guide to Ypres recommended that travellers climb the town ramparts near the Lille gate so they could see a 'magnificent panorama' of the ruins of the city.[98]

The emotions evoked by the devastation encompassed a wide spectrum of responses. In some of the guides there is almost a sense of awe at what has been done to the landscape by modern technology. The Michelin guide to Ypres asserted that 'History furnishes few examples of such grandeur followed by destruction so swift and so complete.'[99] Examples of the power of modern weapons were a popular attraction. The large German gun at Chuignes, known as 'Big Bertha', drew many tourists, as did the huge crater left by a British mine at La Boiselle on the Somme.[100] One guide suggested visits to Bailleul and La Bassée, which had been razed to the ground, because they were good examples of the 'efficacy of British ammunition and efficiency of British gunnery'.[101] At the same time there was a sense of unease at the power of an industrial war. Violet Markham considered that the most horrible sight she saw was the 'heap of tortured iron and steel' that remained of a factory. She felt seized by 'some evil maniacal power' in the presence of the factory: 'whose charred remains bore witness to the fratricidal strife of science applied to gunnery and high explosive . . . of all aspects of modern life the worst is when latter-day warfare and latter-day industrialism make common cause together in one unholy combination'.[102]

Although in the mid-1920s the horrors of war would discourage many travellers, in the immediate aftermath of the war they could become a reason for visiting the battlefields. Anna

97. S. Story, *Present Day Paris and the Battlefields: The Visitors Handbook with the Chief Excursions to the Battlefields* (New York and London, 1920), p. 164.

98. Michelin & Cie, *Ypres and the Battles of Ypres* (Clermont-Ferrand, 1919), pp. 100–1.

99. Ibid., p. 69.

100. B. S. Townroe, *A Pilgrim in Picardy* (London, 1927), p. 194. W. R. Bird, 'From the Things that Are to the Things that Were', *Veteran* 11 (Sept. 1934), p. 7.

101. J. O. Coop, *A Short Guide to the Battlefields: Where to Go and How to See Them* (Liverpool, n.d.), pp. 38, 45.

102. V. R. Markham, 'In a Devastated Area', *Fortnightly Review*, DCXXX (June 1919), p. 941.

Dodd suggested that, as you pass on your travels along the road from Villers-Bretonneux to Hamel, Arras, Albert, Bapaume, Peronne or Amiens, you 'may sup on horrors, and take your fill of the terrorising proofs of what man can endure, and of what man, returned to savagery, can inflict'.[103] Thomas Cook's assured potential travellers to Verdun that 'unforgettable sights meet the eye at every turn in the terribly tortured countryside - scenes of fighting and artillery duels so terrible that whole forests in this region were reduced to what the soldiers called "toothpicks"'.[104]

There was also a moral or educational purpose informing travel in the devastated zone. Travellers were encouraged to come in order to understand the suffering of and the lessons to be learned from the martyred regions of France and Belgium. The focus on the destruction wrought by Germany was most noticeable in the guidebooks produced in France for English tourists. The Michelin guides stressed the grandeur of the churches, towns, and artefacts which had been destroyed in the war. They directed tourists to visit the churches and museums which had been pre-war tourist attractions in Lille, Ypres, Amiens, Rheims and Soissons. For example *Amiens: Before and During the Great War* devotes thirty-two of its fifty-five pages to the Cathedral and the Museum, with particular emphasis on what they were like before the war.[105]

These descriptions of damage to the cities and buildings of Northern France formed part of a wider emphasis in the Michelin guides upon the wartime atrocities perpetrated by the Germans. The Michelin guides stressed the damage to French industry caused 'not so much by the war, as by the systematic pillaging and destructions carried out by the Germans'.[106] A common theme was the role of German frustration at the failure of their attacks as the motivation for the destruction. The guide to Rheims claimed: 'In revenging themselves on Rheims for their disappointments and failures, the Germans seem to have been particularly

103. A. B. Dodd, *Up the Seine to the Battlefields* (New York and London, 1920), p. 380.

104. Thomas Cook, 'How to See Paris and the Battlefields: Automobile Tours', 1922, Thomas Cook Archive.

105. Michelin Tyre Co. Ltd., *Amiens: Before and During the Great War* (London, 1919).

106. Michelin Tyre Co. Ltd., *Lille: Before and During the Great War* (London, 1919), p. 24.

determined to destroy the building which is at once one of the most precious artistic treasures of France and one of the most ancient evidences of her history.'[107] The guides also relied upon individual victims' accounts of German atrocities. This is a particularly notable feature of the guide to the battlefields of the Marne, which was published during the war.[108]

Among British travellers the concentration on the sufferings of France and Belgium both justified the British involvement in the war by providing a warning of what might have happened in Britain and looked forward to the reparations which would be imposed on Germany as recompense for the destruction. In his 1919 guide to the battlefields Atherton Fleming recommended that Ypres 'should be left as it is, untouched by aught but nature surrounded by what is left of its walls - a monument to German *Kultur* and a constant reminder to mankind of the value of the written word of man'.[109] Charles Whibley, after visiting the ruins of the library at Louvain, wrote: 'To gaze upon the wanton ruin and to think of the treasures within the shattered walls, is to condemn to eternal obloquy the Kaiser and all his works . . . The pitiless annihilation of books and manuscripts is a crime from which all but Huns and Vandals shrink in horror.'[110]

One of the recurring themes of travel to the battlefields was that the visit provided an insight into the atmosphere and experience of the soldiers. Wilfred Ewart encouraged the pilgrim to hurry to the battlefields 'where today a certain atmosphere may be recaptured - for the last time since tomorrow it will be gone'.[111] Stephen Graham assured possible travellers to Gallipoli how 'vividly you see all that they saw, the grandeur of Nature, the glimmer of the sea! You can still smell the Dardanelles expedition, and tread in old footsteps which hardly have been worn away', while Graham Hutchison suggested that it is at sunset, particularly in winter 'when the trees are shorn of their leaves, that the landscape seems to give back something of the atmo-

107. Michelin & Cie, *Rheims and the Battles for its Possession* (Clermont-Ferrand, 1919), p. 31.

108. Michelin & Cie, *The Marne Battlefields 1914: An Illustrated History and Guide* (Clermont-Ferrand, 1917), pp. 43, 47, 49–50.

109. Fleming, *How to See the Battlefields*, p. 7.

110. C. Whibley, 'Belgium in 1919', *Blackwood's Magazine*, CCVI (Oct. 1919), p. 529.

111. W. Ewart, 'Auburs Revisited', *Household Brigade Magazine* (1921), p. 15.

sphere which held it during the war'.[112] The direct experience of ex-servicemen was an important feature of many battlefield guides. The guidebook to the Ypres salient published by Toc H emphasised that all the contributors to the guide were ex-servicemen, who speak 'with the fidelity that actual experience alone can give, not so much of the nature of the task itself as of the way and spirit in which it was undertaken, undergone and ultimately achieved'.[113]

The landscape of the battlefields changed as people in Northern France and Belgium returned to and rebuilt their homes. A few guides claimed that travellers would be encouraged by the sights of reconstruction. Henry Parr Maskell suggested in his guide to Picardy that ex-servicemen might 'find encouragement and consolation in revisiting the stricken fields and viewing what in ten short years of peace has been done to restore hearths and homesteads'.[114] Another traveller believed the reconstruction held a message of hope: 'Pageants, empires, wars – all pass, and here are the good crops growing, and the new trees springing to attention where the old once stood, and new homes being made, and the implements of war being turned to farm and domestic uses, and eternal hope on human faces and in human hearts.'[115]

The reconstruction reduced the emphasis on the close links between battlefield tourism and an image of the war which stressed German barbarity. Once the ruins disappeared the landscape was less likely to evoke anger among British tourists at the wartime behaviour of Germany. An account of a visit to Louvain in the 1930s indicates a significant change in attitude. Fletcher Allen found that Louvain 'did not reach any depth of feeling in me, although I followed its streets and byways religiously'.[116] This was part of a wider sympathy with the German war experience

112. S. Graham, *Europe – Whither Bound? (Quo Vadis Europa?): Being Letters of Travel from the Capitals of Europe in the Year 1921* (London, 1921), p. 45. G. S. Hutchison, *Pilgrimage* (London, 1935), p. 77 (Hutchison also wrote under the pseudonyms G. Seton and G. Seton Hutchison).

113. Talbot House, *The Pilgrim's Guide to the Ypres Salient* (London, 1920), p. 84.

114. H. P. Maskell, *The Soul of Picardy* (London, 1930), pp. 172–3.

115. A. T. Sheppard, 'Northern France Revisited', *Spectator*, 5185 (Nov. 1927), p. 809.

116. F. Allen, *A Wayfarer in Belgium* (London, 1934).

in the late 1920s and 1930s. Many ex-servicemen's accounts about their return to the battlefields note the presence of German pilgrims on the battlefields as a means of highlighting the similarity between the people of both countries.[117] In 'Kamarad' a British ex-serviceman described his meeting with a party of German ex-servicemen at the Ypres railway station, stressing that they had returned to pay tribute to old comrades, and that it was 'just that fact which drew us close to them in spirit, for we too had come back to pay homage to brave comrades'.[118]

Baedeker's noted this distinction between the British memory of the war in the late 1920s, and the French and Belgian memory. Both the German and the English editions of their guidebook to Northern France claimed that the towns of Aerschott and Dinant had been razed and hundreds of their citizens shot by the Germans in response to civilian snipers. The French edition made no such claim, and these towns were successful in a court action against Baedeker's, arguing that the English edition of the guidebook had misrepresented what had taken place. They asserted that the guidebooks should state that the German actions were an unprovoked wartime atrocity. Baedeker's were required to include the Belgian version of the events, with its emphasis on German atrocities, alongside their claim that the civilians who had been shot were snipers.[119]

Most British travellers were not interested in reconstruction. The desire to visit a section of the battlefields in their wartime state remained strong despite the small number of sites. In the British battle areas only a few sections of the old trenches were left untouched. These areas were set aside because commercial operators, as at Hill 60 or Sanctuary Wood, realised that travellers would pay to see a battlefield in its 'original state'. Both Hill 60 and Sanctuary Wood near Ypres were extremely popular with tourists, despite frequent criticism of these places for exploiting the battlefields for commercial gain.[120] The other areas of the old British front which remained in their wartime state did so

117. S. Brandt, 'Le Voyage Aux Champs de Bataille', *Vingtième Siècle Revue d'histoire*, 41 (Janvier–Mars 1994), p. 21, notes that German pilgrims first began to travel to the battlefields of the Western Front in the second half of the 1920s.

118. F. J. Lineton, 'Kamarad', *Ypres Times*, 6 (Jan. 1932), p. 20.

119. E. Mendelson, 'Baedeker's Universe', *Yale Review*, 74 (Spring 1985), p. 402.

120. P. R. Butler, 'Twenty-One Years After', *Blackwood's Magazine*, CCXXXVIII (Dec. 1935), pp. 836–7.

thanks to the Dominion Governments, as with the Canadian, South African and Newfoundland Governments at Vimy Ridge, Delville Wood and Beaumont Hamel respectively, or because individual cities such as Sheffield intervened to set aside a small area of the trench line as a reminder of the war.

The Newfoundland Memorial Park at Beaumont Hamel was one of the most important of these sites. Here a small section of the 1918 trenches was preserved in the sectors of the front lines which had been held by the Royal Newfoundland Regiment and the opposing German forces on 1 July 1916. Virtually every account of a tour of the Somme mentions the Park. One traveller described his visit as follows: 'we zig zag along the duck-boards, and here are grim reminders on every side of fierce fighting, nothing altered from the time when war ended, helmets where they fell, many pierced with shrapnel; rifles rusty with mouldering stocks; a rusty machine gun; rusty bayonets, mouldering packs, water bottles, mess tins - just where they fell'.[121] The Park even featured in F. Scott Fitzgerald's *Tender is the Night*, in which the main characters visit it during a holiday in Europe.[122]

The more distant in time the war became, the greater the need among travellers to see evidence of the presence of the war. The *Legionary* described the preserved trenches at Vimy Ridge as the 'only spot in France where a man can feel that he is back again in 1914-1918 . . . where he can stand at a sniper's post and fit the rotted butt of a rusted rifle to his shoulder as he peeps out between the bushes towards the German trenches'.[123] Toc H successfully campaigned to protect one of the craters created by the explosion of mines in the 1917 attack on the ridge at Messines.[124] In 1932 Toc H and the British Legion combined to protect the remaining pillboxes in the Ypres salient from destruction by the Belgian Government. The guide to these pillboxes produced by the Legion described them as 'the chief reminders of the scenes of heroic deeds of comradeship, and of prowess of those who fought in "the Salient" during the memorable years of 1914-18'.[125]

121. Sheppard, 'Northern France Revisited', p. 808.

122. F. Scott Fitzgerald, *Tender is the Night* (London, 1934), pp. 117-18.

123. *Legionary*, II (June 1928), p. 12.

124. B. B., *Over There: A Little Guide for Pilgrims to Ypres; The Salient and Talbot House, Poperinghe* (London, 1935).

125. E. G. L. Thurlow, *The Pill-boxes of Flanders* (London, 1933).

The division of travel to the Western Front into a number of small sites contrasts with the battlefield of Verdun, which was retained in its wartime state and became the central place of memory for the French.[126] Despite a proposal from Winston Churchill to keep Ypres in its wartime state, it was rebuilt in the early 1920s. In any case Churchill's plan was opposed by a number of the commissioners of the IWGC, who believed that the Commission should concentrate on building the war cemeteries. The commissioners maintained their position even though Fabian Ware suggested to them that the Ypres scheme 'in addition to its own intrinsic merits, might be most useful for attracting public attention and withdrawing a good deal of idle curiosity and criticism from the work that the Commission has already undertaken'.[127] However, even if the commissioners had supported the proposal, it would have been difficult for the British Government to persuade the Belgian Government to relocate the people of Ypres, who wished to rebuild their town as it had been before the war.[128]

Also while Ypres was a key site in the British memory of the war, it had to compete with other sites, in particular the battlefield of the Somme, as the focus of the British memory of the war experience. The 1921 Report of the National Battlefields Memorial Committee concluded that to 'some extent the Somme stands for France, much as Ypres stands for Belgium in the eyes of the British soldier'.[129] In towns such as Leeds and Sheffield, where local 'Pals' battalions had been virtually wiped out on the Somme, that battlefield rather than Ypres dominated the memory of the war. The Sunday nearest 1 July was commemorated by a ceremony of remembrance throughout the inter-war period, and parties of pilgrims travelled annually to the cemeteries on the Somme battlefield.[130]

The various battlefield sites evoked a range of images of the war. In a few places it was possible to capture the spirit and

126. Prost, 'Verdun', p. 129.

127. Fabian Ware to Winston Churchill, 26 Feb. 1919, PRO, WO 32 - 5853.

128. Draft Conclusions of a Conference of Ministers, 5 July 1920, PRO WO 32 - 5569.

129. Report of the National Battlefields Memorial Committee, 28 Feb. 1921, p. 7, PRO, WO 32 - 3135.

130. *Leeds Mercury*, 1 July 1928, *Yorkshire Post*, 1 July 1928, *Sheffield Daily Independent*, 25 Apr. 1931.

romance of pre-war heroism. One of the most popular sites for tourists in the 1920s was the port of Zeebrugge. This was the scene of a costly British naval raid on St George's Day, 23 April 1918. The raid was perceived as an epic of British gallantry and heroism in the heroic traditions of pre-war literature. Imbued with the romance of a heroic assault, Zeebrugge was transformed from a small fishing village into a major tourist site. Thomas Cook's guide to Belgium in 1929 noted that it 'is only since the war and the unforgettable engagement off the Mole that the place has attracted tourists at all. Now they do not visit the harbour, and disorderly sprinkling of dwellings which form the village, because of their natural amenities, but because of their desire to set foot on the soil of this historic port.'[131] The war museum at Zeebrugge was described as the most popular of its type because 'it deals mainly with one incident of the war, which is so concentrated and dramatic that the dullest imagination can comprehend the splendid heroism of the attackers'.[132] The battlefields associated with the fighting in 1914 also evoked the heroic ethos of the pre-war period. One traveller who visited Mons argued that it appealed to him because it drew him back to the 'last dying flicker of the war of manoeuvre', where even the uniforms of the French in their 1914 equipment evoked an earlier age.[133]

The wretched conditions and the bloody slaughter on the Somme and at Passchendaele required a different kind of heroism. One guidebook observed that the name Passchendaele 'at once recalls the most heroic efforts and the worst conditions of the War'.[134] Another guidebook claimed that 'nothing could be more withering to the real spirit of romance in war than the wood fighting which took place during the initial stages of the battle of the Somme in 1916. It was ghastly and no other words in the dictionary can describe it.'[135] The guidebooks and travellers' accounts of visits to these battlefields, particularly in the 1920s, stressed that the heroism of the men who fought there

131. R. Elston, *The Traveller's Handbook to Belgium* (London, 1929), p. 14.

132. R. P. Hearne, 'The Battle Museum on Zeebrugge Mole', *Sphere*, XCIX (Oct. 1924), p. xiv.

133. C. H. Johnston, 'Mons: 1914–1934', *Spectator*, 5539 (Aug. 1934), p. 249.

134. T. G. Barman and J. De Geynst, *Guide to Belgium and Luxembourg* (London, 1938), p. 54.

135. Lowe, *The Western Battlefields*, p. 45.

lay in their tenacity and endurance. In the foreword to *The Immortal Salient* Philip Gibbs wrote that the Ypres Salient 'was the ground on which the quality of British manhood was put to the test, most often, in most frightful conditions, against heaviest odds, during the years of war. Every yard of it is sanctified for our race by the heroism of our men who defended it by their bodies and souls.'[136] Beatrix Brice was inspired by the belief that it is 'in the repetition again and again of supreme heroism, the endurance again and again of supreme trial, the sacrifice again and again in supreme agony, that the wonder lies'.[137]

Another important theme of battlefield travel in the 1920s was sacrifice. This was particularly associated with the cemeteries and memorials which came to dominate both the landscape and the imaginative landscape in the 1920s and 1930s. Brice wrote that at Tyne Cot the 'great cemetery and memorial holds the imminent meaning of Ypres. We look out over all the spaces of the Salient; we look down and realise that the earth on which we stand is literally the very substance of man's sacrifice.'[138]

In the early 1920s the theme of sacrifice competed with a more assertive representation of the war experience which stressed the British victory. In 1919 a Committee was set up to erect National Battlefield Memorials. The memorials were primarily to commemorate fighting on the battlefields and the Committee initially rejected Reginald Blomfield's design for the Menin Gate because they were not dealing with memorials to the dead: 'Our task is to erect suitable memorials of the British effort in France and Belgium – the combined effort of the dead and the living which led to victory. Indeed, the Committee are strongly impressed with the necessity of avoiding anything in the nature of tombstones or monuments to the dead.'[139] By 1921 the Battle Exploits Committee had changed its policy. This was primarily because the IWGC was already planning to erect memorials to the missing in similar places to the proposed Battle Exploit Memorials, and thus it would be a waste of both effort

136. W. Pulteney and B. Brice, *The Immortal Salient: An Historical Record and Complete Guide for Pilgrims to Ypres* (London, 1925), p. 3.

137. B. Brice, *The Battle Book of Ypres* (London, 1927), p. ix.

138. B. Brice, *Ypres – Outpost of the Channel Ports: A Concise Historical Guide to the Salient of Ypres* (London, 1929), p. 48.

139. Lord Riddell to Winston Churchill, 12 Nov. 1920, PRO WO - 32 3134.

and money to produce two memorials at these sites.[140] However, it also seems reasonable to assume that the Committee now found it easier to accept that the dominant theme of commemoration should be sacrifice.

The war cemeteries were designed to evoke traditional concepts of sacrifice. Reginald Blomfield prepared a memorandum for the architects who were designing the cemeteries in which he emphasised that they should be an 'abstract expression of the idea of sacrifice and heroic death for a great cause'.[141] The cemeteries relied upon three images of sacrifice. Firstly, the cemeteries transformed into reality Rupert Brooke's immortal lines about the potency of sacrifice:

> If I should die, think only this of me:
> That there's a corner of a foreign field
> That is forever England . . .[142]

The cemeteries created an English landscape on the battlefields of the Western Front. One traveller described her experience in one of these cemeteries: 'I turned my face into the sun, and closed my eyes; the wind came softly to me, full of the scent of wall flowers, and fresh turf. A bee hummed by, a lark sang, and the gardener's mowing machine began its busy chatter. I was standing with my eyes closed, in an English garden.'[143]

Secondly, the cemeteries were symbols of 'the common purpose, the common devotion, the common sacrifice of all ranks in the Empire'.[144] This was achieved by the use of a uniform rectangular headstone for all the dead, no matter what their rank or social class. The decision met with considerable opposition from parents who wanted to erect individual headstones, but their wishes were subordinated to the desire to construct an image of the war which stressed the unity of the nation and the Empire. The report of Frederic Kenyon in 1918 conceded: 'It is necessary to face the fact that this decision has given pain in

140. P. Longworth, *The Unending Vigil: A History of the Commonwealth War Graves Commission 1917–1967* (London, 1967), p. 85.

141. R. Blomfield, *Memoirs of an Architect* (London, 1932), p. 178.

142. R. Brooke, 'The Soldier', in R. Brooke, *The Collected Poems of Rupert Brooke* (London, 1918), p. 9.

143. K. M. Hitchcox, 'A British Cemetery', *English Review*, XLIV (Apr. 1927), p. 462.

144. IWGC, *Report* (1918).

some quarters, and pain which the Commissioners would have been glad to avoid.'[145] However, there were sites associated with individuals whose memory arose above the egalitarian ethos which pervaded the commemoration of the war. The graves of individuals such as the Canadian poet John McCrae who gained fame as the writer of 'In Flanders Fields', the Welsh poet Hedd Wyn and the Irish nationalist Willie Redmond were singled out by travellers.[146]

Finally, it was an unmistakably Christian sacrifice. Kenyon's report recommended that every cemetery should include a memorial stone which would satisfy 'many forms of religious feeling', because for some it would be 'merely a memorial stone, such as those of which we read in the Old Testament', while to others it would be an altar. As the stone would lack a 'definitely Christian character' Kenyon also recommended that the cemeteries should include a Cross.[147] The monuments became known as the Stone of Remembrance and the Cross of Sacrifice respectively. Blomfield and Edwin Lutyens, the architects who designed these monuments, sought to create abstract symbols which would evoke the infinite; but in practice both were usually regarded as Christian.[148] The YMCA handbook for pilgrims uses the Cross of Sacrifice as a symbol for the resurrection of the dead and the Stone of Remembrance was used as an altar for religious services by pilgrims. Lutyens actually wrote to the Archbishop of Canterbury to say: 'I was so glad to see in to-day's papers that the Great War stone in a cemetery was used as an Altar for the administration of Holy Communion.'[149]

145. F. Kenyon, *War Graves, How the Cemeteries Abroad Will Be Designed* (London, 1918), p. 6.

146. *The Times*, 12 Nov. 1931. *British Legion Journal,* XIV (Oct. 1934), p. 179; Hedd Wyn was known as the 'Welsh Rupert Brooke' and his grave was described as the 'Welsh Cenotaph'. S. Gwynne, 'France of the Battle-Zone', *The Nineteenth Century and After*, LXXXIX (Jan. 1921), p. 165.

147. Kenyon, *War Graves, How the Cemeteries Abroad will be Designed*, pp. 10–11.

148. Blomfield, *Memoirs of an Architect*, p. 179. Also see J. M. Winter, *Sites of Memory, Sites of Mourning: The Great War in European Cultural History*, (Cambridge, 1995), p. 107.

149. YMCA, 'Visitation of Graves in France and Flanders', Peter Liddle Collection, Edward Boyle Library, Leeds University. E. Lutyens to R. Davidson, 26 Mar. 1923, Lambeth Palace Library, Davidson Papers, Vol. 202, Item 155. I am indebted to Adrian Gregory for this reference.

The memorials erected on the battlefields extended this traditional theme of sacrifice, because they provided an abstract image of the implications of that sacrifice. One of the most popular of the smaller memorials in the British area of the battlefields was the Canadian memorial at St Julien. It was unveiled by the Canadian Government in 1923 on the spot where 2,000 Canadians were buried who had been with the 18,000 Canadians on the British left who withstood the German gas attacks on 22–24 April 1915. The memorial is the head and shoulders of a Canadian soldier resting over his reversed rifle, which merges into the block of stone from which the figure is carved. One English newspaper found that there was a 'mysterious power in this brooding figure, drawing you from the things that are to the things that were', while Will Bird claimed that the sight of the memorial 'rising from the fog . . . fills the watcher with awe'.[150] Henry Williamson attempted to convey the genius of this memorial, which he believed lay in 'the gravity and strength of grief coming from full knowledge of old wrongs done to men by men. It mourns, but it mourns for all mankind. We are silent before it, as we are before the stone figures of the Greeks.'[151]

The St Julien memorial captured the most important features of the memorials which drew tourists and pilgrims in the mid 1920s and the 1930s. The message was to the imagination. The memorials to the 'missing', particularly the Menin Gate and Thiepval, which contained the names of thousands of soldiers whose bodies could not be found, encouraged travellers to look beyond the veil of death and to embrace the implications of the sacrifice by so many young men in the war. Jay Winter has recently described the Thiepval memorial as 'an extraordinary statement in abstract language about mass death and the impossibility of triumphalism'.[152] A guide to the British memorials produced in the 1930s compared the meaning of the Menin Gate and Thiepval: 'When one has seen the Menin Gate, the Thiepval Memorial compels comparison and we realise that they

150. Canadian Battlefields Memorials Commission, *Canadian Battlefield Memorials* (Ottawa, 1929), p. 21. W. R. Bird, *Thirteen Years After: The Story of the Old Front Revisited* (Toronto, 1932), p. 8.

151. H. Williamson, *The Wet Flanders Plain* (London, 1929), p. 98.

152. Winter, *Sites of Memory*, p. 107.

are complementary; the Menin Gate is intimate and brings grief home to us. The massive Thiepval memorial situated on a hill overlooking the Valley of the Ancre with its history of carnage, emphasises the loneliness and solitude of death.'[153]

One event came to encapsulate this quest for the meaning of the sacrifice, the Last Post at the Menin Gate. The unveiling of the Menin Gate memorial in 1927 provided the inspiration for the ceremony. At the conclusion of the ceremony the Light Infantry Regiment played the Last Post and Reveille, which made a powerful impression on P. Vandenbraambussche, the Superintendent of Police in Ypres. He instituted the practice of sounding the Last Post at the memorial each evening at 9 p.m. in the summer of 1928. The practice was discontinued owing to bad weather in October, but was resumed in 1929. The ceremony tapped a chord among travellers to the battlefields. On Armistice Day 1930 it was broadcast by the BBC. Similar ceremonies were initiated at the other memorials to the missing.[154]

The Last Post ceremony became the focal point of battlefield travel because it symbolically stopped time. It enabled ex-servicemen and bereaved relatives to feel that they were once again with the men who died in the salient. One visitor to Ypres stated that as 'the sad plaintive notes floated softly out of the Gate, the hands of time were turned back for me and the flood-gates of memory opened wide'.[155] More than this, it even enabled the people who participated in the ceremony to reach out to the dead and to reassure them that they were not forgotten, that they did not die in vain. The ceremony was described as 'the most stirring war memorial of all, the voice of the dead armies ringing with mournful triumph along the corridors which separate them from the humanity they died to save'.[156]

An undercurrent in the response of many travellers to the battlefields and war relics in the 1920s was the belief that these sights provided a lesson in the horrors of war and the need to work for peace. A mother who visited her son's grave in 1924

153. Dean and Dawson Ltd, *British Memorials of the Great War 1914–1918* (n.p., n.d.), p. 23.

154. Organising Committee '10,000th Last Post', 'The Last Post Ceremony at Ypres', AWM 27 - 623 [17], pp. 1-3.

155. L. A. Robb, 'Gone the Debris, Gone the Death', *Reveille*, 7 (Jan. 1934), p. 16.

156. *British Legion Journal*, 14 (May 1935), p. 475.

wrote: 'Never before had I thought that so many brave lads had fallen. When I think of the miles of graves in the cemetery, where my boy lies it makes the war seem more terrible than all the accounts and figures I had ever heard or read of it.'[157] Another traveller was prompted by his journey across the battlefields to write that, while human nature means that war will never be abolished, 'that is no reason why right-minded people should not strive steadfastly for the maximum obtainable disappearance of both these gruesome factors of destruction and suffering'.[158]

These sentiments were echoed at the highest levels in Great Britain. When George V stood before the thousands of headstones at Terlincthun cemetery in 1921 he spoke to the Empire of his feelings: 'In the course of my pilgrimage I have many times asked myself whether there can be more potent advocates of peace upon earth through the years to come than this massed multitude of silent witnesses to the desolation of war.'[159] The sentiments expressed by the King were repeated by the Australian Prime Minister in 1924.[160] This was also considered to be one of the purposes of the exhibits in the IWM. The Director-General of the IWM wrote in 1923 that the exhibits 'which from their nature and history had become memorials to gallant men, . . . also put before the public forcibly the horrors of modern warfare and as such the Museum became valuable propaganda for Peace'.[161]

In the late 1920s the construction of war cemeteries and memorials and the reconstruction of the battlefields led a number of writers to wonder if the landscape now emphasised the sacrifice of the soldiers without containing a warning about the horrors of war. Fabian Ware addressed the issue in 1927, deciding that the 'impression created on our own people generally (that made on the relatives of the dead is not for discussion here) by the larger cemeteries containing 10,000 or more graves is undoubtedly one mainly of horror which arouses bitter

157. St Barnabas Society, *Empire Pilgrimage, Scottish Pilgrimage* (London, *c.*1924), p. 26.

158. F. C. Rimington, *Motor Rambles Through France: Some Descriptions and Reflections* (London, 1925), p. 180.

159. F. Fox, *The King's Pilgrimage* (London, 1922).

160. Minutes of Proceedings of the IWGC, 12 Dec. 1923, pp. 2–4, NAC RG 38 Vol. 348.

161. IWM, *Annual Report* (1923/4), p. 1.

reflections. But that is not the effect always produced by the smaller cemeteries.'[162] In 1928 an article in *Country Life* warned that in the cemeteries the 'flowers which now blossom and make everything fair may obscure in our minds the stark fact represented by the graves'. The writer quoted one of the gardeners, who said: 'Yes, it's very beautiful, but it would have been far better if it had not been here at all.'[163]

A few writers such as Vera Brittain believed that the landscape now operated to sanitise the war and even to glorify it. In *Testament of Friendship* she surveyed the monuments erected on the Somme and asked: 'What a cheating and a camouflage was this combined effort of man and nature to create the impression that war was glorious, just because its aftermath could wear an appearance of beauty and dignity when fifteen years of uneasy peace had passed over mankind!'[164] She published two articles about her journey to the Somme in order to stress that its image as a place of peace was an illusion.[165] Seigfried Sassoon criticised the Menin Gate memorial in a similar vein:

> Here was the world's worst wound. And here with pride
> 'Their name liveth for ever,' the Gateway claims.
> Was ever an immolation so belied
> As these intolerably nameless names?
> Well might the Dead who struggled in the slime
> Rise and deride this sepulchre of crime.[166]

Many other writers concluded that on balance the battlefields actually provided convincing evidence of the horrors of war. J. B. Sterndale Bennett decided that while Ypres might be assumed to stand 'rebuilt as a glorification of war', the overriding impression both of the town and the surrounding area is of the 'most complete example that could be imagined of the obliteration of

162. F. Ware, 'War Graves and the British Commonwealth', *The Nineteenth Century and After*, DCIX (Nov. 1927), pp. 639–40.

163. '"For ever England": The Graves in France and Flanders', *Country Life*, XIV (Nov. 1928), p. 661.

164. V. Brittain, *Testament of Friendship: The Story of Winifred Holtby* (London, 1940), p. 362.

165. V. Brittain, 'Somme Battlefield, 1933', *Week-end Review*, VIII (Aug. 1933), p. 157. V. Brittain, 'Illusion on the Somme', in P. Berry (ed.), *Testament of a Generation: The Journalism of Vera Brittain and Winifred Holtby* (London, 1985), pp. 213–16.

166. S. Sassoon, *Collected Poems* (London, 1947), p. 188.

war and all its abominable traces'.[167] This was also a theme in guidebooks published in the late 1920s and 1930s. The 1929 Muirhead guide to Belgium referred to the Cloth Hall as a 'derelict and shattered monument to the horrors of war', while Thomas Cook's guide observed that ruined towns and 'glistening white cemeteries commemorate the misery of the war'.[168] A number of ex-servicemen expressed their belief that a day in the war cemeteries or on the battlefield would do more towards ensuring a permanent peace than disarmament conferences.[169] In his 1937 account of a visit to the Somme Victor Hyde argued that 'more solid progress indeed, would be made in a day on the Somme towards ensuring a permanent peace of the world than a year around the conference table'. He concluded that 'whether on land or air there cannot be another "Somme" we are still paying for the last one - still, as you have seen, trying to heal its sores'.[170]

Conclusion

In the inter-war years the battlefields of the Great War attracted thousands of travellers from Great Britain. While the Western Front drew the majority of tourists and pilgrims, a surprising number of people visited Gallipoli and the war cemetery in Jerusalem. Both places captured a significant aspect of the British memory of the war. Jerusalem evoked a strong identification between the passion of Christ and that of British soldiers. Gallipoli retained an aura of romance, at a time when many of the battlefields on the Western Front were associated with the misery and losses required to defeat Germany.

The popularity of travel to the old Western Front fluctuated in this period, reflecting changes in the level of interest in the war. The boom in travel in the immediate aftermath of the war resulted from a general preoccupation and even obsession with the war. This obsession could not be maintained, and in the mid-

167. J. B. Sterndale Bennett, 'The Return to Passchendaele', *The Nation and Athenaeum,* XLVII (June 1930), p. 346.

168. F. Muirhead, *Belgium and Luxembourg* (London, 1929), p. 37. Elston, *The Traveller's Handbook to Belgium*, pp. xi–xii.

169. B. Newman, *In the Trail of the Three Musketeers* (London, 1934), p. 140.

170. V. Hyde, 'The Greatest No More War Advertisement', *British Legion Journal*, 16 (Feb. 1937), pp. 293–4.

1920s there was a decline in the significance of battlefield travel as tourists were attracted to other destinations. The years of the 'war books boom' were a second high point in interest in travel to the battlefields. Travel was affected by the Depression, but after 1933 the numbers of travellers to the battlefields remained high. In particular the deteriorating international situation encouraged people to return to the battlefields in order to prepare for the coming war or in the desperate hope that somehow the war might be avoided.

In the inter-war years the landscape of the battlefields and the imaginative landscape of the sites which attracted travellers underwent a number of changes. The devastation was the main attraction for travellers in the years immediately after the war. It confirmed the wartime images of German barbarity and justified British involvement in the war. The reconstruction of the battlefields resulted in a small number of sites which catered to a general desire among travellers to see the wartime landscape. These sites told a story of heroism, which particularly emphasised the tenacity and endurance of British soldiers. Allied with the story of heroism was one of sacrifice. The war cemeteries evoked a traditional image of sacrifice which attempted to recreate the English landscape, and stressed equality and Christianity. Popular war memorials went beyond this to provide a glimpse of the wider implications of sacrifice. The reconstruction of the battlefields and the construction of war cemeteries challenged the role of these sites as a lesson in the need to strive for peace, a significant undercurrent in the response of travellers to the battlefields in the early 1920s. A few writers argued that the battlefields no longer provided a warning about the horrors of war. However, in the 1930s for many travellers the very scale of the memorials and cemeteries spoke of the horrors of war and the need to strive for peace.

4

'A Deeper Awareness of the War and its Import': Pilgrimages to the Battlefields of the Great War

> A further setting for reappraisal of the war emerged in the twenties with the pressing vogue of visits and pilgrimages to the battlefields. The legendary prestige of such sites of utter devotion and suffering as those associated with Ypres and the Menin Gate, with Verdun and the Fort de Douaumont, could not be denied. A deeper awareness of the war and its import diffused itself.
>
> – A. Wilder, *Armageddon Revisited: A World War I Journal*[1]

Throughout the 1920s and 1930s the battlefields of the Great War were places of pilgrimage for bereaved relatives and ex-servicemen. These pilgrimages were different from those to memorials in Great Britain because battlefield pilgrims were both in the presence of the dead and, if they were ex-servicemen, the presence of their past. The journey was therefore an opportunity for the bereaved to remember the dead and to come to terms with grief and sometimes guilt. Pilgrimages of the bereaved drew upon religious language and imagery as well as belief for their meaning. Ex-servicemen became pilgrims to remember, relive and often confront their past. The experience of confronting the dead or the past was an individual one which needs to be understood at this level.

These journeys also had significant implications for and reflected aspects of the collective memory of the war. In particular, large pilgrimages, such as the 1928 British Legion[2] pilgrimage, were public journeys which united bereaved relatives and ex-servicemen with political, military and often religious

1. A. Wilder, *Armageddon Revisited: A World War I Journal* (New Haven and London, 1994), p. 154.
2. Referred to as the Legion in this chapter.

leaders in an act of mourning for and homage to the dead. The journey expressed the national and imperial identity, as well as prestige, of Britain. Pilgrimages were part of a conservative reconstruction of the war experience which stressed continuity with the past and the ideals of service and sacrifice exemplified by the fallen. At the public level the acceptance of such a reconstruction, which privileged the fallen, could also create tensions. Increasingly in the late 1920s and 1930s the idealisation of the fallen was subsumed by the broader issue of whether their sacrifice had been worthwhile.

Remembering and Confronting Death

One feature of pilgrimages to places associated with the war, in common with many other types of pilgrimage, was the role of death as a focus for the journey.[3] Even in 1939 a pilgrim asserted that the dead 'dominate the former battlefields of France'.[4] The dead are usually present in the written accounts of pilgrimages. The souvenir of the 1928 Legion pilgrimage imagined the dead responding to the commotion created by the pilgrimage out of fear that war has broken out once again, only to be comforted by learning:

> It is your comrades below who are keeping faith with you. They leave to-day for the scenes of your ordeals, to blaze to the whole of the world - and even to these Heavens - that their promise to remember you is no idle word but the bond of a mighty race, given and kept with a strength, tested often to the limit, but never found wanting.[5]

The dead then join the pilgrims as they conduct their pilgrimage. The importance of the memory of the dead made bereaved relatives the centre of many pilgrimages. On a pilgrimage organised by the Ypres League, one observer commented that it was 'touching to watch the personal interest shown by the other pilgrims of the party and their anxiety to share in some small

3. V. Turner, 'Death and the Dead in the Pilgrimage Process', in V. Turner, *Process, Performance and Pilgrimage: A Study in Comparative Symbology* (New Delhi, 1979), p. 121.

4. E. H. Thompson, 'A Reminiscence of a Recent Visit to France and Flanders', *King's Royal Rifle Corps Chronicle* (1939), p. 73.

5. L. J. D. Gavin and J. Harter (eds), *The Story of an Epic Pilgrimage: A Souvenir of the Battlefield Pilgrimage* (n.p., 1928), p. 11.

way the sorrow endured by the bereaved relatives whenever a particular grave was visited'.[6]

Bereaved relatives travelled to the graves of their loved ones or, if no body could be found, to one of the memorials to the 'Missing'. In either case it was the name on the headstone or the memorial which drew them. Pilgrims took photographs of these names and occasionally they would kiss the name of a loved one or the headstone under which he lay.[7] Many pilgrims also traced a name on paper so that they could take it back with them.[8] A father actually sought compensation from the IWGC on the grounds that the visit to his son's grave 'had been without result' because there was no headstone on the grave.[9] The name on the memorial or the headstone was important because this distinguished the individual from the thousands of dead. It was the last tangible link with the person and the personality that had motivated the pilgrimage.

But it was more than just the name which drew bereaved relatives. The name was the signpost to an individual experience. Pilgrims carried the diaries or letters written by the fallen and used these in an attempt to re-create elements of the experiences of their loved ones.[10] P. E. Goodliffe travelled across the battlefields in 1919 thinking of Esmond, who had been killed during the war. She wrote to her mother that 'Esmond would be pleased to know that I had seen many of the places that he knew, and all the time I was wondering if he had been in this and that place and what he had thought of it.'[11] A father, aged seventy, insisted on walking three miles to and from a cemetery near Ypres, because he said that 'he would never pass that way again and he wanted to feel that he had traversed the same road that his son

6. *Ypres Times*, 3 (Oct. 1934), p. 116.

7. For examples of pilgrims kissing the name of a loved one see: St Barnabas Society, *The Menin Gate Pilgrimage* (London, *c.*1927), p. 36. A. K. Yapp, 'The Western Front Revisited', *Red Triangle*, III (Jan. 1920), p. 213.

8. T. Allen, *The Tracks They Trod; Salonika and the Balkans, Gallipoli, Egypt and Palestine Revisited* (London, 1932), p. 75.

9. Minutes of Proceedings of the IWGC, 12 Oct. 1927, p. 12, NAC RG 38 Vol. 348.

10. St Barnabas Society, *Gallipoli and Salonika* (London, *c.*1926), pp. 23, 25. A. Hickman, 'The Pilgrims to France', *Red Triangle*, V (Sept. 1921), p. 15.

11. P. E. Goodliffe to her family, 22 Jan. 1919, IWM - Documents of P. E. Goodliffe VAD.

had traversed on his last journey on earth'.[12] Another pilgrim wrote that it 'was a great thing for us to tread the roads our beloved ones trod and we felt they were not far away'.[13] Many pilgrims also wore outward reminders of their dead, such as medals or small photographs, during their journey.[14]

The difficulties of walking over the battlefields actually provided consolation for some pilgrims, because they brought them even closer to the experiences of their dead. An elderly woman walked four miles down the steep incline of Chunuk Bair and drew comfort from the fact that she had 'actually walked the way he [her son] went, and been able to share a little of the hardship'.[15] Another pilgrim, after participating in the 1927 pilgrimage for the unveiling of the Menin Gate, explained that the pilgrims 'had been soldiers, and had had our iron rations as our boys had had. They used to be tired, so why not us?'[16]

The pilgrimages made by bereaved relatives were part of the process of coming to terms with the pain of bereavement by confronting the sense of loss. Vera Brittain's description of her visit to the grave of her brother Edward in Northern Italy in 1921 evokes this sense of loss. It is a feeling that the future cannot live up to the past. Standing at the grave of Edward she thinks to herself:

> How trivial my life has been since the War! . . . How mean they are these little strivings, these petty ambitions of us who are left, now that all of you are gone! How can the future achieve, through us, the sombre majesty of the past? Oh Edward, you're so lonely up here; why can't I stay for ever and keep your grave company, far from the world and its vain endeavours to rebuild civilization, on this plateau where alone there is dignity and peace?[17]

Describing a visit to the grave of her brother at Annezin, Frances Stevenson wrote 'it was a terrible moment to see it for the first time. The pathos of it all swept over me, & the regret that

12. St Barnabas Society, *Croydon Pilgrimage, The Second Scottish Pilgrimage, Italian Pilgrimage, The Smaller Pilgrimages* (London, *c.*1925), p. 22.

13. St Barnabas Society, *Empire Pilgrimage, Scottish Pilgrimage* (London, *c.*1924), p. 32.

14. *Our Empire*, IV (July 1928), p. 2. *The Times*, 5 Aug. 1928.

15. St Barnabas Society, *Gallipoli and Salonika*, p. 18.

16. St Barnabas Society, *Menin Gate Pilgrimage*, pp. 39–40.

17. V. Brittain, *Testament of Youth: An Autobiographical Study of the Years 1900–1925* (London, 1933), pp. 526–7.

his young life should have been cut off before it was scarcely begun.'[18]

Pilgrimages enabled relatives to confront their grief for the dead and to let go of the past. This did not mean that the dead were forgotten, but that they took their place in the memory of the bereaved. The bereaved could then continue with their lives. Wilfred Ewart's story of the pilgrimage he made with his sister to the grave of her husband near Bapaume in 1919 illustrates this process. Although his sister was unable to find her husband's grave, her pilgrimage enabled her to leave the darkness of bereavement and to look to the future. Ewart concluded the story of her pilgrimage: 'She went laughing into the world again: and people say, does she care so very much - for she dances and sings, dances to [the] sound of piano and violin. Nor has the dancing light ever left her gay blue eyes. Her heart responds; she loves; she lives.'[19]

The process of coming to terms with grief and the past was a recurring theme in writing about the war and battlefield travel. In 'The Gardener' Rudyard Kipling described the pilgrimage of Helen Turrell to the grave of her illegitimate son as a means of confronting and accepting the past. Helen had never admitted Michael was her son, telling the village that he was her nephew. When she was informed that Michael was missing she withdrew into herself. She gained a second chance when she learned that Michael's body had been found and that she could visit his grave. At the cemetery she met a man she assumed was a gardener. He was actually an angel or Jesus Christ and when she asked him where her 'nephew' was buried: 'The man lifted his eyes and looked at her with infinite compassion before he turned from the fresh-sown grass toward the naked black crosses. "Come with me," he said, "and I will show you where your son lies."'[20] In making the pilgrimage and meeting the gardener Helen begins a new life and moves on from her past. She is ready to acknowledge her son. Helen's confrontation and acceptance of the past contrasts with that of Mrs Scarsworth, who repeatedly returns to the battlefields, ostensibly to visit graves for other people,

18. F. Stevenson, *Lloyd George: A Diary* (London, 1971), ed. A. J. P. Taylor, p. 180.

19. W. Ewart, 'A Pilgrimage', *National Review*, LXXIV (Dec. 1919) p. 523.

20. R. Kipling, 'The Gardener', *Debits and Credits* (London, 1926), p. 414.

but in reality drawn to the grave of a man who was either her unacknowledged son or her lover.

The return of pilgrims each year to the battlefields also helped the bereaved to let go of the dead and to consign them to memory, because it assumed that the dead would not be forgotten and would continue to be honoured in this way. As the dead were unchanging, so the pilgrims would not waver in their resolve to return. H. A. Taylor wrote that 'it may well be that, a hundred years hence, Britons will still come here to meditate upon deeds of valour and self-sacrifice'.[21] Laurence Binyon's immortal lines were popular with pilgrims precisely because they asserted that the memory of the dead would travel into the future with them:

> They shall not grow old, as we that are left grow old:
> Age shall not weary them, nor the years condemn.
> At the going down of the sun and in the morning
> We will remember them.[22]

Reconciliation with the dead was not always easy; in addition to confronting their grief at the loss of a loved one many pilgrims also confronted feelings of guilt and unease at surviving the dead. It is the guilt of the parent who has survived a son, of the soldier who has survived comrades, of a society faced with the death of around one million men throughout Great Britain and the Dominions. The sense of guilt confronted by many people was rarely addressed in the 1920s and 1930s. R. H. Mottram argued that feelings of guilt were linked to the construction of the war cemeteries, suggesting that when confronted by them 'no honest man or woman, now that ten years have permitted the cooling of mean passions, and the elimination of the animal mob psychology of war, can avoid the sense of a share in War Guilt'.[23] The guilt of a mother over the death of her son in the war was explored in John Ford's 1933 American film 'Pilgrimage.' In the film the mother enlists her son in the army in order to keep him away from the girl he has fallen in love with and the son is killed. Later she makes a pilgrimage to the grave of her son and by

21. H. A. Taylor, *Good-bye to the Battlefields: To-day and Yesterday on the Western Front* (London, 1928), p. 54.

22. *Toc H Journal*, II (Jan. 1924), p. 23.

23. R. H. Mottram, *Through the Menin Gate* (London, 1932), p. 23.

confronting her guilt is able to return home renewed and free from the burden of it.[24]

The significance of guilt for the survivors of the war is encapsulated in the story of Emily Causton and Hans Klutzen. They had to decide when to let go of wartime events and what actions could atone for the death of people they loved. Emily's first lover, Harry Leonard Parkes, served in the AIF and was killed in France in 1917. Emily met Hans in the cemetery where her lover was buried when she visited it on the anniversary of Harry's death. Hans was haunted by the figure of Harry, whom he had killed in a bayonet fight. Unable to come to terms with his remorse he visited the cemetery each year on the anniversary of his death. After meeting in the cemetery, Emily and Hans fell in love and were married. Hans had literally replaced the man that he had killed. Emily had to decide what was the legacy of Harry's death and the war. She resolved that 'it would be wrong of me to throw away God's gift of love just because Fate had brought these two men together in deadly conflict. I believe that a union such as I am contracting will do more for the reconciliation of the two peoples than all the efforts of the world politicians.' However, they accepted that many other people would not be able to put aside wartime hatred so easily.[25]

Guilt could also affect ex-servicemen who had to come to terms with their survival while many of those around them were dead. Stephen Graham recalled finding a skull when he visited the Western Front. His account reflects a profound sense of unease before the dead: 'The more you look at the skull the more angry does it seem - it has an intense eternal grievance. This one does not grin, for the mouth has been destroyed. It is just blind and senseless for ever and ever.'[26] Wilfred Ewart confronted these emotions when he returned to the 'Ghosts of Arras'. He concluded that there 'are no regrets for me in this city. I think of my freedom, of my happiness and full life at home; [and] am not disposed to quarrel with Fate's repeated intervention on my behalf.'[27]

24. J. A. Place, *The Non-Western Films of John Ford* (Secaucus, 1979), pp. 25-7.

25. *Brisbane Mail*, 22 Jan. 1923. AWM Newspaper Cuttings - Pilgrimages - British Legion, Miscellaneous anniversaries.

26. S. Graham, *The Challenge of the Dead* (London, 1921), p. 28.

27. W. Ewart, 'Ghosts of Arras', *The Nineteenth Century and After*, LXXXVIII (Dec. 1920), pp. 1104-5.

Pilgrimage, Religion and Belief

Scholars who study the nature of pilgrimages increasingly accept that they are a feature of travel in many different cultures and religious traditions and may even encompass travel to sites which are not normally associated with religious belief.[28] This understanding has flowed from a growing awareness that the rigid distinction between the sacred and the profane needs to be rethought. Pilgrimages are not always linked to an established religion, but are embedded in the religious experience of people and can take place in an ostensibly secular context.[29] Drawing on a more flexible understanding of 'pilgrimages' Tony Walter argues that war graves pilgrimages are analogous to medieval pilgrimages, although he claims that 'the war grave pilgrim's encounter with the sacred, even if accompanied by a short religious service, may appear to be less a religious experience than an emotional catharsis'.[30]

Walter is primarily concerned with explaining war graves pilgrimages in the 1980s and 1990s. While pilgrimages in the inter-war period were also an emotional catharsis, religion often played a central role in the experience, because religion was inscribed in the experience of people to a much greater degree than today. Annette Becker, in her analysis of religious faith in France during the war and the inter-war years, argues that the pilgrimages to places associated with the war were much closer to a religious experience. The Churches were heavily involved in the erection of memorials on the major battlefields of the war, and these memorials closely identified religious belief with the pilgrimages to them. For example, the Ossuaries at Verdun, Notre Dame de Lorette, Dormans and Rancourt included a Roman Catholic chapel for pilgrims to visit, while the Ossuary at Hartmanswillerkopf incorporated an ecumenical chapel.[31]

28. V. Turner and E. Turner, *Image and Pilgrimage in Christian Culture: Anthropological Perspectives* (Oxford and New York, 1978), p. 241. I. Reader and T. Walter (eds), *Pilgrimage in Popular Culture* (Houndsmills, 1993), pp. 1-16.

29. Reader and Walter (eds), *Pilgrimage in Popular Culture*, p. 16.

30. T. Walter, 'War Grave Pilgrimage', in Reader and Walter (eds), *Pilgrimage in Popular Culture*, p. 82.

31. A. Becker, *La Guerre et La Foi: De la Mort à la Mémoire* (Paris, 1994), pp. 113-14.

Religion also played an important role in British pilgrimages. This was despite the fact that by 1914 church attendance was in decline in both the Church of England and the Free Churches.[32] Even the war only briefly encouraged an increase in churchgoing.[33] However, churchgoing was only one aspect of belief in Britain in the period 1914–1939. Religion was an important facet of the educational and cultural life of people. In 1901 52.6 per cent of the population of England and Wales below the age of fifteen years was enrolled in Sunday School. By 1911 the percentage had only dropped to 51.4 per cent, and during the inter-war years it remained higher than 40 per cent.[34] Robin Gill suggests that most 'of the generation of young men that fought in the First World War had eventually been to Sunday School whether or not their parents went to church'.[35] In addition, compulsory religious education was a part of the curriculum, and Jeffrey Cox concludes that it is 'difficult to believe that it did not aid the diffusion of religious knowledge and increase the number of persons to whom Christian symbols and language were meaningful'.[36]

In contrasting tourism with pilgrimages one scholar has noted the importance of 'culturally-supplied language' in determining the way that people conceptualise what they are doing.[37] The expression 'pilgrimage' in Protestant culture includes a variety of meanings, one of which is the spiritual journey of the believer to God. Another is the religious journey of a medieval pilgrim to a shrine. The pilgrims drew upon these images to express the importance of their journey. The members of the 1927 Toc H pilgrimage to the Salient sang 'He who would valiant be', the Pilgrim's Hymn, which identified them with the Protestant tradition of spiritual pilgrimage.[38] Newspapers and magazines

32. R. Gill, *The Myth of the Empty Church* (London, 1993), p. 170.

33. S. P. Mews, 'Religion and English Society in the First World War', Ph.D. thesis, Cambridge University, 1973, pp. 50–1.

34. Gill, *The Myth of the Empty Church*, p. 301.

35. Ibid., p. 172.

36. J. Cox, *The English Churches in a Secular Society: Lambeth, 1870–1930* (New York, 1982), pp. 95–7.

37. B. Pfaffenberger, 'Serious Pilgrims and Frivolous Tourists: The Chimera of Tourism in the Pilgrimages of Sri Lanka', *Annals of Tourism Research*, 10 (1983), p. 72.

38. B. B., 'The Pilgrim's Way', *Toc H Journal*, V (Aug. 1927), p. 346.

frequently likened battlefield pilgrims to medieval pilgrims, while some pilgrims consciously equipped themselves with pilgrim's staves so they looked as though they had stepped out of *Pilgrim's Progress.*[39]

Stories of miraculous coincidences emphasised that the journey was out of the ordinary; a spiritual experience. One told how a father returned to the battlefields each year in the 1920s to search for the body of his son who was 'missing'. The local people, admiring his dedication, presented him with a piece of land near where his son was last seen, so that he could erect a memorial. When the foundations were dug the body of his son was found.[40] The Salvation Army cited the story of a working-class couple who were thrown together with a missionary and his wife on a pilgrimage. The organisers were afraid that they would have nothing in common. However, both couples talked about their sons who had died in the war and how each son had related that a close friend had helped to sustain him. When they compared photographs they discovered that it was their sons who had been such close friends; and, despite their divergent backgrounds, thenceforward they were inseparable during the journey.[41]

Religion provided more than a language and imagery; it was at the heart of the pilgrimages made by the bereaved. The major Churches continued to play a central role in the major rites of passage in British society, particularly funerals.[42] As an extension of this pastoral role religious organisations, such as the St Barnabas Society, the Church Army, the Salvation Army and the YMCA, were directly involved in the organisation of pilgrimages to war graves. The Church Army believed that they provided an opportunity for ministering to people:

> It is desired that everyone who makes the pilgrimage shall look back on it as one of the most sacred and uplifting experiences of his or her life. It is a time when the heart is peculiarly susceptible to good influences . . . It seems worthwhile that at such a moment a C. A. Evangelist or Sister shall be there to voice the feelings of the little

39. *Radio Times*, 3 Aug. 1928. Gavin and Harter (eds), *The Story of an Epic Pilgrimage*, pp. 77, 79.

40. Taylor, *Good-bye to the Battlefields*, pp. 183–4.

41. *All the World*, 1 (Oct.–Dec. 1938), pp. 37–8.

42. Cox, *The English Churches in a Secular Society*, p. 190.

> group at the graveside, and to direct them into channels of permanent spiritual value.[43]

The certificate they gave pilgrims to remind them of their visit to a grave recalled the consolation that Jesus Christ provided for those who mourn [Figure 4]. The St Barnabas Society hostels included a chapel where services of Holy Communion were held for pilgrims. Also funds were raised to build the Anglican Church of St George in Ypres, which Sir John French emphasised would provide pilgrims with a place into which 'they could come for prayer and remembrance of their dead, and there, in peace and spirit, feel that appeal to service and sacrifice of which we are all so conscious today'.[44]

The precise nature of the beliefs held by the majority of people in Great Britain is unclear. A study of servicemen produced in 1919 concluded that the 'men of the British armies, however dim their faith may be, do in the hour of danger, at least believe in God' and that 'the men, though vaguely, believe in the life to come'.[45] Recent studies have tended to support this impression of a belief system which combined a general concept of God and an instinctive spiritualism. Paul Thompson concludes that the Edwardians believed 'if imprecisely, in a Christian God; also in luck, and very likely in Ghosts'.[46] Popular hymns, such as 'Abide with Me', expressed the belief in life after death and the continuing presence of God. The hymn was a favourite of pilgrims to the battlefields. R. H. Mottram recalled the beginnings of the Menin Gate ceremony which concluded the 1928 Legion pilgrimage:

> All was now ready for the Prince (of those days) to come and perform the ceremony, but many of the 11,000 had been standing for an hour or two and somehow felt that the matter was not going forward quite as it should. Some rich North-country voice bellowed: 'Ab-aide with me!' And, with a little quavering, the 11,000 took it up. I have never forgotten the expression on the faces of the military and other dignitaries. They could not make it out. The situation was saved by

43. *Church Army Review*, (Aug. 1924), p. 14.

44. G. French (ed.), *Some War Diaries, Addresses and Correspondence of Field Marshal the Right Honourable The Earl of Ypres KP, GCB, OM, GCVO, KCMG* (London, 1937), p. 343.

45. D. S. Cairns, *The Army and Religion* (London, 1919), pp. 7, 16.

46. P. Thompson, *The Edwardians: The Remaking of British Society* (London and New York, 1992), p. 174.

O LORD, Who didst weep with Mary and Martha over their loved one and Who art afflicted in all our afflictions, comfort us by Thy Presence. Bless our dear one, and grant that we may for ever be joined together in the place which Thou art gone to prepare. Amen.

Figure 4. Church Army Certificate. Miscellaneous Papers, IWM, Misc. 1964, item 1964.

the arrival of the (then) Prince of Wales, in a lounge suit and bowler hat.[47]

Religious belief offered pilgrims a source of strength and the promise that they might meet their loved one in the afterlife. The Salvation Army published a letter from a pilgrim who stated that they had 'begun to doubt that God was love, but at that graveside your officer prayed such a beautiful prayer that I will never doubt God again!'[48] Another pilgrim concluded: 'Can we thank God for the death of our boy? I do not know, but this I do know, that we go home pacified and more content than before, to wait God's good pleasure until he shall reunite us without shadow of further parting.'[49] The parents of William John Williams visited his grave in France in 1926 and wrote that while they were there 'came the burst of tears, *but with* a *hope* to *meet* our *dear brave lad again* in a *far* and *better* sphear [*sic*], than this world where there is no Sorrow, nor tears, nor cruel wars, where we shall enjoy everlasting life, when God will wipe every tear'.[50]

Pilgrims also drew upon an instinctive spiritualism which blurred the divide between the presence of the memory of the dead and their spirits. The feeling that the war areas were a place of ghosts was widely shared. Mrs Humphry Ward found that the 'great army of the dead' seemed to gather round her as she stood on the Menin road, a view echoed by John Bart (the last Lord Chancellor of Ireland) who felt as if 'the spirits of the fallen' were 'hovering' over the road.[51] Stanley Baldwin stated that when he walked the Menin road to Guillemont 'he seemed to be encompassed with a cloud of witnesses. The whole air still seemed pulsating with the life of those who had marched and fought.'[52] The presence of the dead on the battlefields was a key element in Graham Hutchison's war novel *Life Without End*. In the novel the hero is disillusioned by the post-war world and his loss of

47. R. H. Mottram, *Journey to the Western Front: Twenty Years After* (London, 1936), p. 75.

48. *War Cry* (Sept. 1920), p. 8.

49. *Church Army Review* (Feb. 1921), p. 5.

50. D. Williams to A. O'Neil, 17 Aug. 1926, IWM, Miscellaneous Papers, Misc. 100 Item 1556.

51. M. A. Ward, *Fields of Victory* (London, 1919), p. 46. J. R. Bart, *Pilgrim Scrip: More Random Reminiscences* (London, 1927), p. 294.

52. *The Times*, 20 Feb. 1929.

faith, and returns to the battlefields where he fought during the war. On his return to High Wood on the Somme he is spiritually transformed by a vision of the dead who call on him to return to England and to start life afresh. At that moment he sees a vision of the cross and knows that he has become 'a pilgrim possessed of revelation'.[53]

Pilgrimages therefore provided the bereaved with an opportunity to interact with the dead. In a letter to the St Barnabas Society one pilgrim claimed that 'as I was kneeling by my husband's grave one beautiful white rose shed all its petals over me, and I seemed to hear this message: "Do not fret for us, for all is well," and I took comfort from this, for "oh," the years have seemed so long'.[54] Another pilgrim was seen smoking on a gravestone; he remarked 'I was only having a pipe with dear old Ted . . . Just as we used to.'[55] A Salvation Army Major recalled a pilgrim who brought his son's mouth organ to his grave and enquired 'Would they mind if I played him a tune?'[56]

Often the pilgrims brought gifts such as flowers from their gardens or wreaths to place on the graves of their dead relatives or to leave at the memorials to the missing. In return they usually collected something from the grave or battlefield to take back with them. These items included a variety of mementoes, such as flowers, a length of barbed wire, mould from the headstone, stones from the grave or seeds from the plants growing there. Ethel Richardson placed a bottle containing soil and grass from her son's grave under the village war memorial.[57] The souvenirs which the pilgrims collected enabled them to carry home a tangible link with the memory, or even the spirit, of the dead.

The close link between religious belief and the organisation of battlefield pilgrimages was clearly evident in the pilgrimages organised by Toc H.[58] It was founded by the Reverend P. B. 'Tubby' Clayton to perpetuate the spirit of Talbot House, a recreation centre and chapel for British servicemen established in

53. G. Hutchison, *Life Without End* (London, 1932), pp. 271-82.
54. St Barnabas Society, *Ypres/The Somme* (London, *c.*1923), p. 36.
55. St Barnabas Society, *Croydon Pilgrimage*, p. 10.
56. R. Woods, 'War Graves Visitation in France', *Officer's Review*, VII (Nov./Dec. 1938), p. 498.
57. E. M. Richardson, *Remembrance Wakes* (London, 1934), p. 205.
58. For the story of Toc H see: T. Lever, *Clayton of Toc H* (London, 1971).

Poperinghe during the war. The men who visited the club and joined in its fellowship discovered what was described as the Christianity of the BEF, which was expressed through comradeship, unity and service.[59] The chapel at the top of Talbot House became the most sacred place in the Salient to its members, and they were encouraged to make pilgrimages to the House and the battlefields. The organisation's Journal stressed to members that every

> movement with a religious basis has found inspiration in a pilgrimage. We go back to our beginnings to understand our growth and see our objective. The lad who was a baby in the war gains more by going to the old House in Poperinghe and imagining the refreshment of the tired soldiers than by listening to many poor reminiscences of mine or any other.[60]

In the 1930s there was increasing debate over the utility of these pilgrimages, because some members were concerned that the spiritual significance of Talbot House and its chapel might be obscured by the accompanying visits to the battlefields, which were closer to tourism.[61]

Remembering and Confronting the Past

Ex-servicemen who became pilgrims not only returned to visit the graves of their comrades; they also searched for or were confronted by an imagined past. It was a quest either to ensure that their experiences or the individuals that they once knew were not forgotten or, if the nightmare experience could not be forgotten, an attempt to defuse the memory. In 1936 R. H. Mottram decided to write about his journeys to the battlefields because he believed that

> the War that seems the special possession of those of us who are growing middle-aged is being turned by time and change into something fabulous, misunderstood and made romantic by distance, as it recedes into the past. For half the people alive to-day it might almost as well be something that happened to the Ancient Egyptians,

59. Talbot House, *The Pilgrim's Guide to the Ypres Salient* (London, 1920), pp. 80–3.

60. *Toc H Journal*, X (Jan. 1932), p. xiii.

61. *Toc H Journal*, XI (Dec. 1933), pp. 394–5; XVI (May 1938), pp. 119–20; XVI (Sept. 1938), pp. 326–7; XVI (Oct. 1938), pp. 372–3.

> so little can they, who did not experience it conceive, what it was like.[62]

John Gibbons returned to the battlefields in the mid-1930s to 'reconstruct' his memories, because he believed that another war was coming and he wanted to write for his son and others who would read his book about what to expect and how to survive.[63]

The range of responses of ex-servicemen to the past included a sense of nostalgia and the desire to relive the remembered experience or even to act out things which were denied to them during the war. Nostalgia inspired *Twenty Years After: The Battlefields of 1914–1918 Then and Now*, a weekly magazine which was produced to enable ex-servicemen who could not visit the battlefields to compare photographs taken during the war with the scene twenty years later.[64] The magazine included stories about the war, as well as accounts by ex-servicemen of their experiences when they returned to the battlefields. It was very popular, as over sixty issues of the magazine were published in 1936–1937. An important element of the nostalgia of the men was the recollection of the comradeship they experienced during the war. The editorial of the *British Legion Journal* emphasised that ex-servicemen did not return because they were morbid or curious, or out of affection for the war or with pleasure, or out of an interest in military tactics, but out of comradeship.[65]

However, this comradeship did not encompass all ex-servicemen. Most pilgrimages consisted of smaller groups of ex-servicemen with a more immediate tie than the fact that they had served during the war. Thus ex-servicemen who travelled together as pilgrims usually belonged to the same Division, Regimental, Company or even Battalion associations or lived in the same area. For example in June 1928 seventy members of the Leeds 'Pals' battalion returned to Serre, where the battalion had been shattered on 1 July 1916.[66] The Old Contemptibles, inspired by the American Legion visit, travelled to Belgium in 1927 to

62. Mottram, *Journey to the Western Front*, pp. 1–2.

63. J. Gibbons, *Roll On, Next War! The Common Man's Guide to Army Life* (London, 1935), p. 21.

64. E. Swinton (ed.), *Twenty Years After: The Battlefields of 1914–18, Then and Now*, Vol. 1 (London, 1936–7), p. 1.

65. *British Legion Journal*, 14 (Sept. 1934), p. 93.

66. Leeds 'Pals' 1928 Battlefield Tour, Peter Liddle Collection, Edward Boyle Library, Leeds University.

celebrate Armistice Day in Mons.[67] Ex-servicemen might also be united through their place of employment. In 1929 three thousand ex-servicemen who were employees of the Leyland Corporation travelled to Belgium and the battlefields. At the time it was the largest employees' trip to leave England.[68]

The importance of the pilgrimage as a journey for a limited circle of comrades helps to explain why so few national pilgrimages of ex-servicemen were organised. After the success of the 1928 Legion pilgrimage the Legion sent a circular to branches proposing a Sub-department to assist in organising future pilgrimages, as well as announcing plans to prepare a national pilgrimage to Salonika, Gallipoli and Palestine.[69] The General Secretary's Monthly Circular for February 1929 announced that owing to the poor response received from Branches the Sub-department would not be set up.[70] Despite this around five thousand pilgrims participated in smaller pilgrimages organised at the Area, Branch or sub-branch level in 1929.[71] The Legion was unable to organise another national pilgrimage in the 1930s, despite several proposals and in spite of the high level of interest and participation in smaller pilgrimages by ex-servicemen. In part this was because of the confused international situation; but a more important reason was that most ex-servicemen were happier returning in smaller groups of wartime or post-war comrades.[72]

The men not only remembered events in their past, but also sought to recreate fondly remembered wartime experiences. They returned to the *estaminets* to purchase omelettes, just as they used to do during the war, using the old army slang and wartime French, such as ordering drinks by saying 'toot sweet and the tooter the sweeter'.[73] Men wore their brigade badges

67. Old Contemptibles - Plan for a Pilgrimage to Mons, 1927, 2 Oct. 1927, PRO FO 371 - 12621.

68. *The Times*, 22 June 1929.

69. The British Legion, *Special Circular* 7.

70. The British Legion, *General Secretary's Monthly Circular*, Feb. 1929.

71. *British Legion Journal*, 9 (Sept. 1929), pp. 66–7.

72. The British Legion, *General Secretary's Monthly Circular for October 1932*. Resolutions of the Annual Conference of the British Legion, 1937, Resolution 85.

73. A. Behrend, *As From Kemmel Hill: An Adjutant in France and Flanders 1917 and 1918* (London, 1963), p. 150. *Yorkshire Post*, 9 Aug. 1928.

and brought along games such as Crown and Anchor and House as well as singing wartime songs.[74] A number of writers describe acting out scenes from their past. The *Tablet*, a Catholic journal, wrote that the small party of British ex-servicemen who joined the ex-servicemen's pilgrimage to Lourdes in 1934 exercised an influence out of all proportion to their numbers because they followed the practice of marching in columns of four as they had done during the war.[75] Another account of a pilgrimage described how the ex-servicemen instinctively knew that they should form fours and march through Ypres to the Menin Gate.[76]

Some ex-servicemen revelled in the new circumstances which enabled them to fulfil dreams they had held during the war. Many were anxious to see the German, Austro-Hungarian, Bulgarian or Turkish trenches, and those long-desired green fields beyond. One ex-serviceman travelling to Gallipoli expressed a desire 'to stand on Achi Baba and feel as Johnny Turk must have felt when he was perched on top there, blasting us all to hell. What a day to live for!'[77] An ex-prisoner of war recalled the long days of hunger he had endured and had dinner in an *estaminet* he used to pass as a starving prisoner.[78] John Gibbons made a point of travelling first class on the steamer from Southampton because he wished to be waited on by a steward on a journey he made during the war in cramped conditions. He also had a beer in an *estaminet* which was closed to him during the war because it was 'Officers Only'.[79]

Other ex-servicemen felt an inexplicable sadness when they discovered that the battlefields they remembered had disappeared. One ex-serviceman followed 'the footsteps of the battalion - up to the battle trenches' in 1921 and was shocked to discover that 'it was as though I had never been there'.[80]

74. *Daily News and Westminster Gazette*, 6 Aug. 1928. *The British Legion Pilgrimage Handbook* (n.p., 1928), pp. 82-91, reproduced the words of many of the popular wartime songs for pilgrims.

75. *Tablet*, 164 (Oct. 1934), p. 450.

76. 'The Visit to Ypres', *City of London Rifles and Quarterly Journal*, 1 (Jan. 1931), p. 12.

77. Allen, *The Tracks They Trod*, p. 16.

78. G. H. Johnson, 'An Ex-prisoner Returns', *Ypres Times*, 5 (Apr. 1931), pp. 169-70.

79. J. Gibbons, *I Wanted to Travel* (London, 1938), pp. 234-5.

80. H, 'The Old Road, September 1916-1921', *New Statesman*, XVIII (Oct. 1921), p. 74.

Edmund Blunden, who returned to the battlefields in 1930, wrote: 'It is ridiculous to be depressed by the triumph of life, but I feel a little grey as I move in this vernal world, marvellously re-flourishing. I am grateful to the low drumfire of the thunder, and the sudden, cold slashing, thorough rainstorm which makes us crouch under an outhouse wall in Zillebeke.'[81] Another ex-serviceman found himself 'nursing a dawning resentment as it becomes more and more evident that we are nothing better than strangers on our own ground . . . these trees, these telegraph posts, the road we foot have blotted out the past'.[82]

The desire shared by a number of ex-servicemen who returned to relive the events of the war reflects one of the paradoxes of their wartime experience. For many of them it was a nightmare consisting of long periods of monotony punctuated by moments of intense fear, pain and sadness. However, they were also participating in a titanic event, and one which left an indelible impression upon them. The experience helped to define their youth, and so it was difficult to believe that images and landscapes which had been seared into their memories had disappeared, often without a trace. They found it hard to accept that the world in which they lived during the war had vanished.

After surveying writing about returning to the battlefields of the Great War, Modris Eksteins suggests that it is in the traveller to the battlefields 'we may find a figure symbolic of our century'. This is because the traveller who is a stranger on the battlefields is emblematic of modernism. Eksteins equates modernism with disconnectedness, with a 'journey into the unknown, to a new frontier or into darkness'.[83] His suggestion superficially appears attractive. Many ex-servicemen clearly did feel that they were strangers on the old battlefields. But the source for this feeling lies squarely in their past. They are strangers because they journey to the known, to the places in their memories, and find that

81. E. Blunden, 'We Went to Ypres', in E. Blunden, *The Mind's Eye* (London, 1934), pp. 46–7.

82. 'A Sub-lieutenant RN Looks Back', in Swinton (ed.), *Twenty Years After*, Vol. 1, p. 287.

83. M. Eksteins, 'Michelin, Pickfords and the Great War: Tourism on the Western Front 1919–1991', Paper presented at Histoire Culturelle Comparée du Premier Conflit Mondial: La Guerre et La Mémoire de la Guerre, Colloque, Péronne (1992). French translation in J. J. Becker *et al.*, *1914–1918. Guerre et Cultures* (Paris, 1994).

these places no longer exist. Ironically, what they discover instead are the normal everyday scenes of a rural countryside at peace. They are strangers because what they sought was an aberration, a brief moment of the past.

The past and memories of ex-servicemen were often more than something to be recalled and relived; many returned to the battlefields with a strong sense of foreboding and unease. The journey for them was a confrontation with their past. An ex-serviceman who returned to the river Lys found himself unable to walk up the river to the places he once knew because: 'I should stand naked before my past . . . The very permanence of the beauty is too sharp a reminder of the pain and waste, the slaughter and the fury, the long-drawn waiting for the dawn.'[84] In 1934 P. R. Butler wrote that he would like to revisit the old farmsteads and inns of the Western Front if 'going back were not so certain to be painful'.[85] Despite his forebodings he returned to Ypres in 1935, explaining that while it was 'not surprising that the thought of revisiting "the battlefields" should be repugnant, even at this date', it was only the behaviour of his fellow Englishmen in Ostend which sent his party to the battlefields 'in spite of our reluctance to evoke the ghosts of Ypres!'[86]

Many ex-servicemen baulked at confronting places which they could only recall as a nightmare, and chose never to visit the battlefields. Unfortunately, these men have disappeared from the history of battlefield pilgrimages. The response of a few surviving Australian ex-servicemen to the offer of a free trip to Gallipoli in 1990 suggests just how difficult it could be to contemplate returning to the battlefields. One veteran refused to join the pilgrimage, explaining that as he had huddled aboard the evacuation craft in 1915 he had made a vow that he would never return. Another stated 'I hate the place. I've seen enough of it already', while another exclaimed 'Once was more than sufficient. Who wants to revive horrors I've spent a lifetime trying

84. 'A Welshman Returns to the Lys', in Swinton (ed.), *Twenty Years After*, Supplementary Volume, pp. 302–3.

85. P. R. Butler, 'Farmsteads and Inn-Names of Picardy and Artois', *English Review*, LIX (Aug. 1934), p. 212.

86. P. R. Butler, 'Twenty-One Years After', *Blackwood's Magazine*, CCXXXVIII (Dec. 1935), p. 832.

to forget?'[87] Such strong emotions after seventy-five years suggest that many ex-servicemen may have been unable to contemplate a return to the battlefields.

For some ex-servicemen, such as Henry Williamson, the pilgrimage to the battlefields was a chance to exorcise the war. He described himself as 'a foreigner among the living, and half a foreigner to myself - a man who had lost part of himself . . . For years the lost part had lurked in the marsh, seeing wraiths of men in grey with coal-scuttle helmets and big boots.' Unable to let go of the war, he found that it continued to visit him in the form of a wraith. His pilgrimage provided the means for him to find a new part of himself, by learning that the war had been lost for ever. He awoke on the final day of his pilgrimage 'filled with longing for my home; to see again the lanes, the sea, the barns, the hills, the eyes of my wife, the smile of my little boy listening to the bells on the wind of heaven, - the new part of myself overlaying the wraith of that lost forever'.[88] Williamson returned to the battlefields again and again in his fiction. Each time they are a place where his protagonists can confront their past and be reborn. He concludes the *Sun in the Sands*: 'I went to Amiens, thence to Albert, and walked over the old battlefields I had known on the Somme, with aching heart for all things remembered in ancient sunlight, but with hope for the future.'[89]

Public Ceremony – A Case Study of the British Legion Pilgrimage

Pilgrimages were also a public experience, which united groups and the nation in remembrance. There was widespread interest in pilgrimages to the battlefields, and correspondents accompanied the major pilgrimages, so that they were widely reported in the press. These accounts, together with those of the returning pilgrims, contributed to the collective memory of the war. The largest British pilgrimage was the 1928 Legion pilgrimage to the Western Front. A case study of the pilgrimage illustrates how

87. *Mercury*, 26 Apr. 1990; *Adelaide News* 11 Apr. 1990; *Sunraysia Daily*, 28 Apr. 1990. AWM, Newspaper Cuttings, Anzac Day 1990, Box 2, file 70, Box 1 files 9(1) and 9(2).
88. H. Williamson, *The Wet Flanders Plain* (London, 1929), pp. 145–8.
89. H. Williamson, *The Sun in the Sands* (London, 1945), p. 250.

issues of national identity and prestige could influence large pilgrimages. They were also an expression of the continuing need, particularly among women, for a public ceremony for mourning the dead. Large pilgrimages stressed the communities of the nation and of the Empire and among the pilgrims; however, they also revealed tensions in these communities.

The Story of the Pilgrimage

In the period from 3 to 8 August 1928 eleven thousand people took part in the Legion pilgrimage, which reporters claimed represented only 'a tithe' of those who would have gone if the accommodation had been available.[90] Other groups toured the battlefields at the same time as the pilgrimage, and there was a Jewish memorial service at the Menin Gate in the afternoon of 8 August. Many contemporaries considered the Legion pilgrimage to be the 'greatest and most remarkable of the battlefield Pilgrimages', overshadowing the remarkable scenes in July 1927 when the memorial at the Menin Gate was opened.[91]

There was a widespread feeling that the pilgrims were engaged in more than an ordinary journey. In many places 'ex-service men, friends and well-wishers' gathered to watch the pilgrims depart. The belief that this was a special journey was also reflected in the pilgrims' actions. They sent delegations to lay wreaths at the tombs of the Unknown Soldier in both Paris and Brussels. They also participated in a memorial service at Zeebrugge and in a wreath-laying ceremony to honour the French war dead in the Ossuary at Notre Dame de Lorette. In addition, each group of pilgrims conducted a wreath-laying ceremony in honour of the dead of the town where the group was billeted, as well as at memorials of particular significance to the group. For example, both the Irish Free State party and the Ulster party laid wreaths at the memorial to the Ulster Division at Thiepval.

The pilgrims were carried to the Continent by seven steamers. The first left England on 4 August and was followed by the remaining six the next day. They were billeted with families, in schools and army barracks in towns such as Amiens, Lens, Arras, Ypres and Poperinghe where the British Army had been billeted

90. *Ypres Times*, 4 (July 1928), p. 85.

91. *The Times*, 5 Aug. 1928; *Ypres Times*, 4 (Oct. 1928), p. 107; *Daily Mail*, 1 Aug. 1928.

during the war. Most spent a day touring the battlefields and cemeteries at Beaumont Hamel and a day touring those on and around Vimy Ridge. Ex-servicemen found the journey an emotional experience. They saluted whenever they passed a cemetery, and many of them had to gulp back tears. At Vimy Ridge the British Legion band played 'God Save the King' amidst the 'rapturous enthusiasm' of the vast crowd. In addition more than four thousand pilgrims went on special visits to the graves of relatives or friends.

The pilgrimage culminated in a large memorial service held at the Menin Gate in Ypres on Wednesday 8 August. As the morning of 8 August dawned the pilgrims marched through Ypres in four columns through cheering crowds. At the Menin Gate a ceremony was held in memory of the dead. It included an address by the Archbishop of York, who stressed that today it was clear that the war had been 'worthwhile'. Following the service the pilgrims marched past the Prince of Wales. After the service the pilgrims wandered around the battlefields and cemeteries of the Ypres Salient.

In addition to the eleven thousand pilgrims, people from England went independently to France and Belgium to visit individual graves and to attend the memorial service in Ypres. Excursions were organised by the London, Midland and Scottish Railway Company in connection with the pilgrimage and the service in Ypres. Many English people who were on holiday at Belgian and French seaside resorts also attended the memorial service, as did some of the local inhabitants of Northern France and Belgium. It is difficult to estimate how many people were in Ypres for the memorial service. The figures of the railway administration referred to in *The Times* state that 25,000 tickets were collected at Ypres Station on 8 August (not including those of the pilgrims).[92] This, combined with the fact that all the hotel accommodation in Ypres was booked on 7 August, suggests that many other people joined the pilgrims in Ypres.[93] The *Daily Express* estimated that there were 50,000 people present in addition to the pilgrims, while *The Times* stated that as many as 20,000 people from Great Britain were in Ypres.[94]

92. *The Times*, 13 Aug. 1928.
93. *The Times*, 9 Aug. 1928.
94. *Daily Express*, 8 Aug. 1928. *The Times*, 9 Aug. 1928.

The potential audience for the memorial service was even greater, as the BBC broadcast the service from all its stations. An article in the *Evening Standard* referred to a 'reverent little crowd in the Strand; the men bareheaded, gathered outside a small wireless shop, whose loud speaker on the doorstep, reproduced the service of the Menin Gate'.[95] The leading article in the *Eastern Daily Press* confidently stated that the ceremony 'found a response in the hearts of millions of the British people of whom the pilgrims . . . were the representatives'.[96] The impact of the pilgrimage would also have been furthered by the eye-witness account of Sir Ian Hamilton broadcast by the BBC on the Friday following the pilgrimage.[97]

The pilgrimage was primarily organised by the Legion with the BESL. However, the significance of the event was reflected in the heavy involvement of other groups. *La Fédération Interalliée des Anciens Combattants*, the international organisation for ex-servicemen, helped to organise billets for the pilgrims in Northern France and Belgium. French and Belgian ex-servicemen's associations were also involved in the provision of billets and in the conduct of memorial services throughout Northern France and Belgium. The Ypres League provided the pilgrims with a free descriptive and historical guide of Ypres and the neighbourhood. The IWGC helped to plan the itinerary, organised the visits to individual graves and provided 200 gardeners to act as guides. There was also government assistance. Through the Foreign Office the Legion was able to arrange for the Belgian and French Governments to exempt the pilgrims from customs duties. Concessions on French and Belgian railways were also provided.

It is difficult to know how the pilgrims responded to the events during the pilgrimage. Mrs Ralph Blewitt, who helped organise the special visits, quoted some of the letters she had received from participants. These included statements such as: 'we have had a great yearning fulfilled', 'our life's ambition satisfied', or 'the dearest wish of my life fulfilled'.[98] A number of contributors to the Souvenir commented that the pilgrimage was one of the

95. *Evening Standard*, 8 Aug. 1928.
96. *Eastern Daily Press*, 9 Aug. 1928.
97. *Radio Times*, 3 Aug. 1928.
98. Gavin and Harter (eds), *The Story of an Epic Pilgrimage*, pp. 134–5.

most exciting times of their lives.[99] For others the memory of the loss of a near relative could be too much even ten years after the war. A week after the pilgrimage the *Eastern Daily Press* carried the story of a man who had committed suicide. The man's brother-in-law felt that his mind had been affected by his recent pilgrimage to the battlefields in France, where his brother had been killed.[100]

However, there is some evidence to suggest that the pilgrimage did not leave the tremendous impression on participants that the rhetoric of the Legion claimed. The Legion printed a limited number of books as souvenirs of the pilgrimage; however, these did not sell as well as expected. The General Secretary in June 1929 announced that the price of the souvenir would be reduced from 5s. to 3s. In December the General Secretary announced that the price would be further reduced to 2s.6d.[101]

The Conception and Form of the Pilgrimage

Both the conception and the form of the pilgrimage were closely tied to issues of national identity and how the war should be remembered, in particular by the need to ensure that Britain's contribution to the Allied victory should not be ignored or forgotten. The Legion organised its first pilgrimage in 1927, but the response was 'somewhat disappointing', with only 150 people participating. The Chairman of the Legion blamed the failure of the 1927 pilgrimage on the high cost, about £5, and the novelty of the idea of a pilgrimage.[102] The first of these factors would also have been significant in 1928. Although the cost had been reduced to £4.5s., it would still have been beyond the means of many people. The Legion claimed that the 1927 pilgrimage provided the inspiration for the 1928 pilgrimage, an explanation which is accepted by the official historian of the Legion.[103] This claim ignores the significant role played by the Annual Conference of the American Legion, which was held in

99. Gavin and Harter (eds), *The Story of an Epic Pilgrimage*, pp. 40, 90.

100. *Eastern Daily Press*, 16 Aug. 1928.

101. The British Legion, *General Secretary's Monthly Circular*, June 1929, Dec. 1929.

102. Gavin and Harter (eds), *The Story of an Epic Pilgrimage*, p. 13.

103. Ibid.; G. Wootton, *The Official History of the British Legion* (London, 1956), p. 104.

Paris from 19 to 24 September 1927, as a motivating factor behind the pilgrimage. The Legion only planned to organise further small pilgrimages in 1928. In August 1927 the National Executive Council sanctioned a tour for June 1928, which would be a small affair involving a trip from London to Ostend with three days and two nights in Ostend.[104] Motivated by the American Legion visit, however, proposals were later put forward for a British pilgrimage on the scale of the American Legion visit.

On 19 August 1927 the *Daily Mail* printed an article entitled 'Take the Troops Back to France' by an 'English Resident in France'. The article suggested that under the Legion the men who fought in the war with their relatives and dependants should 'make a pious pilgrimage with a great march past in Paris'. The writer stressed that 'the moment is particularly opportune in view of the fact that the American Legion is bringing over its veterans to visit the former battlefields'. The suggestion was also supported in the leading article of the same day.[105]

The idea was taken up in the French newspaper *Le Temps*, which published extracts from the *Daily Mail's* leading article.[106] M. Poincaré, the French Prime Minister, sent an official message to the *Daily Mail*, stating that: 'France would be extremely happy if, in a few months the British Legion were to organise with the Canadians, South Africans, Australians and New Zealanders a voyage similar to that which the American Legion is about to make in France.'[107] The Prime Minister's proposal was particularly directed at the Old Contemptibles who had constituted the original BEF in 1914. The *Daily Mail* claimed on 22 August that the idea of a pilgrimage had the unanimous agreement of the Old Contemptibles, who had been interviewed while at a wreath-laying ceremony at the Cenotaph.[108] The proposal led to a letter from Sir Ian Hamilton on behalf of the Legion agreeing with the idea of sending the Old Contemptibles back to France, but regretting that it was not possible because the Legion lacked the financial resources of the American Legion.[109]

104. British Legion, *General Secretary's Monthly Circular*, Aug. 1927.
105. *Daily Mail*, 19 Aug. 1927.
106. *Le Temps*, 20 Août 1928.
107. *Daily Mail*, 20 Aug. 1927.
108. *Daily Mail*, 22 Aug. 1927.
109. *Daily Mail*, 23 Aug. 1927.

The idea of a Legion pilgrimage was also pursued in an article in the *Sphere* in September 1927. The author referred to the American Legion visit, warning that the Franco-American celebration will 'tend to relegate the British land effort on the continent still further into the background from its already dim degree of recognition'.[110] According to the *Daily Mail* the decision of the Legion to organise a major pilgrimage was taken in a committee meeting of the Legion on 7 October.[111] On 12 October the French Minister of War, M. Painlevé, stated that he was 'deeply touched by the decision to organise a pilgrimage to the old battlefront' and that he hoped that the pilgrims could visit Paris.[112]

Surprisingly, the fact that 1928 was the tenth anniversary of the Armistice does not appear to have been a motivating force behind the pilgrimage, and the writing about it made almost no reference to this anniversary. The plan proposed in the *Daily Mail* did not put forward a specific date for the pilgrimage, and the proposal in the *Sphere* suggested May as the best month, as 'both London and Paris are full while May is usually an ideal interlude up the old frontline'.[113] The initial Legion proposal was for a tour to be held in June. The first date suggested for the expanded pilgrimage was 16 August, on which a memorial service in Ypres was proposed because it was the fourteenth anniversary of the landing of the BEF in France.[114] Eventually two dates came to dominate planning. The first was 4 August, the fourteenth anniversary of the British declaration of war. This was the day the pilgrimage commenced with the departure of the first steamer for France. The second date was 8 August, which was chosen as the day for the memorial service in Ypres. This was the tenth anniversary both of the date Haig considered to have been the beginning of the British march to victory and of that which the German commander Ludendorff had described as the 'black day' of the German Army.

110. F. Tuohy, 'Shall the B.E.F. March in Flanders Fields Again?', *Sphere*, CX (Sept. 1927), p. 449.

111. *Daily Mail*, 8 Oct. 1927.

112. *Daily Mail*, 12 Oct. 1927.

113. *Daily Mail*, 19 Aug. 1927. Tuohy, 'Shall the B.E.F. March in Flanders Fields Again?' p. 449.

114. *Daily Mail*, 8 Oct. 1927.

The form the pilgrimage took was also influenced by the American Legion visit, because there was a determination to avoid the lack of solemnity which had been perceived as characterising it. Both the suggestion for the proposed pilgrimage in the *Daily Mail* and those of Poincaré and Painlevé envisaged that, like the American Legion, the British Legion would march through Paris. However, the Foreign Office was determined that the British Legion pilgrimage would take a very different form. In a letter to the British Legion the Foreign Office discouraged holding the pilgrimage soon after the American Legion visit; and in a memorandum on the pilgrimage Lord Crewe deprecated any ostentation or a visit to Paris. The letter and memorandum have not survived.[115] However, Austen Chamberlain referred to the memorandum in a meeting on the proposed pilgrimage, stating:

> When the pilgrimage scheme was first mooted last Autumn Paris was included in the itinerary. Lord Crewe wrote officially deprecating very strongly the arrival of any large number of British Legionaries in Paris in view of the possibility of a repetition of the preposterous opera-bouffe scenes which attended the visit to Paris of the American Legion. Subsequently it was decided that very small detachments only should, before the pilgrimage proper begins, visit Paris and Brussels in order to lay wreaths on the tombs of the Unknown Soldiers.[116]

Lord Crewe was referring to the behaviour of the members of the American Legion, which an American reporter referred to as 'the obviously arrogant, the obviously drunk, giving vent to the opinion that all Paris is a bar and a brothel - and that the town is ours!'[117]

The same explanation was given to the Prince of Wales when he enquired if there would be any Foreign Office objection to his taking the salute of the Legionaries at the march past at the Menin Gate ceremony. The reply to the Prince stated that there was no objection to his taking the salute '*at Ypres*'.[118] The concern of the Foreign Office to avoid any ostentation was also

115. There is a short reference to the letter in *Index to the Correspondence of the Foreign Office for the Year 1927*, Part 1, (Nendeln/Liechtenstein, 1969), p. 242.

116. Foreign Office Minute - 9 Feb. 1928, PRO, FO 371 - 13346.

117. R. Robin, *Enclaves of America: The Rhetoric of American Political Architecture Abroad, 1900–1965* (Princeton, 1992), p. 61.

118. W. H. M. Selby to A. F. Lascelles, 9 Feb. 1928, PRO, FO 371 - 13346.

expressed at a meeting to consider the Legion proposal to invite the President of France to participate in the pilgrimage. The Foreign Office opposed the idea. P. H. Broadmead with the agreement of G. H. Villiers and Austen Chamberlain wrote: 'We have all along tried to keep the Pilgrimage as free from show as possibl(e) to be a Pilgrimage . . . The more external issues are involved the more it will lose its character.'[119]

The Foreign Office's concern that the pilgrimage should be a more solemn occasion than the American visit was shared by many others. The writer in the *Sphere* referred to the American visit as more of a 'Big Party', and stated that what had gone before should be forgotten.[120] The President of the Legion, Earl Haig, on hearing of the plan to hold a pilgrimage 'before giving his consent, desired to know whether the undertaking was to be a mere tour to France and Belgium - a joy ride in fact - or a real Pilgrimage to the Battlefields.'[121] The intention to make the pilgrimage a solemn and pious act was reaffirmed whenever the pilgrimage was described in the newspapers. A writer in the *Irish Times* stated that 'this pilgrimage, if it is to be made worthy of its name, must be regarded by all participating in it as something far greater than the usual trip abroad, or the yearly holiday for rest and recreation'.[122] The *Catholic Times* contrasted the spirit of the pilgrimage, which was 'the true spirit for such an occasion', with the London Music Hall, which advertised the chief attraction for the week as 'August 1914 - A Military Burlesque Comic Review'.[123]

The view that the pilgrimage should be a pious undertaking was also shared by many of the pilgrims. The East Midland Party arranged for an impromptu service while they were on the boat crossing to France.[124] The solemn mood of the pilgrims would have been prompted by the visits to cemeteries. It was also fostered by the Legion, which sent out a reminder, just prior to leaving England, that the pilgrims 'should bear themselves in no mere holiday spirit'.[125]

119. Foreign Office Minute 21 May 1928, PRO, FO 371 - 13346.
120. Tuohy, 'Shall the B.E.F. March in Flanders Fields Again?', p. 449.
121. Gavin and Harter (eds), *The Story of an Epic Pilgrimage*, p. 13.
122. *Irish Times*, 3 Aug. 1928.
123. *Catholic Times and Catholic Opinion*, 10 Aug. 1928.
124. Gavin and Harter (eds), *The Story of an Epic Pilgrimage*, p. 72.
125. *Catholic Times and Catholic Opinion*, 10 Aug. 1928.

Another influence behind the decision to emphasise solemnity was the belief that this accorded with the British character. The *Yorkshire Post* commented: 'The Pilgrimage conducted with the reverent dignity and absence of fuss that are characteristic of assemblies carried out under British auspices, is likely to be of the most memorable kind, and to leave a deep impression on all those taking part in it.'[126] The *Sunday Times* stressed that the departure from England was 'typically British; there was no demonstration, no band, no cheering'.[127] Also the dignity and patience of the women on the pilgrimage were closely identified with the qualities which had enabled their sons and husbands to triumph during the war.[128] One concern of British writers about the pilgrimage was that the French would fail to appreciate this aspect of the event. In a sense the British national character was on trial. More than one account of the pilgrimage stressed that the French were particularly impressed by its simplicity and dignity.[129]

In reality the obsession with ensuring that the pilgrimage to the battlefields was dignified and solemn was shared by people who made pilgrimages from all the combatant nations. There were moments on the American Legion visit when the participants solemnly recalled the dead, just as the British Legion pilgrimage included occasions when the pilgrims behaved more like tourists.[130] The photos from the Legion pilgrimage show pilgrims playing with the rusted remains of helmets and rifles and picnicking in trenches.[131] R. H. Mottram recalled that he saw within Ypres 'a horrid business of hotels hastily run up, of streets and roads hardly passable, of profiteering in "relics" of the battlefield'.[132] In this respect it is remarkable that the commitment to ensuring that the pilgrimage was not a 'joy-ride' was actually believed to reflect the national character of the participants. That such a belief was current suggests the extent to which the res-

126. *Yorkshire Post*, 1 Aug. 1928.

127. *Sunday Times*, 5 Aug. 1928.

128. *Morning Post*, 6 Aug. 1928.

129. *Manchester Guardian*, 9 Aug. 1928; Gavin and Harter (eds), *The Story of an Epic Pilgrimage*, p. 144.

130. D. Kennedy, *Over Here: The First World War and American Society* (Oxford, 1980), pp. 364–5.

131. *Daily Sketch*, 7 Aug. 1928.

132. Mottram, *Journey to the Western Front*, p. 74.

ponse of some groups in Britain to the war changed the concept of national identity to encompass the sense of obligation felt to the dead.

The death of Earl Haig in January 1928 changed the form of the pilgrimage. Haig was insistent that 8 August should be emphasised.[133] On this date in Ypres he would take the salute of the ex-servicemen as they marched past him. The plan for a review of ex-servicemen reflects the identification of the pilgrimage with a victory parade to commemorate the British victory. Not only would the pilgrimage emphasise the victory, rather than just the need to pay homage to the dead, but it would concentrate upon the British and Dominion, rather than the Allied, contribution to the victory. The journals of both the Legion and the BESL stressed that one object of the pilgrimage was to enable the ex-soldiers to 'tour the Battlefields under Field Marshal Earl Haig's leadership on the tenth anniversary of the launching of the Victory Offensive'.[134] The journal of the BESL stated that this was 'perhaps the greatest object of the Pilgrimage'.[135]

Support began hesitantly. In early February only a thousand people had registered, and the Legion called on its branches to encourage members to register before the end of February and to guarantee one or more pilgrims from the Branch.[136] By 25 February the Legion was forced to extend eligibility to all ex-servicemen and women and to the wives and bereaved relatives of ex-servicemen.[137] The reason for the poor initial response is not clear, but from March onwards interest began to increase. This was not just the result of the Legion's extending the categories of eligible people. It may be that many Legionaries were not interested in a pilgrimage which was too closely identified with a victory parade. The death of Haig, followed by the decision of the Prince of Wales to become a pilgrim, established the pilgrimage as primarily a national act of homage to the dead. The popularity of the Prince of Wales may also have persuaded some people to participate.

The increase in the number of pilgrims was also due to the growing involvement of women. This had a significant influence

133. Gavin and Harter (eds), *The Story of an Epic Pilgrimage*, p. 13.
134. *British Legion Journal*, 7 (Dec. 1927), p. 155.
135. *Our Empire*, III (Mar. 1928), p. 43.
136. *The Times*, 10 Feb. 1928.
137. *The Times*, 25 Feb. 1928.

upon the form of the pilgrimage. When the plan for a pilgrimage was first put forward, a minimal role was envisaged for women. The scheme in the *Daily Mail* provided for the men to be accompanied by their relatives and dependants. The proposal in the *Sphere* provided even less of a place for women, arguing that when the ex-soldiers marched along the battleline there were to be no family or relations unless they lined the pavement as the men marched past.

The Legion plan proposed in October 1927 provided for 5,000 pilgrims, who would be mainly ex-servicemen.[138] There would be potential space for 500 women; but in actual fact there would not have been that many places, as this figure included married couples.[139] By January the plan was for 1,250 women to be included amongst the 8,000 pilgrims.[140] However, the women's desire to participate in the pilgrimage far outweighed these plans. Among the 11,000 pilgrims who finally went to the battlefields, more than 3,000 were women.[141] The space which had been provided for the women was all taken up, and the women of the Irish Free State, the North-East party and the South-West party had to travel with their respective parties rather than as part of a women's party. Despite the increase in the space allocated for women, many applications still had to be denied.[142]

The increasing involvement of women changed the tone of the pilgrimage by placing an even greater emphasis on the need for solemnity, and further stressed the role of the memory of the fallen in setting the tone of the journey. A female official of the Legion commented:

> Where we have had free tickets we have given them to those absolutely poverty stricken women who have lost many sons in the War and are anxious to see their graves. We feel that the women who go will realise that this is not to be in any sense a holiday or a tour, but is an extremely solemn occasion, and that they will help us to maintain the right atmosphere.[143]

138. *Daily Mail*, 8 Oct. 1927.
139. Gavin and Harter (eds), *The Story of an Epic Pilgrimage*, p. 51.
140. *Our Empire*, III (Jan. 1928), p. 24.
141. Gavin and Harter (eds), *The Story of an Epic Pilgrimage*, p. 49.
142. *British Legion Journal*, 7 (Apr. 1928), p. 306.
143. *Daily Express*, 7 Aug. 1928.

With the greater involvement of women came also a demand for visits to individual graves. In the end over 4,000 pilgrims were taken on these visits. The number of people who shared this intention was probably even greater, as some people travelled independently to visit graves and then came to Ypres for the memorial service. Clearly in the initial stages of planning the Legion had underestimated the extent to which many women still desired a public means of mourning their dead, and their longing to visit the places where their sons, husbands and brothers had died.

The Community of Pilgrims?

A record of the people who became pilgrims does not appear to have survived; it is therefore difficult to ascertain exactly who took part. The pilgrimage was portrayed as comprising people from all of Great Britain, if not the British Empire. For instance, *The Times* claimed: 'It has attracted men from the towns and glens of the North, from the mines of South Wales and the shipyards of the Clyde and Tyne, out of the factories of Lancashire and Yorkshire, up from the pastures of East Anglia and the Moors of Devon.'[144] The 11,000 pilgrims included about 6,000 ex-servicemen. Among the ex-servicemen were those who had been crippled by the war, including twenty-five men who had been blinded. The pilgrims also included bereaved relatives. Amongst them were twenty-five boys who had been orphaned by the war, as well as more than 3,000 women.[145] While some of the 3,000 women were ex-servicewomen, many had lost a relative during the war. In one of the companies of pilgrims in the women's section 125 of the 130 women had lost someone.[146]

The pilgrims came not only from England, but also from Scotland, Wales, Ireland, Ulster and the other Dominions. In some parties most came from rural areas. The *Yorkshire Post* noted that the villages and hamlets would be supplying a large proportion of the members of the Yorkshire Party.[147] It would appear that the majority of the pilgrims were over fifty. The *Daily Herald* correspondent wrote that 'white haired women and elderly

144. *The Times*, 5 Aug. 1928.
145. *Daily Sketch*, 4 Aug. 1928.
146. Gavin and Harter (eds), *The Story of an Epic Pilgrimage*, p. 55.
147. *Yorkshire Post*, 1 Aug. 1928.

men have been most conspicuous amongst the mourners - the women with tired eyes and the men with toil worn hands'.[148] One participant stated that he missed those 'faces once belonging to the Army of the Somme, and which should show thirty-five to forty years today'.[149] He suggested the reason they were not present was unemployment. The group which surprised the organisers was the Irish Free State Party. Provision had been made for 500 persons. Seven hundred people eventually made up the party, and the applications of hundreds of others had to be denied.[150] In addition, when the Irish Free State and the Ulster parties departed from Dublin and later Kingston Harbour thousands came out to cheer them.[151]

The involvement of two pilgrims, the Prince of Wales and Lady Haig, dominated reporting. A recurring theme was the fact that they were here as 'ordinary' pilgrims. The Legion souvenir of the pilgrimage stated that the 'outstanding fact' was that the Prince was 'from first to last a pilgrim like the rest of us, an ex-serviceman travelling to France and Belgium to pay homage to his Comrades who slept on foreign soil. Like the rest of us he wore throughout the same lounge suit with his Legion badge and medals.'[152] Similarly, when the souvenir referred to Lady Haig it stated that here 'had been pilgrims of every rank without distinction. Among them came a Lady, a simple pilgrim, the wife of that great gentleman who led the British Armies to Victory.'[153]

Not only were the Prince and Lady Haig representative of the equality of the pilgrims, but they also symbolised the belief that the loss of so many young men was shared by the nation. The *Evening News* called the Prince the pilgrim who is regarded 'by the mourning women as a symbol of the new manhood which is to carry on the work left the nation by the armies of the dead'.[154] The *Morning Post* commented that the person of the Prince seemed to represent to the pilgrims 'all the youth of England who prodigally laid down their lives in defence of a

148. *Daily Herald*, 7 Aug. 1928.

149. F. Tuohy, 'The Return to Flanders Fields', *Sphere*, CXIV (Aug. 1928), p. 299.

150. *British Legion Journal*, 8 (Sept. 1928), p. 63.

151. *Irish Times*, 6 Aug. 1928.

152. Gavin and Harter (eds), *The Story of an Epic Pilgrimage*, p. 28.

153. *The British Legion Pilgrimage Handbook*, p. 46.

154. *Evening News*, 8 Aug. 1928.

neighbour's land'.[155] For many people Lady Haig seemed to symbolise the widows of England. She conducted the pilgrimage in mourning for Earl Haig, who had died in January 1928, and her courage and example was noted by many journalists.[156]

Benedict Anderson has suggested that pilgrimages are one of the shared experiences which can provide the basis for an 'imagined community' of nation-ness.[157] The idea of the pilgrimage's being a community is a constantly recurring theme of the Legion souvenir. The front pages carried the statement that 'Prince and ploughman, general and private soldier, mother and widow found unity in something greater even than the discipline of War.'[158] The concentration on the status of the Prince of Wales and Lady Haig as ordinary pilgrims also expressed this theme of a community which transcended the hierarchy and divisions of British society. This feeling of unity extended to a belief that the pilgrimage had affirmed the pride of ordinary British people in their country and had fostered a new spirit. The Chairman of the pilgrimage Committee wrote that the pilgrimage 'has shown that the people who bore the heat and burden of the day during the War are still proud of their country and are willing to give of their best. With such a spirit the future of the British Empire is assured.'[159]

The image of the community of pilgrims was more difficult to realise in practice. There were two difficulties: firstly, the attempt to incorporate into the pilgrimage an imperial act of commemoration which included ex-servicemen from the Dominions and, secondly, the problem of combining the shared pilgrimage of ex-servicemen and the bereaved in mourning for the dead with the pilgrimage which ex-servicemen made in search of their past.

The party from the Dominions was much smaller than the organisers had anticipated. The BESL party was to have been 1,000, but was only 300.[160] The sheer expense and time needed

155. *Morning Post*, 8 Aug. 1928.

156. Tuohy, 'The Return to Flanders Fields', p. 298; *Daily News and Westminster Gazette*, 7 Aug. 1928.

157. B. Anderson, *Imagined Communities: Reflections on the Origins and Spread of Nationalism* (London, 1983), p. 57.

158. Gavin and Harter (eds), *The Story of an Epic Pilgrimage*, p. 6.

159. Ibid., p. 9.

160. *Our Empire*, III (Jan. 1928), p. 24. *Daily Telegraph*, 3 Aug. 1928.

to travel from countries such as Australia militated against a large involvement by pilgrims from the Dominions. More importantly, the Legion pilgrimage sought to merge the British commemoration of the war into an imperial act of commemoration. The original Legion plan included a ceremony near Amiens which would be closely identified with the Dominions and would commemorate the victory offensive launched on 4 August 1918.[161] In Canada this conflicted with the desire of the Canadian Legion to organise a purely Canadian pilgrimage in response to the American Legion visit to France. The organisers of the Canadian pilgrimage advertised the planned British Legion pilgrimage, but also reminded potential pilgrims of the proposed Canadian pilgrimage.[162] Thus the poor Canadian response may also be due to the desire of pilgrims for a national rather than an imperial act of remembrance.

In Australia, the response of the Federal Executive of the RSSILA was very different. The American Legion visit to France in 1927 led to an RSSILA resolution to organise a national pilgrimage of Australian ex-servicemen in 1928.[163] However, the Federal Executive believed that the planned pilgrimage should be replaced by involvement in an imperial pilgrimage.[164] In *Reveille* ex-servicemen were assured that the 'British Empire which bore the heavy burdens of war from start to finish, though not given to the spectacular, will reveal to an amazed world her splendid strength and unity when her sons from lands bordering on the seven seas go swinging in triumphal procession through the Menin Gate'.[165] Not all the State branches and sub-branches supported this proposal. The Western Australian branch passed a resolution that the Australian pilgrimage should go ahead, and the Melbourne sub-branch actually began to advertise an Australian pilgrimage which would leave in 1930–1931.[166] Again,

161. *Argus*, 22 Feb. 1928. AWM Newspaper Cuttings - Pilgrimages - British Legion, Miscellaneous anniversaries.

162. *Legionary*, II (Feb. 1928), p. 21.

163. General Secretary of the RSSILA to Sir Neville Howse, VC, 29 Feb. 1928, ANL, MS 6609, Series B, Box 32, file 3476.

164. General Secretary of the RSSILA to D. M. Benson, 5 Apr. 1928, ANL, MS 6609, Series B, Box 32, file 3476.

165. *Reveille*, 1 (Mar. 1928), p. 2.

166. D. M. Benson to General Secretary of the RSSILA, 17 Apr. 1928; *Sun News Pictorial*, 18 Feb. 1928, ANL, MS 6609, Series B, Box 32, file 3476.

national aspirations were in tension with an imperial commemoration of the war.

Another source of tension which threatened to undermine the shared community of pilgrims was the issue of what experiences could be shared by all the pilgrims. A central feature of the Legion pilgrimage, in common with most other British pilgrimages, was the combination of veterans, widows and parents. This is in contrast to the organised French pilgrimages to Verdun, because the French appear to have drawn a distinction between a private pilgrimage which would involve the widows and families of the dead and the pilgrimages of ex-servicemen.[167] The *Daily Telegraph* noted that on the Legion pilgrimage the fact that 3,000 of the pilgrims were women struck a 'peculiarly sympathetic chord' in France and Belgium.[168] Women were given a place of honour in the centre at the memorial service in Ypres, supposedly at the request of the men.[169]

Many accounts of the pilgrimage concentrate on the experience of the female pilgrims. There were headings such as 'British Mothers on the Battlefields' and 'March of Widows - A Sad Procession to Tragic Park'.[170] The underlying assumption was the belief that it was the special role of women to mourn the dead. The *Evening Standard* printed an article entitled 'My Son: By a Pilgrim Mother' in which the mother describes the pain of bereavement and the experience of visiting the place where her son died. She finds it hard to believe that he died 'here where thousands of my fellow pilgrims are picnicking'; however, she concludes that even though her son's body was never found 'his memory will not die'.[171] Bereaved relatives and ex-servicemen were therefore united in their common experience of mourning the dead.

However, this shared experience of mourning was undermined by the exclusive wartime experiences of ex-servicemen. A number of accounts referred to the gulf between the understanding and experiences of the war of ex-servicemen and those of their families. At Vimy Ridge, some reporters on the Legion

167. A. Prost, 'Verdun', in P. Nora (ed.), *Les Lieux de Mémoire*, Vol. II *La Nation* (Paris, 1984), p. 129.

168. *Daily Telegraph*, 4 Aug. 1928.

169. *Daily Express*, 2 Aug. 1928.

170. *Daily Express*, 6 Aug. 1928. *Irish Independent*, 7 Aug. 1928.

171. *Evening Standard*, 8 Aug. 1928.

pilgrimage found it was the 'strangest sight in the world to see women and girls walking up and down those old trenches following the windings and picking bunches of the gaily coloured flowers'.[172] An account of the visit by female pilgrims to Thiepval Ridge stated that 'very few knew over what terrible ground they had passed and fewer still understood just where it was they were so contentedly munching ham sandwich and tomatoes'.[173] In his poem 'Pilgrimage' J. B. Salmond emphasised this gulf between a veteran's experiences and those of his family. In the poem the ex-soldier becomes increasingly separated from his son and then his wife as they enter Ypres for the Memorial Service at the conclusion of the Legion pilgrimage, because he cannot share his memories of the war and, in particular of his dead friend Ginger, with them.[174]

The Search for Meaning

The practice of pilgrimage was part of the process through which people after the war sought to reconstruct history and values. Samuel Hynes has explored the ways in which English art and thought in the 1920s produced what he sees as a new culture out of the broken images left by the war. He concludes that 'only at the end of the decade was the war remade, the vast loss described and mythologized, in the prose narratives that became the war-book canon'. The myth of the war which he argues arose from this process was modernist. It stressed the discontinuity of the war and the break from the old high rhetoric.[175] Hynes' concentration on the 'war books boom' obscures the vitality of alternative reconstructions of history and values which drew upon continuity with the past and which modified, yet retained, the old rhetoric emphasising sacrifice and service. There was an ongoing debate about the lessons and implications of the war, of which the 'war books boom' was merely one of the most notable periods. In the 1920s middlebrow writers offered an

172. *Daily News and Westminster Gazette*, 7 Aug. 1928.

173. Gavin and Harter (eds), *The Story of an Epic Pilgrimage*, p. 43.

174. J. B. Salmond, 'Pilgrimage: Being Thoughts of an Ex-soldier at Ypres 8/8/28', in J. B. Salmond, *The Old Stalker and Other Verses* (Edinburgh and London, 1936), pp. 85–6.

175. S. Hynes, *A War Imagined: The First World War and English Culture* (London, 1990), pp. 439, 459.

alternate view of the war experience which did not attempt to 'camouflage the horror of war', but instead sought to 'soften the impact of the break it represented by reasserting links with the past'. They looked forward to a post-war regeneration which would draw upon morality, religion and tradition.[176]

Pilgrimages were part of this second conservative reconstruction of English history. One successful middlebrow writer, John Buchan, was even enlisted to write the preface to the handbook of the Legion pilgrimage and to write about the pilgrimage for the *Yorkshire Post*.[177] The values of the middlebrow writers were affirmed in the explanations of the meanings of pilgrimages. For example, the *Yorkshire Post* explained that the memories which are being recalled by the Legion pilgrimage

> are not deadening but vitalising, as is any memory of human courage and idealism - national sacrifice, cheerful disregard of private interest, fellowship . . . they are not memories to be ashamed of when we carry them over from time of War to time of peace, but of which to be proud. The British Legion deserve well of this country for keeping them green.[178]

The *Daily Telegraph* described Ypres as 'holy ground to the British race, a place to be approached with solemn prayer and thankfulness, a shrine at which to chasten pride and to cast out all thoughts but those of pure service to humanity'.[179]

Pilgrimages to the battlefields were suggested as an antidote to the 'war books boom'. The Reverend Tubby Clayton suggested that a large pilgrimage for schools was needed to counteract the influence of recent war novels. He argued: 'The stains have got to be taken off the War Memorial, which, for many boys, was now a thing at which they could not look without thinking of one of those pestilential books that had got into their hands. The one historical ideal of their lives had been smirched.' Clayton claimed that Toc H had conducted small parties of schoolboys over the battlefields each year since they had started, and he 'did not know a single case of irony, shallowness, or anything approaching contempt or small mindedness among the thousands

176. R. Bracco, *Merchants of Hope: British Middlebrow Writers and the First World War, 1919–1939* (Oxford and Providence, 1993), pp. 12–13, 197.
177. *The British Legion Pilgrimage Handbook*, pp. 9–13.
178. *Yorkshire Post*, 4 Aug. 1928.
179. *Daily Telegraph*, 9 Aug. 1928.

who had gone there as pilgrims'.[180] In Graham Hutchison's *Life Without End* the novels produced during the 'war books boom' are included as an example of the 'insidious, soul-destroying paralysis [which] was creeping over the civilized world'. They are among the disillusioning things which the novel's protagonist Hugh Richmond is only able to overcome by returning to the Somme in order to rediscover his beliefs through the return of the dead.[181]

Many of the ex-servicemen who wrote about their visits to the battlefields also noted that they did not agree with what they perceived as the worst excesses of the 'war books boom'. Generally writers state that they hated the war, but that this should not be allowed to detract from the qualities of the men themselves and their comradeship. Bernard Newman stressed that because he condemned war he should not be classed with those writers of war books during the 'war books boom'. He said that they only told of the 'filth, lice and debauchery' without mentioning the 'courage of the men - the thrill of danger - . . . above all, that great sense of comradeship which made horror endurable and death easy'.[182] F. Yeats Brown used his account of a visit to the battlefields to attack the arguments of Beverley Nichols' *Cry Havoc!* He visited Zeebrugge and asserted that you 'can feel the glory of sacrifice that haunts these places, and you can praise the courage of our men without minimising that of the enemy'.[183]

At the heart of this alternative vision of the war experience was the example of the dead: their spirit, service, sacrifice and memory. This is why pilgrimages played an important role in the construction of the memory of the war. They brought individuals and communities into the presence of the dead to pay homage and to renew their commitment to follow the example they had set. These values were closely linked to religious beliefs. The definition of a pilgrimage used by Brunel Cohen in a broadcast to the people of Belgium at the beginning of the Legion pilgrimage reflects its roots in traditional religion. He described it as

180. *The Times*, 7 Jan. 1930.

181. Hutchison, *Life Without End*, pp. 264-8, 271-82.

182. B. Newman, *In the Trail of the Three Musketeers* (London, 1934), p. 142.

183. F. Yeats Brown, *Dogs of War!* (London, 1934), p. 220.

> a journey undertaken from religious motives to some place reputed to be sacred. That definition dates back to the earliest days of Christendom or even before. There is no doubt that no more sacred place can exist than where one's loved one laid down his life for his country. Consequently the Pilgrimage has been undertaken from the holiest of motives in a most solemn and orthodox manner.[184]

Also, all the major and even many of the smaller pilgrimages included a service of remembrance as a central feature of the journey.

Pilgrimages merged the secular rhetoric of service to the State with the religious language of sacrifice. In the early 1920s this centred on the domestic turmoil in Great Britain. One traveller claimed that the pilgrim 'stands by the small crosses with a sense of being uplifted to a higher plane than that on which quarrels and class bitterness prevail'.[185] The St Barnabas Society called on people to remember the example of the dead, because only then could the world find the peace from political, industrial and social stress which it was crying out for.[186] It was also a central theme of the Archbishop of York's address on the Legion pilgrimage. He emphasised that now 'as then, we must think more of duty than of comfort, more of what we can give than of what we can get. Now, as then, we must banish the spirit of faction, of class struggle, and bring in a spirit of devotion to the whole community. For our country's sake we must work hard and together.'[187]

Bob Bushaway argues that the development of a language of remembrance during the war operated in the inter-war period to deny people in Great Britain a critique of the war, because it elevated the war to a sacred event through its concentration on the sacrifice of the fallen.[188] However, the emphasis on the sacrifice made by the dead assumed that such a selfless act should be justified by clear evidence that it had not been in vain. In the 1920s and 1930s this belief created considerable unease among pilgrims. Ian Hay wrote in 1926 that 'until history has turned

184. *Glasgow Herald*, 4 Aug. 1928.

185. M. M. Moore, 'Our Buried Caesar's', *United Empire*, XII (Nov. 1921), p. 735.

186. St Barnabas Society, *Ypres/The Somme*, p. 4.

187. *British Legion Journal*, 8 (Sept. 1928), p. 67.

188. B. Bushaway, 'Name Upon Name: The Great War and Remembrance', in R. Porter (ed.), *The Myths of the English* (Cambridge, 1992), p. 137.

over a few more pages we cannot say whether or no our million dead died in vain'.[189] H. W. Allinson visited Ypres in the same year and suggested that the survivors of the salient 'watch the dancing in the hostels and estaminets, and contemplate the silent cemetery just over there, where many dear old pals lay, and wonder if the price we paid to defend Ypres was worth it after all'.[190]

The Address of the Archbishop of York at the memorial service which concluded the Legion pilgrimage brought this uncertainty over the issue whether the war had been in vain into the centre of public debate about the war. He posed the question 'Was it all worthwhile?', answering it by saying 'Here at this Gate let there be no faltering in the answer - yes, a thousand times yes.'[191] Many newspaper editorials concluded that it was worthwhile, although for different reasons. Some claimed that it was worthwhile because England kept her pledge to Belgium, others because of the need to defeat the threat of militarism. Another newspaper stressed the spirit in which the volunteers went forward to fight, while other common arguments centred on the fact that it was a war to end all wars.[192]

Despite this chorus of affirmation there was no unanimous agreement that the war had been worthwhile. While the pilgrimage took place, the No More War Movement held a series of rallies throughout Britain. The *Daily Herald* criticised the Archbishop for his comments at the ceremony. On the day after he had given his address, the leading article commented 'History, we are confident, will note his address as a revelation of his utter failure to appreciate the stupendous tragedy of the War.'[193] On 14 August the newspaper again attacked the address, warning: 'But time is already touching those dreadful memories with the rosy finger of romance. A young generation is growing up which is learning more about the thrills and the heroism of War than its bestialities. Even many of those who fought in 1914–1918 would rush to the recruiting offices tomorrow if hostilities

189. I. Hay, *The Ship of Remembrance* (London, *c.*1926), p. 34.

190. H. W. Allinson, 'August Pilgrimage to Ypres', *Ypres Times*, 3 (Oct. 1926), p. 105.

191. *The Times*, 9 Aug. 1928.

192. *The Times*, 9 Aug. 1928 *Irish Times*, 9 Aug. 1928. *Daily News and Westminster Gazette*, 9 Aug. 1928.

193. *Daily Herald*, 9 Aug. 1928.

broke out.'[194] The question whether the war had been worthwhile was taken up by many correspondents to the *Daily Herald*, which printed excerpts from thirty letters and extravagently claimed that there had been thousands more.[195] One pilgrim from the Lancashire party wrote to the Archbishop in the following terms: 'As one just returned from the battlefields I should like to ask His Grace, did he see the scores of armless and legless men not a hundred yards from where he was speaking soliciting alms?'[196]

The editorials of some other papers also questioned whether the war had been worthwhile, although they did not directly attack the Archbishop. The leading article in the *Eastern Daily Press* pointed out that the prospects were not as optimistic as the Archbishop had suggested. The writer commented:

> Such a celebration as that of which the world has been a sympathetic witness this week can only have its greatest value to humanity if it brings home to this and to future generations the character and the dreadful consequences of such a war as that into which the peoples of Europe plunged 14 years ago. Time is apt to accentuate the triumph and the glory.[197]

The Anglo-Catholic newspaper, the *Church Times*, also questioned the Archbishop's arguments as to why the war had been worthwhile, even though they were purporting to defend him from the accusations in the *Daily Herald*,[198] while another newspaper felt there were no grounds for the certainty needed to answer 'yes' with the same confidence expressed by the Archbishop.[199]

Despite the attacks, the desire for the bereaved to believe that there was a purpose to the sacrifices of the war remained. The Archbishop returned to the question whether the war was 'worthwhile' in his 1928 Armistice Day address in St Paul's Cathedral, saying that to answer other than yes to the question 'would be to wrong not only the memory of the dead but the heart of the living'. He quoted the words of a man who had told him that 'to think otherwise would be enough to drive me out of my

194. *Daily Herald*, 14 Aug. 1928.
195. *Daily Herald,* 11–16 Aug. 1928.
196. *Daily Herald*, 14 Aug. 1928.
197. *Eastern Daily Press*, 9 Aug. 1928.
198. *Church Times*, 17 Aug. 1928.
199. *Reynolds Illustrated News,* 12 Aug. 1928.

mind. It would mean that my fine son was thrown away.'[200] In 1934 Ethel Richardson concluded her war memories by asking whether any good will have come out of the war, and asserting that, as the cutting of a diamond releases its beauty 'so, surely, will those Sacrifices, offered so freely in four awful years of War, find at last in God's good time, their due and meet reward'.[201]

However, it could be difficult to convince yourself and others that the war was worthwhile when confronted by the sea of white crosses in a cemetery or the lists of names on the memorials to the missing. Dirk Bogarde recalls that he and his sister were overcome with sadness when they visited a war cemetery in France in the 1930s. He recollects that his nanny sought to cheer them up, saying:

> 'You ought to be very happy that you're both here on such a lovely day as this, because all these poor men here died just so that you could be walking about in the sun without a care in the world . . . You see what it says on top of that big stone cross there? Their Sacrifice Was Not in Vain. So just you remember that. And show your manners.'[202]

In the late 1920s and 1930s both the doubts about and the desire of bereaved relatives to believe that the death of so many young men in the war was not in vain merged into a consensus that the war would be made worthwhile if it led to a lasting peace. This consensus dominated the discourse surrounding Armistice Day in this period, and it was also the message which pilgrims found on the battlefields.[203] W. E. Stanton Hope described a woman who stood staring with tear-filled eyes at the peninsula of Gallipoli; as the ship carrying the 1934 Naval Division pilgrimage left the Narrows, she turned to him and said 'I pray to God that my own sons may never have to go through the hell of warfare!'[204] In 1932 R. H. Mottram recalled the ceremony at the Menin Gate in 1928, and asserted that it 'would be a mockery indeed if instead of marching past, we are merely

200. N. Branson, *Britain in the Nineteen Twenties* (London, 1975), p. 243.

201. Richardson, *Remembrance Wakes*, p. 206.

202. D. Bogarde, *A Postillion Struck By Lightning* (London, 1977), pp. 95-6.

203. A. Gregory, *The Silence of Memory: Armistice Day 1919-1946* (Oxford and Providence, 1994), pp. 118-26.

204. W. E. Stanton Hope, *Gallipoli Revisited: An Account of the Duchess of Richmond Pilgrimage Cruise* (London, *c.*1934), p. 56.

marching toward some other catastrophe . . . Not until the actual fact forces me to such a conclusion will I believe that a ceremony so heartfelt, reverent and attended by the great and holy, as that I witnessed that day, is a mere piece of sentiment and glory.'[205]

Throughout the 1930s the memory of the dead and the sacred were invoked to emphasise the need to ensure that a world war would not happen again. Fabian Ware wrote that pilgrims to the battlefields returned with a message from the million dead to future generations, and particularly to the statesmen of Great Britain, France and Germany: 'You have failed to achieve your ends by other means than war and we have expiated your failure - fail not again, accept our atonement and give new faith and life to the world.'[206]

In 1938, as war became increasingly likely, a pilgrimage of all the ex-combatant nations was proposed to the *Comité International Permanent des Anciens Combattants*. It foundered because of British plans to hold a national pilgrimage to the battlefields in 1939.[207] The British plans were overtaken by international events, and this became a march of British ex-servicemen down the Champs Elysées on 4 August 1939, twenty-five years after the outbreak of the Great War and eleven after the equivalent proposal had been discouraged by the Foreign Office in 1928.[208] Within a month of the march, the Second World War broke out, and in its shadow future generations would have to address the issue of whether the sacrifice made by the dead both in the Great War and in a second world war had been in vain.

Conclusion

In the 1920s and 1930s pilgrimages combined the individual experiences and memory of the bereaved and ex-servicemen with a public act of commemoration. Both elements were central to the nature of battlefield pilgrimages. Bereaved relatives travelled to see the headstone or the name of a loved one. Their journey was a part of the process of coming to terms with grief

205. Mottram, *Through the Menin Gate*, p. 5.

206. F. Ware, 'The Empire's Homage: Memorials of a Million Dead', *Listener*, VIII (Nov. 1932), pp. 651-2.

207. British Legion, *Comité International Permanent des Anciens Combattants, Résumé of Work Accomplished* (n.p., 1939), p. 12.

208. B. Cohen, *Count Your Blessings* (London, 1956), p. 122.

and consigning the dead to memory. Religion played an important role in this process. In particular, the beliefs held by many pilgrims in God and the afterlife, as well as an instinctive spiritualism provided them with the strength to face the journey and enriched its meaning for them. Ex-servicemen were drawn back to the battlefields in search of their past. Many of them searched in vain for their memories, and felt alienated because their war had disappeared from a land at peace. For others the journey was a confrontation with their memories and a chance to exorcise the war.

The Legion pilgrimage provides a case study of how people in Britain used pilgrimages as a public ceremony of remembrance. The form which the pilgrimage took was influenced by the American Legion visit to France and in particular by the determination of Foreign Office officials to ensure that, unlike the American Legion visit, it was a solemn and dignified event. The dignity and simplicity of the pilgrimage was also felt to convey the essence of British national character – an extraordinary assumption given that these same factors also dominated remembrance ceremonies in other countries. The fact that it was made reflects the growing identification of national identity with the memory of, and sense of obligation felt towards, the dead. Two other elements also closely identified the pilgrimage with a national act of homage to the dead: the participation of the Prince of Wales and the increasing involvement of women in the journey. The pilgrims were described as a community which united the nation and the Empire. However, the community of pilgrims faced a number of tensions. These included the desire of people in the Dominions for their own national pilgrimages and the difficulty of reconciling the exclusive wartime experiences of ex-servicemen with the experience of bereavement they shared with the relatives of the dead.

In the inter-war years there was an ongoing debate about the memory of the war and its meaning. Pilgrimages were a part of an alternative reconstruction of the memory of the war which emphasised the achievement of the dead and the traditions of service and sacrifice. The discourse surrounding the meaning of pilgrimages merged the secular value of duty with the religious concept of sacrifice. In the 1920s this focused on the need to look beyond domestic troubles and to work for the whole community. However, the concentration on the sacrifice made by the dead raised a potentially divisive note in the memory of the war, because it assumed that the sacrifice was not in vain. The question was the war 'worthwhile' was a key issue in a debate concerning whether the war had achieved anything in proportion to the terrible sacrifices which had been required to win it. In the 1930s this issue was resolved in a consensus that the war would not be in vain if it taught the lesson that all energies needed to be devoted to working for peace and to ensure that there would never be another world war. This resolution to the debate was shattered by the outbreak of the Second World War.

5

Tourism, Pilgrimage and the Commemoration of the Great War in Australia and Canada, 1919–1939

The role of tourism and pilgrimages in the commemoration of the Great War in Australia and Canada provides an interesting comparison with Great Britain.[1] Travel was an important facet of the experience of Australian and Canadian servicemen during the war, because they had to journey to the battlefields of Europe and the Near East, and in many instances they remained away from their homes for its duration.[2] People also anticipated that the Australian and Canadian battlefields would become places of pilgrimage after the war. An Australian serviceman, Hector Dinning, wrote that the 'day is far off (but it will come) when splendid mausolea will be raised over these heroic dead. And one foresees the time when steamers will bear up the Ægean pilgrims come to do honour at the resting place of friends and kindred, and to move over the charred battlegrounds of Turkey.'[3] Similarly the journalist John Dafoe anticipated the '1000s of Canadians [who] will make the pilgrimage each year visiting in turn Flanders, Vimy, the Somme battlefields and finally step by step the Canadian advance in the hundred days'.[4]

1. This study does not consider Newfoundland, which was a separate Dominion in the period 1914–1939. However, Newfoundland does raise some interesting issues, for which see D. Macfarlane, *The Danger Tree: War, Memory, and the Search for a Family's Past* (Toronto, 1992).

2. R. White, 'The Soldier as Tourist: The Australian Experience of the Great War', in A. Rutherford and J. Wieland (eds), *War: Australia's Creative Response* (St Leonards, 1997), pp. 117–29.

3. C. E. W. Bean (ed.), *The Anzac Book: Written and Collected in Gallipoli by the Men of Anzac* (London, 1916), p. 21. I am indebted to Ken Inglis for this reference.

4. J. W. Dafoe, *Over the Canadian Battlefields: Notes of a Little Journey in France in March, 1919* (Toronto, 1919), p. 17.

There were many similarities between Australia, Canada and Great Britain, in addition to the shared expectation that after the war pilgrims would visit its battlefields. Firstly, they all participated in the war from August 1914 until November 1918, they fought in many of the same battles and their servicemen were under the overall command of British generals. Although none of these countries was invaded, their servicemen who fought on the Western Front and in the Near East suffered high casualty rates. Great Britain and Ireland lost 730,000 killed out of a total pre-war population of approximately forty-five million, Canada lost 61,000 killed out of a total pre-war population of approximately eight million, and from Australia 60,000 were killed out of a total pre-war population of nearly five million.[5] They were also similar because their dead were not brought home, but instead, with a few exceptions, were buried in the countries where they fell. This meant that bereaved relatives had no choice but to travel overseas to visit the graves of the dead. Finally, all three countries were predominantly Anglo-Saxon and Protestant, so that pilgrimages did not play as important a role in religious belief as they did in predominantly Catholic France.[6]

Despite these similarities, there were significant differences between Australia and Canada on the one hand and Great Britain on the other. Firstly, Canada and particularly Australia were much further away from the main battlefields. This restricted the numbers of tourists and pilgrims who could afford the high cost in both time and money to travel from Canada and the even higher costs of travel from Australia to Europe or the Near East. As a result there was a lower expectation that bereaved relatives would be able to visit the graves of their dead, which may have placed an even greater importance on local forms of commemoration. This was despite wartime predictions of pilgrims' visiting the battlefields. Also, the experience of the war and its memory were different in Canada and Australia because they were new countries and Dominions of the British Empire. In both countries, but particularly in Australia, the war was perceived as a rite of passage to nationhood. Throughout the war and in the 1920s and 1930s political leaders, writers and journalists in these

5. J. M. Winter, *The Great War and the British People* (London, 1986), p. 75.

6. For a study of the role of religious faith in pilgrimages in France see A. Becker, *La Guerre et La Foi: De la Mort à la Mémoire* (Paris, 1994).

nations claimed that their men had not only passed the test of war, but had excelled to such a degree that they were the best troops not only in the British Army but in the conflict.[7] The military prowess of Australian servicemen was a key component of what became known as the Anzac tradition.[8] National pride in the soldiers' achievements therefore had an additional meaning in both Australia and Canada. Finally, the issue of conscription proved more divisive in both countries than in Britain. In Canada this issue divided English- and French-speaking Canadians, while in Australia it split the Labor Party, as well as exacerbating the tensions between Irish Catholics and other Australians.[9]

Local Tourism and Pilgrimage

Places associated with the Great War in Canada and Australia drew large numbers of tourists and pilgrims. In the 1920s exhibitions of war relics and paintings were very popular. The most successful exhibitions either drew upon the need of the bereaved for a place where they could remember their loss or re-created wartime scenes and memories. Travel to a war memorial provided a further means of recalling and mourning the dead. In Canada the act of travelling to a memorial to lay a wreath on 11 November was closely identified with the loss felt by the bereaved, although it was rarely described as a pilgrimage. In Australia war memorials were often referred to as sacred places, and the people who visited them were described as pilgrims. Although the bereaved made pilgrimages to memorials, their role in the commemoration of the war was increasingly of secondary importance by comparison with the emphasis in the major commemorative ceremonies on the wartime achievements of Australian servicemen.

7. P. Berton, *Vimy* (Toronto, 1986), pp. 293–5. N. McLachlan, *Waiting for the Revolution: A History of Australian Nationalism* (Melbourne, 1989), pp. 187–208. R. White, *Inventing Australia: Images and Identity 1688–1980* (Sydney, 1981), pp. 125–39.

8. There are a number of studies of the Anzac tradition. The seminal article is K. S. Inglis, 'The Anzac Tradition', *Meanjin Quarterly*, XXIV (Mar. 1965), pp. 25–44. Also see J. Beaumont, 'The Anzac Legend', in J. Beaumont, *Australia's War 1914–18* (St Leonards, 1995), pp. 149–80.

9. In Australia, since 1907 the Labor Party has officially used the American spelling for its title. For a brief account of the conscription issue in Australia and in Canada see J. Beaumont, 'The Politics of a Divided Society', in Beaumont, *Australia's War 1914–18*, pp. 35–63 and R. Bothwell *et al.*, *Canada, 1900–1945* (Toronto, 1987), pp. 126–33.

Exhibitions

One way of satisfying the desire of those who stayed at home to understand the wartime experiences of servicemen was through exhibitions of war paintings and relics. In Canada the exhibition of war paintings collected by the Canadian War Memorials Fund was shown in Toronto in August and Montreal in October 1919. The exhibition also included photographs, war trophies, souvenirs and larger artefacts, such as artillery pieces and aeroplanes. It was advertised as an opportunity to 'live 2 hours with the Canadians behind the lines, and before the lines - review the war's tremendous moments - see a great conflict as it has never been granted home folks to see it heretofore'.[10] The editorial of the *Toronto Globe* claimed that it 'seems to express on canvas the thousand emotions which have thrilled Canadians through years of war, as they saw, heard or read of the heroism, the horror, and the never-ending destruction of Armageddon'.[11] In just one day in Toronto more Canadians visited the exhibition than during the month the paintings had been on display in New York, and after two weeks 107,865 people had seen it.[12] Successful exhibitions of the paintings were held in 1923, 1926 and 1934.

There was also an extraordinary response in Australia when the relics and artefacts collected during the war under the inspiration of C. E. W. Bean for a proposed war museum and memorial were exhibited. A selection of photographs from the collection were first shown in Melbourne in 1921, and within five weeks 82,998 visits were made to the exhibition. An exhibition of some of the other artefacts opened in Melbourne on Anzac Day 1922; and when it closed on 26 January 1925, 780,000 visits had been made to it.[13] The exhibition met with similar success when it was moved to Sydney. In the period from April 1926 to December 1928 around 1,350,000 visits were made to it.[14] The museum was described as a place where Australians could go to under-

10. Cited in M. Tippett, *Art at the Service of War: Canada, Art and the Great War* (Toronto, 1984), pp. 89-90.

11. *Globe*, 23 Sept. 1919, NGC, War Memorials file.

12. *Globe*, 5 Sept. 1919, NGC, War Memorials file. Tippett, *Art at the Service of War*, p. 90.

13. M. McKernan, *Here is Their Spirit: A History of the Australian War Memorial 1917-1990* (St Lucia, 1991), pp. 69, 88.

14. *Reveille*, 2 (Dec. 1928), p. 16.

stand something of the war and to which 'parents of fallen men' could visit 'in grief and come away in pride'.[15]

In both countries there were moments when a particular event was able to capture the imagination of thousands of people because it crystallised an aspect of the memory of the war which had widespread appeal. In Australia there was an extraordinary public response to William Longstaff's painting the *Menin gate at midnight (Ghosts of Menin gate)* [Figure 5]. The painting was the result of an inspiration which struck Longstaff when he attended the opening of the Menin Gate memorial in 1927. That night he walked along the Menin road and imagined the ghosts of the dead rising out of the surrounding fields, and he recreated this image in his painting.[16] The painting was purchased by Lord Woolavington and given to Australia, and in the period 1928 to 1929 it was exhibited along with a scale model of the Menin Gate memorial in major cities throughout the country. People travelled in large numbers to see it; Michael McKernan estimates that 35,000 people saw it in Melbourne, 23,000 in Sydney, 29,000 in Brisbane and 8,500 in Hobart and Launceston combined.[17] Eric George recollects visiting the painting when it was in Sydney when he was thirteen years old, and remembers that all the men removed their hats on entering the building in which it was shown. Solemn and subdued music was playing in the background, and he recalls that the painting was positioned so that onlookers needed to bow to see the painting correctly.[18] The response to the painting in Sydney was so great that it was exhibited for a second time from September to October 1929.

The primary motif of the painting was the dead, and by emphasising their presence it captured the feelings of thousands of bereaved relatives who sought a place where they could recall their loved ones. One writer claimed that no one could see Longstaff's vision of a 'deathless army . . . without being deeply impressed with a deep and abiding realisation of what the war meant to civilisation'.[19] A reporter in the *Herald* wrote that Australia had accepted the gift of the painting as 'a product of the Great War that bears to many people a little heartsease, and

15. *Herald*, 25 Apr. 1922, AWM Newspaper Cuttings, Australian War Memorial.

16. A. Grey, 'Will Longstaff's *Menin Gate at Midnight*', *Journal of the Australian War Memorial*, 12 (Apr. 1988), pp. 47–9.

17. McKernan, *Here is Their Spirit*, p. 133.

18. Private information given to me by Eric George, 3 Nov. 1993.

19. *Reveille*, 3 (Sept. 1929), p. 39.

Figure 5. Will Longstaff *Menin gate at midnight (Ghosts of Menin gate)* 1927 Oil on Canvas 140.5 × 170.2 cm (sight) AWM (9807).

a grain or two of comfort which they can lay to their great sorrow'.[20] In this sense the response to the painting moved beyond the commemoration of Australia's wartime achievements and closer to a pilgrimage of the bereaved.

By contrast the 1934 Canadian Corps Reunion in Toronto was a moment of nostalgia which stressed the comradeship of the men of the Canadian Corps. The *Legionary* described it as 'the joyous abandoned, uproarious culmination of a three-day triumph - the outburst of a comradeship which had lain dormant for 16 years'.[21] The Reunion was initially planned for 15,000 ex-servicemen who would come together as part of the celebrations of the centennial of Toronto; but in excess of 100,000 ex-servicemen actually joined in the events from 4 to 6 August. Ex-servicemen walked, hid in box-cars and hitch-hiked from all over Canada in order to take part. They wore armbands, badges and berets which divided them according to their wartime units.

A mock French village built with *estaminets* was widely considered to be the highlight of the event. The village was a nostalgic window into the past, and included chalked inscriptions on the walls such as 'Nellie doesn't live here any more' and 'The beer's no bon', while signs in German were included on the outskirts of the village such as 'Nach Bapaume'. The decision to build the village reflects the desire of many ex-servicemen to remember the positive elements of their wartime experiences and to relive them. The men engaged in a series of pranks such as disrupting traffic in the centre of town by replacing policemen with ex-servicemen and staging mock attacks on hotels by seizing artillery pieces and trying to push them into the foyer.[22] It was also an opportunity for the public to experience a piece of wartime France. Under popular pressure the village was opened to the public for two days prior to the Reunion, and 52,000 people visited it.[23]

War Memorials

Local and national war memorials also provided a focal point for the commemoration of the war and a place to remember and

20. *Herald*, 14 Feb. 1929.
21. *Legionary*, IX (Sept. 1934), p. 6.
22. *Legionary*, IX (Sept. 1934), pp. 6-7.
23. *The Story of the Canadian Corps* (Toronto, 1934), pp. 11-12, 14, 16, 26, 28.

mourn the dead. These memorials often played an important role in the major ceremonies to commemorate the war, such as Armistice Day, later renamed Remembrance Day in Canada, which was officially celebrated on 11 November in both countries, and Anzac Day, which was celebrated annually in Australia on 25 April.[24]

In Canada the example of the temporary Cenotaph erected in Whitehall in 1919 was copied for the celebration of Armistice Day on 11 November 1920. A temporary Cenotaph was erected in Toronto in front of the City Hall, and for an hour after the ceremony at 11 a.m. men, women and children filed past the memorial, leaving wreaths and flowers.[25] Processions past a temporary cenotaph or, once it was built, the war memorial were a central feature of the commemorative ceremonies in many Canadian cities on 11 November during the inter-war period. The practice reached its height in 1928 for the tenth anniversary of the Armistice. In Ottawa 40,000 people gathered before the temporary cenotaph, and it was surrounded with wreaths and flowers. Similarly large numbers of people thronged the memorials in Toronto, Montreal and Winnipeg, leaving flowers and wreaths throughout the day and even into the night.[26] Even in 1938 Canadian newspapers noted that in the major cities war memorials continued to draw large crowds of people who placed wreaths and flowers there.[27]

Although the practice was similar to the pilgrimages of the bereaved to the Cenotaph in Whitehall, it was rarely described in Canadian newspapers as a pilgrimage. It is difficult to know why this was the case, particularly as Robert Shipley notes that religious symbolism and imagery were an integral feature of many Canadian war memorials.[28] The absence of the language of pilgrimage appears to suggest a level of understatement in the tone of commemoration in Canada. Perhaps the concentration of these

24. D. Thomson, 'National Sorrow, National Pride: Commemoration of the Great War in Canada 1918–1945', *Journal of Canadian Studies* 30 (Winter, 1995/6), pp. 9–10, describes the story of the celebration of Armistice Day in Canada.

25. *Globe*, 12 Nov. 1920.

26. Armistice Ceremonial Committee, *Armistice Ceremonial* (Toronto, 1928), pp. 3, 27–35.

27. *Globe*, 12 Nov. 1938.

28. R. Shipley, *To Mark Our Place: A History of Canadian War Memorials* (Toronto, 1982), pp. 141–59.

ceremonies on the bereaved and the feelings of the community provided a context in which understatement became the most appropriate tone.

In Australia many war memorials were described as places of pilgrimage. The writer of a description of the new Brisbane war memorial asked his readers to 'come with me on a pilgrimage – a pilgrimage to a shrine; a shrine that is beautiful in form and rich in symbolic meaning wherein is embodied and portrayed a nation's remembrance'.[29] The Shrine of Remembrance in Melbourne, which was dedicated in 1934, actually declared that the site was sacred: 'Let all men know that this is holy ground.' Journalists also used this language to depict the popular response to Anzac Day. As late as 1936 a writer described how on Anzac Day in Sydney from 'the earliest hour people were pouring into the city on a pious pilgrimage'.[30]

Some memorials were closely linked with the pilgrimages of the bereaved. In Sydney during the war the centre for Soldiers' Wives and Mothers began the practice of meeting before the gates at Woolloomooloo wharf for a service of remembrance and to place wreaths in memory of the dead. The gates were often the last place where relatives had seen the men who died. In 1921 a memorial drinking fountain was unveiled near the gates.[31] Each year floral wreaths in memory of the dead were placed there and the drinking fountain was filled with flowers. In 1930 a reporter for the *Sydney Morning Herald* noted that the crowd consisted mostly of mothers and widows of fallen soldiers, many with tear-stained cheeks, who 'forlornly gathered at the place hallowed by them and others as the place of poignant parting. Years pass by, but the Gates of Remembrance become more and more definitely a link between the living and the departed.'[32]

In Melbourne on Anzac Day in 1926 a temporary cenotaph was erected in the city square in front of the Parliament building. The decision to erect the temporary cenotaph was taken by the Anzac Day Commemoration Committee, which was chaired by Sir John Monash, who had commanded the Australian Corps in 1918. The Committee believed that it would 'greatly add to the

29. Anzac Day Celebration Committee, *Anzac Day 1937* (n.p., c.1937), p. 22.
30. *Sydney Morning Herald*, 27 Apr. 1936.
31. *Sydney Morning Herald*, 26 Apr. 1921.
32. *Sydney Morning Herald*, 26 Apr. 1930.

solemnity of the occasion' by providing a saluting point to the dead for the march by ex-servicemen, as well as a place where 'comrades, relatives and the general public' could pay tribute to the dead by leaving wreaths and flowers.[33] It was at the heart of the ceremony that year, and on 26 April groups of men and women made 'special pilgrimages' to place wreaths and flowers on the monument. There were calls for a permanent Cenotaph to be erected; however, they failed in the face of opposition from ex-servicemen led by Monash.[34]

The opposition to the temporary Cenotaph should not be exaggerated. The Victorian branch of the RSSILA received numerous letters from the parents of soldiers expressing their support for the temporary Cenotaph, and the RSSILA ensured that the structure was protected so that it was available for future Anzac Days.[35] In 1934 the Victorian branch even proposed that a permanent Cenotaph should be erected to accompany the Shrine of Remembrance, arguing that the readiness of men to remove their hats when passing the temporary Cenotaph showed that a permanent Cenotaph would be given a place in the daily life of the community.[36] The temporary Cenotaph remained an important feature of Anzac Day in Melbourne even in the first years after the Shrine of Remembrance was unveiled on 11 November 1934.[37] In 1936 the Anzac Day march changed its route so that it ended at the Shrine of Remembrance, and the temporary Cenotaph was moved from its usual place in front of the Parliament building, so that the ex-servicemen would still be able to salute it during the march.[38] The practice was discontinued in 1937, and instead a dais was constructed as a saluting point for the marching ex-servicemen.[39]

Another focus for Australian remembrance was introduced in 1928, when the first dawn service was held on Anzac Day in Sydney. The idea for a service at 4.30 a.m., the time when the

33. *Argus*, 26 Apr. 1926.

34. *Argus*, 27 Apr. 1926. K. S. Inglis, 'Monuments in the Modern City: The War Memorials of Melbourne and Sydney', in D. Fraser (ed.), *Cities, Class and Communications: Essays in Honour of Asa Briggs* (London, 1990), p. 93.

35. *Duckboard*, 2 (July 1927), p. 6.

36. *Argus*, 27 Apr. 1934.

37. *Argus*, 26 Apr. 1935.

38. *Argus*, 27 Apr. 1936.

39. *Age*, 9 Apr. 1937.

first troops landed at Gallipoli, was proposed by the Association of Returned Sailors and Soldiers' Clubs. A few hundred ex-servicemen and bereaved relatives met at the Cenotaph to observe two minutes' silence and to lay a wreath in memory of the dead.[40] By 1939 the service had become a major ceremony, with 30,000 people participating.[41] In Melbourne, on Anzac Day 1933, the idea became a dawn pilgrimage of 7,000 ex-servicemen who gathered at the Shrine of Remembrance at 6 a.m. A single note on a bugle called them to observe a two-minute silence, after which the Last Post and Reveille were played. The Governor of Victoria then placed a wreath on the stone of remembrance and the men filed past the stone, bowing to it as they passed.[42] The pilgrimage to the Shrine became an annual event on Anzac Day in the 1930s.

The pilgrimage to the Shrine of Remembrance implied that the most important link was between the dead and ex-servicemen, because the bereaved were only allowed to join the ceremony once the ex-servicemen had passed. Many Australian war memorials also evoked the special place of ex-servicemen in the memory of the war, because they included the names of all those who had served, not just those who died. This distinguished Australian memorials from those of other countries, and it provided a constant reminder of the achievements of all Australian servicemen.[43] In addition, the march of ex-servicemen during Anzac Day usually included a salute to the dead at the local memorial, which served to privilege further the relationship between ex-servicemen and the dead. Even the temporary Cenotaph in Melbourne was successful, because it served as a site both for the bereaved to mourn and the marching ex-servicemen to salute the dead on Anzac Day.

The privileged place of ex-servicemen in the Australian memory of the war in this period was most clearly evident in the increasingly significant role of the march by ex-servicemen in the ceremonies on Anzac Day in the mid-1920s and 1930s. In Melbourne the numbers of marchers rose from 7,000 in 1925 to

40. *Sydney Morning Herald*, 26 Apr. 1928.

41. *Sydney Morning Herald*, 26 Apr. 1939.

42. *Argus*, 26 Apr. 1933.

43. K. S. Inglis and J. Phillips, 'War Memorials in Australia and New Zealand: A Comparative Survey', in J. Rickard and P. Spearritt (eds), *Packaging the Past? Public Histories* (Melbourne, 1991), p. 186.

15,000 in 1926, after Anzac Day was made a holiday, and to 28,000 in 1927.[44] There was a similar pattern in Sydney. The number of marchers rose from 4,000 in 1927 to 20,000 in 1930, and peaked in 1935, when there were 60,000 marchers. As the march became the key element of the day it tended further to identify the commemoration of the war with the achievements of Australian servicemen, their comradeship and the bond between them and the dead. The march was an opportunity for ex-servicemen once again to be divided from the community and to rejoin their wartime comrades. Increasingly, the role of the bereaved in the rituals of Anzac Day became subordinate to that of the ex-servicemen and the tradition they represented. Ken Inglis observes that the bereaved were 'welcome, even necessary, silent, still, rather like statues themselves at the foot of the war memorials that were the monuments of the Anzac tradition, passive participants in its ceremonies, auxiliaries in the rituals of an Australian civil religion'.[45]

The increasing stress on the achievements of the servicemen rather than the grief of the bereaved distinguished Australian commemoration from the commemoration of the war in Great Britain and Canada. One reason for the difference between the nature of commemoration in Australia and Canada may have been the reluctance of successive Canadian governments to emphasise the memory of a war which had split Canada between its English- and French-speaking parts. It was better to concentrate on the sense of loss felt by each community. Desmond Morton contrasts the pride of Australians in Anzac with the response of Canadians, who 'knew only that war had divided their country, and even their own proud achievements were drowned out by American self-congratulation about the Argonne or St Mihiel'.[46] By contrast, in Australia commemorative ceremonies were dominated by conservative groups who were able to appeal to other ex-servicemen by concentrating on their achievements during the war.[47]

44. M. Wilson, 'The Making of Melbourne's Anzac Day', *Australian Journal of Politics and History*, XX (Aug. 1974), pp. 206–7.

45. K. S. Inglis, 'Anzac and the Australian Military Tradition', *Revue Internationale d'Histoire Militaire*, 72 (1990), p. 14.

46. D. Morton, *Canada and War: A Military and Political History* (Toronto, 1981), p. 1.

47. A. Thomson, *Anzac Memories: Living with the Legend* (Melbourne, 1994), pp. 131–9.

More importantly, the divergence in the nature of commemorative ceremonies in the two countries reflected a different emphasis in the way the war was remembered. Many Canadians believed that they were 'an "unmilitary people" living in "the peaceable Kingdom"'.[48] They believed that they were a civilian force who had been reluctantly called to fight, but who had excelled in spite of their civilian backgrounds.[49] The stress on the civilian background of the Canadians therefore assumed that their military achievements should be appreciated, but should not be given precedence over their civilian identities. This differs in one vital respect from the Anzac tradition, which assumed that Australian soldiers excelled precisely because of their civilian 'bush' background.[50] C. E. W. Bean particularly emphasised the role of the bush, and even suggested that it was easy to train the men of the First AIF because of this background. The fact that most servicemen were from an urban background, rather than the bush, did not lessen the influence of this belief. This tradition left greater scope to privilege the military achievements of the men in Australian commemorative ceremonies.

Finally, this divergence indicates the greater significance of the role of the war in separating the men who served from their civilian backgrounds and from the women who stayed behind in Australia. Stephen Garton argues that Anzac Day served to perpetuate this divide, because it drew upon a distinction between the front, which represented male comradeship, and the stifling feminised world of the home front.[51] It was a practical expression of wartime language which many scholars argue highlighted the role of Australian men in founding the nation and thereby excluded or marginalised women.[52] However, it

48. Morton, *Canada and War*, p. 1.

49. Dafoe, *Over the Canadian Battlefields*, p. 76, 'Our sure defence is not the soldier in his uniform but the patriot citizen in his plain civilian attire.'

50. C. E. W. Bean, *The Official History of Australia in the War of 1914–1918*, Vol. 1 *The Story of Anzac* (St Lucia, 1981, first published 1921), p. 46.

51. S. Garton, *The Cost of War: Australians Return* (Oxford and Melbourne 1996), pp. 20–7, 71.

52. A. Cooper, 'Textual Territories: Gendered Cultural Politics and Australian Representations of the War of 1914–1918', *Australian Historical Studies*, 25 (Apr. 1993), pp. 403–21. M. Lake, 'Mission Impossible: How Men Gave Birth to the Australian Nation – Nationalism, Gender and Other Seminal Acts', *Gender & History*, 4 (Autumn, 1992), pp. 305–22. C. Shute, 'Heroines & Heroes: Sexual Mythology in Australia 1914–1918', *Hecate*, 1 (Jan. 1975), pp. 18–20.

is important not to overstate the extent that ex-servicemen identified with their wartime comrades against those who stayed behind. Joanna Bourke has shown that in Britain the overall impact of the war was not to encourage male bonding, but rather a return to domesticity, because most ex-servicemen largely rejected the wartime comradeship offered by ex-servicemen's associations.[53] A closer examination of the Australian situation shows significant similarities. Although the RSSILA and other ex-servicemen's organisations were able to recruit at least two-thirds of the men who served overseas on their return to Australia, the numbers of active participants in these organisations quickly fell from 167,000 members in 1919 to only 24,000 members in 1924. Thereafter the numbers rose slowly.[54] These figures suggest that, like their compatriots in Great Britain, Australian servicemen also sought a return to domesticity and their civilian lives, and therefore that the divide between the front and the home front may have existed as much in rhetoric as in reality.

Battlefield Pilgrimages

Despite the difficulties and costs of travel to the battlefields, many people from both Australia and Canada visited them during the 1920s and 1930s. In the 1920s pilgrimages were mainly journeys by individual bereaved relatives or family groups to the graves of the fallen. The First Australian War Graves pilgrimage in 1929 was the only large pilgrimage organised in either Australia or Canada in this period. In the 1930s larger pilgrimages were organised, which became national events. Pilgrimages were made to the unveiling of the Canadian National Memorial to the Missing at Vimy Ridge and the Australian Memorial at Villers Bretonneux. The visit of a contingent of Australian servicemen to Great Britain for the Coronation of George VI also became a pilgrimage, because it recreated key themes in the Anzac tradition.

53. J. Bourke, *Dismembering the Male: Men's Bodies, Britain and the Great War* (London, 1996), pp. 153–68.

54. G. L. Kristianson, *The Politics of Patriotism: The Pressure Group Activities of the Returned Servicemen's League* (Canberra, 1966), pp. 26–7, 36–7.

Pilgrimages of the Bereaved

In the first years after the war bereaved relatives predominated in pilgrimages to the battlefields. Despite the difficulties created by the distances involved and costs of travel to the battlefields in the Near East and on the old Western Front pilgrims received minimal official assistance. Australian and Canadian pilgrims travelled to the battlefields in the early 1920s alone or in small groups. Their journey was often reported in their local or even in the London press. Henry Williamson contributed an article to the *Weekly Dispatch* describing the pilgrimage of a poor and elderly couple from Canada who travelled to France even though the only description they had of their son's grave was a letter from his company commander saying that he had been buried 'in an old trench by some trees 500 yards north of a farm house, five miles from Cambrai'. An officer from the Graves Registration section helped them to locate the farmhouse, and near the stumps of some trees they discovered a 'small dark cross' on which the name of their son was inscribed.[55] Tourists also visited the battlefields from Australia and Canada. The magazine of an Australian travel agent described the attractions of a tour of the battlefields, stressing that 'you live through the whole gamut of human emotions from mental excitement to physical exhaustion'.[56]

Organisations were founded to assist individual pilgrims from Australia and Canada. H. H. Chanter MC, who had been the Officer in Charge of the Canadian War Graves Section, set up an organisation with some members of his former staff, based in Ypres, to assist Canadians to visit graves in France and Belgium.[57] In Australia Susan Sellheim, the wife of General Victor Sellheim and the secretary of the Friendly Union of Soldiers' and Sailors' Wives, proposed, in 1923, that bereaved relatives should be helped to visit the graves overseas as a 'humble tribute from citizens of Australia to the bereaved mothers of AIF soldiers'.[58]

55. H. Williamson, '7000 Miles to a Grave: Battlefield Quest of Poor Parents', in *The Weekly Dispatch: Articles Contributed by Henry Williamson in the Years 1920–21* (n.p., 1983).

56. *B.P. Magazine*, 1 (Mar. 1929), p. 19.

57. *Canada*, 4 June 1921, newspaper clipping in J. M. Ross MM papers, IWM 92/19/1.

58. *Herald*, 1 Nov. 1923, AWM Newspaper Cuttings - Pilgrimages - British Legion, Miscellaneous anniversaries.

The proposal received influential support, and Elizabeth Deakin, the wife of a former Prime Minister, became the President of the organisation. Monash, Harry Chauvel and Victor Sellheim became Vice Presidents.[59] Elizabeth Deakin argued that through the organisation of pilgrimages of bereaved mothers it 'should be possible to achieve the peace of the world by a union of mothers. The movement would strengthen the bonds of Empire and keep the memory of the Australian forces green.'[60] Despite this, only one group of four mothers were actually assisted to visit the battlefields, leaving in 1924.[61]

The largest pilgrimage which was dominated by the bereaved was the First Australian War Graves Pilgrimage from July to August 1929. The pilgrimage grew out of a series of concurrent schemes which were planned as a response to the 1927 American Legion visit to Paris. Plans for an Australian pilgrimage were proposed by a private individual, Charles Peel, and two small ex-servicemen's groups, the Association of Returned Sailors' and Soldiers' Clubs of New South Wales and the Imperial Ex-Servicemen's Association (which became the United Services Association).[62] About a hundred pilgrims took part, visiting the war cemetery in Jerusalem and following the route of the victorious Australian troops as they marched to Damascus. While at Gallipoli they held a service of remembrance at the memorial to the Australian missing at Lone Pine and visited the New Zealand memorial at Chunuk Bair, before travelling to the battlefields of Belgium and France. The pilgrimage concluded in England, where they were received at Australia House by the Australian High Commissioner, Sir Granville Ryrie.

The involvement of bereaved relatives included those who remained in Australia. The pilgrims carried sprigs of wattle to place next to a headstone or at the base of a memorial to the missing on behalf of those who could not afford the journey. Sprigs of wattle were a popular national symbol, and had been

59. *Age*, 1 Nov. 1923, AWM Newspaper Cuttings - Pilgrimages - British Legion, Miscellaneous anniversaries.

60. *Argus*, 1 Nov. 1923, AWM Newspaper Cuttings - Pilgrimages - British Legion, Miscellaneous anniversaries.

61. *Herald*, 7 Aug. 1924, AWM Newspaper Cuttings - Pilgrimages - British Legion, Miscellaneous anniversaries.

62. See documents in AA A1608/1 - F27/1/7 Part 1.

sent by relatives to Australian soldiers during the war.[63] The proposal was promoted by the *Herald* in Melbourne, the *Mercury* in Hobart and the *Register* in Adelaide. Patriotic organisations of the bereaved, such as the Fathers' Association, the Soldiers' Mothers' Association, the Sailors', Soldiers' and Nurses' Relatives Association and the War Widows' Association, also supported it.[64]

The Australian Government was reluctant to be too closely associated with the pilgrimage, because it was organised by an ex-servicemen's group which was a rival to the RSSILA. They refused to send a representative on the pilgrimage and rejected the suggestion of the organisers that the opportunity should be taken to unveil the memorial to the missing on Gallipoli at Lone Pine. The Department of Defence advised the Prime Minister's Department that 'it is considered that it would be unwise for the Commonwealth Government to be associated in any way with the Pilgrimage. It is apparently a private venture by the United Services Association, and is not in any way connected with the Imperial League of Returned Sailors and Soldiers.'[65] The suggestion was rejected, even though it was supported by many bereaved relatives. In a letter to the editor of the *Herald* one relative argued: 'I should like to know that while the mothers, fathers and sisters who do go are paying homage to their own who fell that they would be doing the same to my own boy. I feel sure the Prime Minister has only to realise this point of view for him to act.'[66] The reluctance of the Government to support the pilgrimage is indicative of the role which successive governments played in endeavouring to ensure that the RSSILA remained the sole voice of ex-servicemen and provides further evidence of the significant position held by ex-servicemen, and in particular those associated with the RSSILA, in the commemoration of the war.[67]

63. White, *Inventing Australia*, pp. 117–19. Also see A. H. Scott, 'A Little Sprig of Wattle', in Bean (ed.), *The Anzac Book*, p. 67.

64. *Mercury*, 17 May 1929; *Register*, 18 May 1929; *Herald*, 19 May 1929: AWM Newspaper Cuttings - Pilgrimages - Gallipoli; Europe.

65. Secretary of the Department of Defence Memorandum to the Secretary of the Prime Minister's Department, 7 Mar. 1929 AA A1608/1 - F27/1/7 Part 1.

66. *Herald*, 2 Jan. 1929, AWM Newspaper Cuttings - Pilgrimages - Gallipoli; Europe.

67. Beaumont, 'The Anzac Legend', in Beaumont, *Australia's War*, pp. 170–1.

When the pilgrims reached France they were caught up in a controversy which was created by their belief that as the relatives of the men who helped to save France they should be welcomed with open arms. The pilgrims were incensed when customs officials at Marseilles were rude to them - an anger compounded by the fact that they were searched before they crossed the border from France to Belgium. While they waited, a French factory worker purportedly called them 'moneymaking foreigners who have prospered as a result of French sacrifices'. An ex-serviceman among the pilgrims was reputed to have replied: 'Then it is a pity we ever fought.'[68] Relations between the pilgrims and French officials deteriorated further when they became embroiled in a quarrel between the Mayor of Villers Bretonneux and the IWGC over the burial of the bodies of two British soldiers and a French soldier which had recently been discovered in the village. The Mayor supposedly told a delegation from the pilgrims that they should have given money to the village rather than laying a wreath in the Adelaide cemetery.[69] This comment inflamed the pilgrims, who approached the High Commissioner for Australia in London, Sir G. Ryrie, with a request that he make an official protest, but were persuaded to let the matter rest.[70] Surprisingly, the IWGC report on the pilgrimage made no reference to the difficulties the pilgrims encountered, and even suggested that the Mayor of Villers Bretonneux had cordially received the delegation.[71]

The Vimy Pilgrimage

The most important and the largest Dominion pilgrimage was the Canadian pilgrimage to Vimy Ridge in 1936, which involved 8,000 pilgrims.[72] As an act of commemoration the pilgrimage

68. *Guardian*, 2 Aug. 1929, AWM Newspaper Cuttings - Pilgrimages - Gallipoli; Europe.

69. *Age*, 7 Aug. 1929; *Herald*, 7 Aug. 1929: AWM Newspaper Cuttings - Pilgrimages - Gallipoli; Europe.

70. *Age*, 8 Aug. 1929, AWM Newspaper Cuttings - Pilgrimages - Gallipoli; Europe.

71. Extracts From Report Made to Fabian Ware. AA A461/1 - E337-1-9 Part 1.

72. Despite the significance of this pilgrimage it has yet to be studied in detail, although there are brief accounts in Berton, *Vimy*, pp. 303–4; J. Pierce, 'Constructing Memory: The Vimy Memorial', *Canadian Military History*, 1 (Autumn 1992), pp. 5–14; Thomson, 'National Sorrow, National Pride', pp. 16–20.

reflected many of the key themes of the memory of the Great War in Canada. Firstly, it remembered the dead, the achievements of Canadian servicemen and the loss felt by the bereaved. In the name of these groups the pilgrims made a desperate call for peace. At the same time the pilgrimage and the unveiling ceremony of the Vimy Ridge memorial merged the assertion of the new status of Canada as a nation with the memory of the imperial cause for which Canadians had fought.

The Vimy pilgrimage was first proposed in 1927, following the American Legion visit to France. A resolution was carried at the Dominion Convention of the Canadian Legion in St John in June 1928 that the Dominion Council should make enquiries about organising a pilgrimage of ex-servicemen and women and bereaved relatives to be present at the unveiling of the Vimy memorial, which was expected to be in 1931 or 1932.[73] The Depression and delays in completing the memorial resulted in the pilgrimage's being postponed; but it remained an aspiration of the Canadian Legion. A pilgrimage was widely considered to be an important feature of any ceremony to unveil the memorial. The Canadian Battlefield Monuments Commission wrote to the Department of National Defence in 1934 about the possible unveiling ceremony of the memorial, noting that it 'seems obvious that if some thousands of Canadians - largely ex-soldiers and their relatives - are to be in France at any given time, that is the appropriate time to hold such a ceremony as the one in contemplation'.[74] When it was finally determined that the memorial would be completed early in 1936 plans were made to hold the pilgrimage in July of that year.

The pilgrimage commenced with the assembling of the 6,000 pilgrims in Montreal to board the six liners which would carry them to Europe on 16 July. Another 2,000 pilgrims travelled from Great Britain to join them at the memorial. Many major companies as well as the Federal and provincial Governments and local communities were involved in making it easier for ex-servicemen and women and bereaved relatives to join the pilgrimage. The Hudson Bay Company gave its employees who became pilgrims special leave of absence with full pay.[75] Similar arrangements

73. *Legionary*, III (July 1928), p. 19.

74. Col. H. C. Osborne to the Deputy Minister (Department of Defence), 11 May 1934, NAC RG 24 Vol. 6298.

75. *Beaver*, 267 (June 1936), p. 13.

were made by the Federal and Provincial administrations for civil servants.[76] In many communities sweepstakes were held to raise money to send ex-servicemen on the pilgrimage, although these were frowned upon by the leadership of the Canadian Legion.[77]

There were scenes reminiscent of the fanfare which had sent the first contingent of the Canadian Expeditionary Force to Europe in 1914 in Montreal as the liners prepared to leave. Florence Murdock wrote in her diary: 'My, but what a send-off we had . . . Such crowds filled the sheds at Montreal, bands played, aeroplanes flew overhead, they threw flowers, streamers and it was such a beautiful day, really the wharf was filled. The pipe bands of the Highland regiments paraded the sheds playing the bag pipes.'[78] As the liners moved down the St Lawrence river to Quebec and the North Atlantic, crowds gathered to see them pass at Sorel and Three Rivers as well as in smaller towns and villages. In Quebec thousands waited to see the ships in the darkness. The liners were escorted by the Canadian destroyer HMCS *Saguenay*, which further emphasised the similarities with the departure of the first contingent. Once they arrived in France groups of pilgrims participated in a number of smaller ceremonies in places such as Arras, Mons and Ypres before assembling at Vimy Ridge for the unveiling ceremony.

The unveiling of the Vimy memorial on 26 July by King Edward VIII was the highlight of the pilgrimage. The pilgrims spent the morning looking at the trenches which had been preserved and filing through the Grange tunnel located near the memorial. In addition to the 8,000 pilgrims, about 100,000 people from France and Great Britain came to watch the unveiling ceremony and to see the new memorial. The ceremony commenced with the arrival of King Edward VIII at 2.15 p.m. It was held in the afternoon rather than at 11 a.m. so that Canadians at home did not have to listen to the broadcast of the ceremony in the early hours of the morning. The King inspected the Canadian Guard of Honour, which was provided by the sailors from HMCS *Saguenay* and 100 ex-servicemen who made up the 'Pilgrim's Guard of Honour'. The King was presented to the Canadian

76. *Globe*, 22 July 1936.

77. *Legion Circular* No. 35/3/7, 29 July 1935, NAC MG 28 I 298 Vol. 8.

78. D. P. Beatty (ed.), *The Vimy Pilgrimage, July 1936 from the Diary of Florence Murdock, Amhurst Nova Scotia* (n.p., 1987), pp. 18–19.

dignitaries who had been invited to the ceremony, and then descended to the foot of the memorial, where he showed himself to the majority of the pilgrims for the first time. He then walked among the pilgrims for thirty minutes, speaking to bereaved relatives and to many ex-servicemen who were blind or amputees. The ceremony was dominated by a series of addresses which highlighted the need to work for peace and sorrow at the loss of so many men, as well as pride in Canada and the achievements of the Canadian Corps. Addresses were given by the King, representatives of the Anglican, United and Roman Catholic Churches of Canada, and President Lebrun of France, as well as by two Canadian ministers, Ernest Lapointe and Ian Mackenzie. In addition, a message from Prime Minister MacKenzie King was read to the crowd.

Thousands of people in Canada also shared in the unveiling ceremony through the radio broadcast of it. War memorials in all the major cities were the centres for ceremonies of remembrance, and services were held in churches throughout the country. For many of the bereaved the broadcast recalled their memories of the dead and increased their desire to visit the battlefields one day. A relative wrote to the Department of National Defence saying 'I heard the broadcast of the service, and hope to go one day to Vimy to see the Memorial and to find my brother's name.' Another relative wrote that as she listened to the ceremony on the radio 'my thoughts were with him, also my other brothers as I lost 4 in 18 months so I think we gave our share, and I am sure we all hope and trust there will not be another war'.[79]

After the memorial was unveiled, the pilgrims travelled to England, where they stayed from 27 to 31 July. On 29 July they gathered in Westminster Hall for an address by the British Prime Minister, Stanley Baldwin, who spoke about his experiences when he visited the battlefields in 1928. Baldwin recalled his sense that at Gheluvelt he was in the presence of the dead, a topic which was met by what the pilgrimage souvenir described as 'profound silence'.[80] Following the address, the pilgrims marched through crowds of Londoners to the strains of 'Land of

79. F. G. Goddard to Department of National Defence, 9 Sept. 1936; L. Staines to Department of National Defence, 22 Sept. 1936, NAC RG 24 Vol. 6298.

80. W. Murray, *The Epic of Vimy* (Ottawa, 1936), p. 119.

Hope and Glory' to the Cenotaph, where a ceremony of remembrance was held. The pilgrims also paid homage to the grave of the Unknown Warrior, where a wreath was laid on behalf of the bereaved mothers of Canada. A garden party was held in the grounds of Buckingham Palace for the pilgrims, at which Edward VIII was a surprise visitor. The arrival of the King was met by wave after wave of cheers, and when Edward made a brief address it was greeted by the pilgrims' singing 'For He's a Jolly Good Fellow' and 'God Save the King'. Although the pilgrimage concluded with the events in England, about 5,000 pilgrims accepted a French invitation to tour France as the guests of the French people from 1 to 5 August.

Although the organisers of the pilgrimage emphasised the unity of the pilgrims and the involvement of ex-servicemen from throughout Canada, this overlooked a number of significant divisions among them. Firstly, different ex-servicemen's organisations were in competition with each other. This played an important role in encouraging the Canadian Legion to proceed with its plans to hold a pilgrimage at Vimy Ridge after the delays following the initial proposals in 1927–1928. A statement about the plans for the pilgrimage was given to the public in August 1934 in order to forestall other veterans' groups.[81] The Legion pilgrimage came under considerable criticism in Toronto, and initially the numbers of ex-servicemen who enrolled in it from that city were low. The Committee was forced to agree to co-operate with its main rival, the Canadian Corps Association, which had a strong following in Toronto. The Association had in fact suggested a pilgrimage to Vimy in July 1934, once it became clear that the Canadian Corps Reunion was going to be successful, and it was probably this proposal which worried the Canadian Legion and led them to issue the public statement.[82] The decision to co-operate with the Corps Association paid off, as much of the criticism died down and ultimately at least 20 per cent of the enrolment in the pilgrimage came from Toronto.[83]

Participation in the pilgrimage was also divided by language. It was predominantly a pilgrimage of British Canadians, despite the identification of Vimy Ridge with the unity of British and

81. *Legion Circular*, No. 35/3/2, 19 Feb. 1935, NAC, MG 28 - I 298 Vol. 8.
82. *Veteran*, 11 (July 1934), p. 3.
83. *Legion Circular*, No. 37/3/1, 2 Apr. 1937, NAC, MG 28 - I 298 Vol. 8.

French Canada.[84] The memory of the war in French Canada was one of division and disharmony, which was reflected in their response to both the pilgrimage and the unveiling ceremony. By far the smallest numbers of participants came from the city of Quebec; only seven pilgrims, compared to between 100 and 200 people from each of the other major cities.[85] *Le Devoir* calculated that altogether between sixty and seventy-five French Canadians joined the pilgrimage.[86] The interest shown by the French-language newspapers in the pilgrimage and the unveiling of the memorial was correspondingly small. The organisers were aware of this difficulty, and sought to involve French Canada in the unveiling ceremony as much as possible. Despite criticism from the British Foreign Office they ensured that the religious ceremony included participation by representatives of the Anglican, the United and the Roman Catholic churches, as well as providing for two ministerial speeches, so that one of the speeches could be in French. The second speech was given by Ernest Lapointe, an important figure in the Liberal Party in Quebec. Also, a bilingual announcer was seconded to the BBC, who broadcast the ceremony, so that the ceremony could be conducted and broadcast in both languages.[87]

Although the Vimy pilgrimage has been described as an exercise in nostalgia, which was certainly an important motivation for the ex-servicemen and women, it was also a ceremony of mourning.[88] Like the pilgrimages in Britain, the Vimy pilgrimage combined both ex-servicemen and bereaved relatives. About half the participants were bereaved relatives. In April 1935 the editorial in the *Veteran* supported a call that 'special provision should be made for the transportation of widows and widowed mothers of deceased soldiers, as part of the pilgrimage' stressing that this 'rightfully is an obligation on the part of the country'.[89] Ex-servicemen and women and bereaved relatives were distinguished by the colours of the berets that they wore during the

84. *Ottawa Citizen*, 25 July 1936.

85. *Legionary*, XI (Jan. 1936), p. 13.

86. *Le Devoir*, 16 Juillet 1936.

87. Notes on Letter of I. A. Mackenzie to W. L. MacKenzie King, 3 Apr. 1936, NAC RG 25 G1 Vol. 1778.

88. D. Morton and G. Wright, *Winning the Second Battle: Canadian Veterans and the Return to Civilian Life 1915–1930* (Toronto, 1987), p. 220.

89. *Veteran*, III (Apr. 1935), p. 2.

pilgrimage, with the former wearing a khaki beret and the latter a blue beret. When the pilgrims arrived in France the first free afternoon was set aside for the bereaved to visit graves and memorials to the missing.

The awareness of the pain and loss caused by the war added extra impetus to the message of the pilgrimage, which was a reiteration of the need to work for peace. In the guide which was presented to pilgrims before they left Canada they were warned that the pilgrimage was 'being made while the world again moves under the shadow of bewildering crises' and therefore that 'nothing should occur that might jeopardize this great opportunity to demonstrate to European nations the cheerful good will, tolerance and understanding which characterize the Canadian attitude towards the world, and the desire of Canadians to live in peace and friendliness with all peoples'.[90] Ministers in the religious services held in Canada to coincide with the unveiling ceremony described Vimy Ridge as the 'symbol of humanity's aspiration towards peace'.[91] The appeals for peace united Canada with Great Britain and France, as well as statesmen from Canada's two major political parties. The editorials in all the major Canadian newspapers stressed the importance of the pilgrimage for the cause of peace. Often they suggested that they were bringing a message of peace from North America to Europe. The editorial of the *Halifax Chronicle* concluded: 'There is a lesson to be learned in this peace-time example; whether or not Europe's leaders will heed is another question. But if the Vimy pilgrimage serves to advance the cause of peace, it will be a Canadian achievement ranking with the part this nation played in the Great War.'[92]

One of the most significant features of the pilgrimage and the unveiling of the memorial was the interrelationship between a sense of Canadian and Imperial identity. The imperial tie played an important role in the motivation of many of the pilgrims. The presence of King Edward VIII was believed to have encouraged many pilgrims to join the pilgrimage. The visit to England was also an important feature of the pilgrimage, because it confirmed

90. *Guide Book of the Pilgrimage to Vimy and the Battlefields* (Ottawa, 1936), p. 18.

91. *Ottawa Citizen*, 27 July 1936.

92. *Halifax Chronicle*, 17 July 1936.

that Canada was part of the Empire and that the memory of the war included the sacrifice which was made to protect it. While the structure of the pilgrimage assumed the importance of Canada's place within the Empire, the unveiling ceremony marked a further stage in the assertion of a separate Canadian identity.

The Vimy Ridge Memorial helped to foster a strong sense of Canadian identity. The site for the memorial was changed to Vimy Ridge from Hill 62, near Ypres, because Vimy was considered to be a 'more distinctly Canadian spot'.[93] In accepting the French gift of the site to Canada MacKenzie King alluded to the many battles fought during the war, and said:

> This possibly may be said of Vimy which could not be said of the others: that it was at Vimy that the Canadian corps first fought as a unit, composed of men from every part of Canada. It was at Vimy that the Canadian army was welded into an efficient fighting organisation, so strong that no opposing armies could resist it; and that Canadian soldiers were able to achieve what no other army had been able to do in the meeting of the enemy at that point.[94]

The Memorial itself was designed by a Canadian architect, Walter Allward, and it was intended to stand as an example of Canadian artistic achievement, in addition to its role as the national memorial and a memorial to the missing. One Member of Parliament in the Canadian House of Commons stated that 'as regards grandeur, simplicity and reverence combined there is nothing to equal the masterpiece that Allward, a Canadian, has produced'.[95]

King Edward VIII was believed to be unveiling the memorial in his capacity as 'King of Canada', rather than as the King of Great Britain who ruled over the Dominions. The Canadian High Commissioner in London considered that the visit of the King represented the first time that the Sovereign had visited a foreign country on the invitation of a Dominion Government. V. Massey sought to ensure that this distinction was made clear to other countries, particularly France. He intervened when King Edward's Private Secretary suggested that the French Govern-

93. H. C. Osborne to F. Ware, 6 Feb. 1922, NAC RG 25 A-2 Vol. 330. For a discussion of the initial plans for the Canadian memorial and the decision to select Vimy Ridge see Pierce, 'Constructing Memory', pp. 5–6.

94. Dominion of Canada, House of Commons Debates, I, 9 Feb. 1923, p. 181.

95. Dominion of Canada, House of Commons Debates, III, 22 May 1922, p. 2100.

ment should be notified of the King's acceptance of the invitation to unveil the memorial by the British Embassy in France. Instead, he argued that, because the King was responding to a Canadian invitation, the French Government should be informed through the Canadian Minister, or in his absence, the Canadian Chargé d'Affaires.[96] The under-secretary for External Affairs, O. D. Skelton, thanked Massey for his intervention, saying that if he had not done so 'a good deal of the value of the episode would have been lost'.[97]

The attempt to ensure that the unveiling ceremony was a major Canadian event brought the Department of External Affairs into conflict with the British Ambassador to France and the private secretaries of the King. In order to emphasise that the occasion was 'distinctly Canadian' officials insisted that when the King arrived in France he should be met by both the Canadian Minister to France and the British Ambassador, even though this would offend the Ambassador. This was because if the King were met by the Ambassador alone this would imply that the Ambassador was the primary diplomatic representative of Canada in France. For the same reason, the King would be met by a Canadian Cabinet Minister at the memorial.[98] The British Ambassador acceded to the Canadian proposal, and his secretary wrote to the Canadian Legation explaining that he was 'only coming to Vimy in *personal* attendance upon his Majesty, and that he considers himself as enjoying no official status whatever at the ceremony', which he considered to be 'a purely Canadian one'.[99]

A number of other changes were made to the arrangements for the ceremony to ensure that it was clearly Canadian. A proposal that the Guard of Honour and the buglers should come from Great Britain was rejected on the grounds that it was inappropriate and that these roles 'above all others should be filled by Canadian veterans'. Similarly, a Canadian announcer was sent to broadcast the ceremony, because it was believed that many Canadians would 'object to the broadcast being performed by an English announcer with a BBC accent'.[100] The question of

96. V. Massey to O. D. Skelton, 4 June 1936, NAC RG 25 G1 Vol. 1778.
97. O. D. Skelton to V. Massey, 17 June 1936, NAC RG 25 G1 Vol. 1778.
98. Memorandum Regarding the Vimy Ceremony, NAC RG 25 G1 Vol. 1778.
99. Charles Peake to M. Jean Désy, 22 July 1936, NAC RG 25 G1 Vol. 1778.
100. Notes on Letter of I. A. Mackenzie to W. L. MacKenzie King, 3 Apr. 1936, NAC RG 25 G1 Vol. 1778.

where 'O Canada' should be used in the ceremony was also raised because of the Canadian determination to ensure that it was a Canadian event. The King's Private Secretary suggested that it should be played immediately after 'God Save the King' upon the arrival of the King at the memorial. L. R. La Fleche objected to this proposal, suggesting that once the King and the French President had moved to the dais then the ceremony proper could begin 'with the distinctively Canadian, "O Canada"'.[101] The Private Secretary to the King was able to get his way on this issue by arguing that placing the song immediately after 'God Save the King' would give 'O Canada' 'the character of a National Anthem instead of incidental music'.[102]

Despite the success of the 1936 pilgrimage it was never repeated on this scale. The Canadian Legion concluded that smaller tours to Vimy should be organised, because if 'a general demand arises for Annual Pilgrimages to Vimy, other organisations may become interested if the Legion is not'.[103] The eventual plan was for a 'Vimy Reunion' in 1937, which would consist of a series of small tours to France meeting at Vimy on the anniversary of the unveiling ceremony, 25 July.[104] The pilgrimage was not successful, and few Canadians were present at the memorial on the first anniversary of its unveiling.[105] In 1938 the Canadian Legion proposed another large national pilgrimage to Vimy for 1940; however, the Second World War intervened.[106]

The Pilgrimage of the Australian Coronation Contingent

The two Australian pilgrimages organised in the 1930s were much smaller in scope than the Vimy pilgrimage. The first was the pilgrimage which developed out of the visit of a contingent of Australian servicemen to the Coronation of George VI. The visit was the result of a proposal that a contingent of ex-servicemen should be organised by the RSSILA to attend the Coronation of Edward VIII. The proposal included a pilgrimage

101. L. R. La Fleche to O. D. Skelton, 15 June 1936, NAC RG 25 G1 Vol. 1778.
102. High Commissioner for Canada in Great Britain to the Secretary of State for External Affairs, 23 June 1936, NAC RG 25 G1 Vol. 1778.
103. *Legion Circular*, No. 36/2/28, 10 Dec. 1936, NAC, MG 28 I 298, Vol. 8.
104. *Legion Circular*, No. 37/2/11, 12 Mar. 1937, NAC, MG 28 I 298, Vol. 8.
105. G. McMoran, 'A Visit to Vimy', *Legionary*, XIII (Dec. 1937), p. 44.
106. *Legion Circular*, No. 38/3/2, 5 Oct. 1938, NAC, MG 28 I 298, Vol. 8.

to Belgium and France after the Coronation.[107] It was argued that the contingent would be an emphatic expression of Australia's loyalty to the new King as well as an opportunity to recapture the spirit of the AIF.[108]

When the difficulties of organising the contingent became clear, the Government was asked to provide assistance. This altered the nature of the contingent, because the Government preferred to select a contingent from men serving in the Defence forces. The Defence Committee stressed that for 'disciplinary and other reasons, it would be undesirable to send a contingent of ex-service men who are no longer under service control'.[109] In the end the contingent included a large number of serving veterans, along with men from the Australian militia. When Edward abdicated it became a contingent for the Coronation of George VI. The main body of the visitors left from Melbourne, and the men marched through the streets to the Shrine of Remembrance as an act of homage to the dead just prior to their departure. Their march was accompanied by scenes which were described as reminiscent of the departure of the First AIF.[110]

While the participants obtained the approval of the Department of Defence to visit the battlefields once the Coronation was over, the entire journey was a pilgrimage. This was because the veterans recalled and wished to relive their wartime experiences in England in addition to revisiting the battlefields.[111] It reflected the importance of wartime leave in England in the memories of many ex-servicemen.

The pilgrimage of the Coronation contingent was not beset by the controversy which surrounded the First Australian War Graves Pilgrimage, and came closer to the heart of the Australian memory of the war, because it emphasised the achievements of Australian servicemen and the Anzac tradition. It also looked to the future of that tradition, which was represented by the militia, and reiterated the close relationship between the Anzac tradition

107. *Listening Post*, 16 (Apr. 1936), p. 5.

108. *Courier-Mail*, 6 Feb. 1936, AWM Newspaper Cuttings - Coronation Pilgrimage 1936–1938.

109. Defence Committee Minute No. 47 29 Oct. 1936, AA A5954 - 1552/7.

110. *Argus*, 15 Feb. 1937, AWM Newspaper Cuttings - Coronation Pilgrimage 1936–1938.

111. *Sun*, 13 Jan. 1937, AWM Newspaper Cuttings - Coronation Pilgrimage 1936–1938.

and loyalty to the King and the British Empire. Men were selected who 'by their physique, discipline, bearing and appearance in England, will draw praiseworthy attention to themselves as representing Australia's best manhood'.[112] They could have no physical disability and had to be at least 5' 7" high. In pursuit of this policy the Defence Committee decided not to accept a proposal from the Blinded Soldiers' Association that two disabled ex-servicemen should be included.[113]

The contingent therefore maintained the Anzac illusion of a nation of natural warriors who were all tall and strong. One newspaper commented that a committee of artists and sculptors could not have selected men more characteristic of the accepted AIF type . . .. That lean face, bronzed and lined, direct of gaze, big-nosed, large, clean-shaven mouth, stern in repose, yet with an underlying suggestion of sardonic humour - practical men, outdoor men.'[114] Another newspaper described them as a 'perfect cross-section of Australian manhood', while the editorial of the *Australasian* claimed that the contingent 'will prove to people of the world that the physique and the bearing of the men who fought at Gallipoli have not declined'.[115] The image was also promoted by comparisons which were made between the contingent and the Coldstream Guards. A private in the Guards was reported to have said that he had 'never seen such easy discipline and we all wish we could join the Australian forces'.[116]

The initial plans for the contingent conceded no role for the nurses who had been a part of the First AIF, reflecting the masculine bias of the tradition and the ambiguous position of nurses within it. The Minister of Defence, Sir Archdale Parkhill, expressed his regret that the nurses would be excluded, but said he believed that a line needed to be drawn somewhere. There was an immediate outcry against the Government's refusal to

112. Coronation Contingent - Military Board instructions, AA A664 - 462/401/253.

113. Cabinet Decisions Regarding the Coronation Arrangements, 13 Nov. 1936, AA A 6006 - 1936/11/13.

114. *Herald*, 4 Feb. 1937, AWM Newspaper Cuttings - Coronation Pilgrimage 1936–1938.

115. *Argus*, 15 Feb. 1937; *Australasian*, 20 Feb. 1937: AWM Newspaper Cuttings - Coronation Pilgrimage 1936–1938.

116. *Herald*, 10 Apr. 1937, AWM Newspaper Cuttings - Coronation Pilgrimage 1936–1938.

include the nurses, particularly from women's organisations such as the Army Nurses' Club, the National Council of Women, the Housewives' Association of Victoria, the Australian Federation of Women Voters and the Victorian Women Citizens' Movement. The Victorian State President of the Sailors' and Soldiers' Womenfolk, Mrs M. E. Prendergast, wrote to the editor of the *Herald*, saying: 'As a representative of wives, mothers, sisters and daughters of soldiers and sailors of the AIF, I feel that we can never forget the service given to those men by the returned army nurses. They are truly a part of the AIF.'[117] Popular pressure forced the Government to reconsider, and seven nurses were included.[118] The response to the decision to exclude the nurses reveals the complexity of the Anzac tradition. Although it was predominantly associated with the image of the 'digger', it merged with a belief in the minds of many people that the nurses had been an integral component of the AIF.

The Pilgrimage to Villers Bretonneux

On 22 July 1938 a pilgrimage by 400 Australian ex-servicemen, most of whom now lived in England, travelled to Villers Bretonneux for the unveiling of the Australian Memorial to the Missing in France by King George VI. The pilgrims provided the Guard of Honour at the ceremony, standing in six sections, each representing one of the five AIF divisions and the Australian Corps.[119] When the plans for the unveiling ceremony were first considered attempts were made to persuade the Australian Government to provide funds to send a party of ex-servicemen from Australia to the unveiling ceremony, but with little success.[120] The Government made two concessions. They paid for a representative of the RSSILA to travel to the unveiling ceremony; and to encourage ex-servicemen in England to attend the

117. *Herald*, 15 Jan. 1937, AWM Newspaper Cuttings - Coronation Pilgrimage 1936-1938.

118. J. Bassett, *Guns and Brooches: Australian Army Nursing from the Boer War to the Gulf War* (Melbourne, 1992), p. 108; they were the Matron in Chief and the Principal Matrons of the six military districts.

119. Official Secretary (Australia House) Memorandum to Secretary (Prime Minister's Department), 7 Sept. 1938, ANL MS 6609 Series B Box 64 file 8180.

120. J. Black (State Secretary, NSW RSSILA) to E. V. Ramont (General Secretary, RSSILA), 19 Feb. 1938, ANL MS 6609 Series B Box 64 file 8180.

unveiling ceremony they agreed to pay £1 towards the cost of travel to Villers Bretonneux from England.[121] The Government would not accede to the request of the Queensland branch of the RSSILA that they should pay for an ex-serviceman from each state to be present at the unveiling.[122]

The pilgrimage is remarkable because it remains the largest pilgrimage by Australian ex-servicemen, although it was largely ignored at the time and has since been forgotten. This was because the pilgrimage did not fit into the Anzac tradition and thus failed to capture the imagination of the Australian public. The men did not journey from Australia, and therefore were not perceived as 'diggers' returning to their old battlefields. L. C. Robson, the Headmaster of Sydney Church of England Grammar School, travelled to the unveiling ceremony and commented on the ex-servicemen who made up the Guard of Honour:

> We passed first through a guard of honour of Australian ex-soldiers. Where they had come from, goodness knows. They were a motley crowd; probably many of them were odds and ends who had jobs in England. It would perhaps have been better if a smart guard of British troops had been brought over, but no doubt room had to be made for Australians. They were all in civilian clothes.[123]

While Robson's comment was exceptional, the lack of interest in the pilgrimage reflects the importance of the journey itself in creating the atmosphere of a pilgrimage.

The story of the Villers Bretonneux memorial illustrates both the national pride in the achievements of Australian servicemen and the lack of importance which was attached to the role of the memorial in the 1930s in promoting a distinctive Australian identity. The press release for the competition in 1926 to select the design for the memorial stressed that the site would be

> near the scene of the most momentous battles in which Australians took part in 1918 - those of 4th and 24th April, when German attacks were hurled back from these slopes overlooking Amiens, and the tremendous Allied assault of 8th August, when five Australian, four

121. *RSSILA Circular* No. 115/38 16 Mar. 1938, ANL MS 6609 Series B Box 64 file 8180. *Sun*, 7 Apr. 1938, AA A663 - 0100/1/102 Attachment E.

122. Secretary (Prime Minister's Department) to E. V. Ramont, 25 Mar. 1938, ANL MS 6609 Series B Box 64 file 8180.

123. L. C. Robson to Mr Board (Chairman of the Soldiers' Children Education Board) 24 July 1938, ANL MS 6609 Series B Box 64 file 8180.

> Canadian, and three British infantry divisions, with a French army on their flank, dealt what proved to be the decisive blow to the German armies.[124]

The War Memorials Committee suggested that the memorial should cost around £100,000, which would be appropriate 'to do justice to Australia', and that 60 per cent of the materials used should be Australian.[125] The design, by an Australian architect, William Lucas, was selected following the competition in August 1927.

The Depression led to the memorial scheme's being postponed and then abandoned in 1931. The IWGC encouraged the Australian Government to reconsider the plan to build the memorial, because the 11,000 Australian missing in France were the only British and Commonwealth dead who had not been commemorated. The Australian Government decided to replace the design of Lucas with a design by the British architect, Edwin Lutyens. They justified the decision by arguing that Lutyens had designed the entrance to the Villers Bretonneux cemetery which led to the site for the memorial, and therefore should be asked to design the memorial itself.[126] The Australian Prime Minister, Joseph Lyons, also contended that since most of the funding for the memorial was coming from the IWGC (they contributed £30,000, while the Australian Government provided £10,000) the construction of the memorial should be left in their hands.[127] His statement led Lucas to argue that the memorial was 'entirely non-Australian' and therefore 'humiliating for the Commonwealth and the Empire'.[128] Whatever the reasons for the decision to use the design of a British architect, the decision itself suggests that the memorial was not perceived as an opportunity to assert a distinctive Australian identity. This contrasts with the Canadian attitude to the Vimy memorial.

The unveiling ceremony for the Villers Bretonneux Memorial provides a further example of the lack of importance which the

124. Press Statement - Villers Bretonneux Memorial, ANL MS 6609 Series B Box 28 file 2535.

125. Recommendations of the War Memorials Committee, 2 May 1924, AA A6006 - 1924/05/02.

126. *RSSILA Circular* No. 133/36, 8 May 1936, ANL MS 6609 Series B Box 64 file 8180.

127. *Sun News Pictorial*, 8 June 1938, in AA A663 - 0100/1/102 Attachment E.

128. *Sun News Pictorial*, 10 June 1938, in AA A663 - 0100/1/102 Attachment E.

Australian Government attached to the need to assert a distinct Australian identity, particularly by comparison with the attitude of the Canadian Government. There was no equivalent to the use of 'O Canada' in the ceremony, while both the band and even the bugler who played the Last Post were provided by Britain.[129] Surprisingly, the only speaker at the ceremony who stressed that Australia had become a nation during the war was George VI, who described the memorial as a symbol 'marking the first entry into history of a young and vigorous nation - the gateway through which Australia passed from youth to manhood'. By contrast Sir Earle Page's address concentrated on the men themselves and the sense of obligation Australians felt towards them, describing the Memorial as 'a permanent symbol of the intense gratitude which those of their generation who remain and those who came after, feel for the men and women who sacrificed themselves for the ideals on which the Empire is founded . . . In this monument is incorporated the personal love, admiration and homage of the Australian people.'[130] While the point should not be overstated, as many Australian newspapers perceived the unveiling as a sign of Australian nationhood [Figure 6], in effect the nationalist emphasis of the Anzac tradition was linked almost exclusively to the qualities of the men themselves. The tradition was indicative of an Australian identity which had little to say about the remainder of the nation. It also reflected widely held assumptions about the continuing importance of the British Empire to the meaning of Australian nationalism.

Conclusion

Tourism and pilgrimage were also elements of the commemoration of the Great War in Australia and Canada. Exhibitions of war paintings and relics played an important role in the aftermath of the war by providing an opportunity for people who had stayed at home to see and understand something of the experiences of the men who served. They could also capture elements of the memory of the war. Longstaff's *Menin gate at midnight* expressed the sense of loss felt by many people, while nostalgia

129. Order of Ceremonial at the Unveiling of the Villers Bretonneux Memorial, 22 July 1938, AA A663 - 0100/1/102 Attachment C.
130. *The Times*, 23 July 1938.

THE AGE, SATURDAY, JULY 23, 1938
THE HOMAGE OF TWO GREAT NATIONS

Figure 6. 'The Homage of Two Great Nations', *Age*, 23 July 1938.

and the memory of wartime comradeship motivated the Canadian Corps Reunion in Toronto. War memorials were also places of pilgrimage, as well as centres for ceremonies to commemorate the war. There were differences in the role of war memorials and the nature of ceremonies of commemoration between Canada and Australia. The focus in Canada remained on civilians, because it was assumed that while Canadian servicemen had excelled during the war, they had done so as civilians who were reluctant soldiers. By contrast, the Anzac tradition stressed the military achievements of Australian servicemen, who were successful because their civilian, primarily bush, background fitted them for their role as soldiers. Thus, while memorials were places of pilgrimage for the bereaved, in the late 1920s and 1930s this role was increasingly subordinate to the place and importance of ex-servicemen in Australian ceremonies of remembrance.

In the first years after the war, Australians and Canadians who had lost a relative in the war travelled to the battlefields individually or in small groups. Only one large pilgrimage of bereaved relatives was organised, the First Australian War Graves Pilgrimage. The largest and most significant Dominion pilgrimage was the Canadian pilgrimage to Vimy Ridge. This pilgrimage was similar to British pilgrimages in that it combined both the bereaved and ex-servicemen. The presence of the bereaved gave an added impetus to the message of peace which the pilgrims carried to Europe. The Vimy pilgrimage combined a strong attachment to the King and the British Empire with a growing sense of Canadian identity. In particular, the unveiling ceremony at Vimy Ridge was consciously crafted by government officials to ensure that it was a distinctively Canadian event. The visit of the Australian Coronation contingent and the unveiling of the Villers Bretonneux memorial also illustrate the interrelationship between national identity and imperial identity. The visit by the Coronation contingent to England and the battlefields was the most successful Australian pilgrimage, because it was firmly rooted in the Anzac tradition. One facet of this tradition was a largely unacknowledged assumption that when the Australians excelled in the war they did so while fighting on behalf of the Empire. The Anzac tradition and the Imperial themes which were factors in the Australian memory of the war help to explain why the Government accepted the design of a British architect for the Villers Bretonneux memorial and why they did not attempt to make the unveiling ceremony a distinctively Australian event.

Conclusion

The Great War was a traumatic experience which was felt by individuals, communities and nations. It was remembered and commemorated at each of these levels in Great Britain, Australia and Canada. One of the most important acts of individual remembrance was the journeying of tourists and pilgrims to battlefields, cemeteries and memorials. Not only ex-servicemen and bereaved relatives were moved by the impulse to travel to these places, but also many other people who were touched by the war experience, even though they did not fight or lose a close relative. For tourists and pilgrims, remembering was not a passive activity. They assumed that at particular places and moments it was possible to renew or recapture something of the past. At the heart of their journeys were the beliefs that they could rediscover their wartime memories, feel closer to the memory and spirit or even spirits of the dead or recreate the experience of the war itself. The impulse to travel to these sites of memory arose out of the continuing presence of the memory of the war in the private lives of many people. Private memory transformed these sites into places of pilgrimage and helped to define their meanings.

The context within which the memory of the war was created and recreated is central to the study of the cultural impact of the Great War. That memory was neither static nor one-dimensional. Its complexity was reflected in the changing popularity of travel to places associated with the war. In 1919 and the early 1920s it was impossible to escape the memory of the war; thousands of travellers visited the battlefields on the Western Front, over a million people made a pilgrimage to the Cenotaph and the grave of the Unknown Warrior in November 1920, and over a million visits were made to the Imperial War Museum in 1921. This obsession with the war could not be maintained, and the mid-1920s represent a brief hiatus, which was followed by a return of the widespread interest in the war in 1927–32. Scholars identify this period with the 'war books boom'; but there was also a marked growth in the numbers of people travelling to the battlefields. After 1932 the popularity of travel to the battlefields remained high, particularly during the late 1930s, as the international situation deteriorated.

Concepts such as tradition and modernity, high and low culture, the sacred and the profane, the search for mentalities and the manipulation of meaning by elites cannot adequately explain the motivations for or the implications of the impulse to travel to places associated with the Great War. When the emphasis is placed on the individual response of people to the war it becomes clear that their experiences were multifaceted and changing. The cultural history of commemoration needs to be sensitive to the variety and ambiguity of individual experience.

The experience of loss was a universal feature of the interwar years. It transcended the distinction between high and low culture which underlies the assumption that the tourist trivialised the places which he or she visited. For the individual traveller, travel was a discourse between an imagined landscape and the landscape itself. When ex-servicemen returned to the battlefields they searched for evidence of their memories of the past. Civilians searched for sites which gave meaning to their memories of an imagined war. In Great Britain the memory of the war was infused with a strong sense of loss, and the feeling that an obligation was owed in response to the sacrifice offered by the dead. Travellers viewed the battlefields within this context, remote from the trivialisation of the memory of the war experience.

A study of the concurrent development of a modern tourist industry and the renewal of pilgrimages in the period 1860–1939 reveals the inadequacy of strict application of the distinction between the persistence of tradition and the rise of modernity. Tourism and pilgrimages represented alternate and overlapping modes of perceiving a journey. Both forms of travel were often seen as having a moral purpose. The distinction between the tourist and the pilgrim replicated a wider dichotomy between tourists, who were identified with the lower classes, and travellers, who represented the middle and upper classes. The Great War accentuated the divide between tourists and pilgrims. Tourists were portrayed as an illustration of the inequality of wartime sacrifice: they were the people who did not respect the sacrifices made by the fallen, ex-servicemen and the bereaved. While it was possible to define the characteristics of this group, in practice it was difficult to isolate specific individuals, as there were few people who were not touched by the war.

The story of how individuals and communities turned to the sacred also illustrates the inappropriateness of a rigid distinction between the sacred and the profane, sacralisation and secularisation. In the aftermath of the war battlefields, cemeteries and memorials, which were ostensibly profane sites, were often described as sacred places, and the people who visited them as pilgrims. The commemoration of the war in Great Britain was not characterised by the secular appropriation of the sacred in the form of a cult of the fallen soldier or a civil religion. Instead, traditional religion continued to play a central, though not an exclusive, role in the mourning process. There were moments when a more instinctive sense of the sacred competed with traditional religion. There seems to have been a widely held belief that pilgrims would feel closer to the spirit or even spirits of the dead at particular memorials or on the battlefields. Also, the Cenotaph was transformed by pilgrims into a sacred place, despite the disapproval of many Church leaders, who even sought to replace it by encouraging the plan to bury an Unknown Warrior in Westminster Abbey.

The active role of individuals in the construction of memory explains why it defies analysis from the perspective of mentalities or the collective unconscious. Individual memory is often defined and perpetuated within collective groups; but this should not mask the extent to which individual needs and perspectives infuse this memory.[1] There were many different memories and experiences of the war. Bereaved relatives travelled in search of tangible traces of the experiences, spirit and even spirits of their dead. Their journey could be a confrontation both with loss and also with guilt. Ex-servicemen returned to their past; sometimes with a sense of nostalgia, particularly for the comradeship they had known during the war. Some returned to confront their past; others could not face the journey to a place they only recalled as a nightmare. The battlefields also reflected the variety of images of the war. Gallipoli, Zeebrugge and the fighting in 1914 were associated in Great Britain with the romanticism of the war. The cemetery in Jerusalem evoked the crusading spirit of the men and the passion of their sacrifice, while the battlefields of the Somme and Ypres were identified with their tenacity, as well as with the heavy loss of life which accompanied the victory.

1. D. Lowenthal, *The Past is a Foreign Country* (Cambridge, 1985), p. 196.

Pilgrims distinguished themselves from tourists in order to stress their special links with the fallen and the war experience. However, the pilgrims were not a homogeneous community. Ex-servicemen generally travelled in groups which reflected a more limited comradeship. The men who participated in the pilgrimages usually belonged to the same Division, Regiment, Company or Battalion or lived in the same area. They might also be united through their place of employment. More importantly, the shared experience of loss which united bereaved relatives and ex-servicemen was often undermined by the gulf between the experiences of civilians and those of the soldiers during the war. Thus the divide between the front and the home front was both submerged within a wider unity of sacrifice and stubbornly persisted in this period.

The extent to which the divide was submerged or persisted varied between different countries. In Canada the emphasis on the civilian identity of the soldiers reflected a concentration on civilians in the ceremonies on 11 November. Despite this there were moments, such as the 1934 Canadian Corps Reunion and the Vimy pilgrimage, when ex-servicemen gathered publicly to recall their unique experiences. By contrast in Australia the achievements of ex-servicemen and the dead remained central to the memory of the war. The bereaved made pilgrimages to memorials and to see Longstaff's *The Menin gate at midnight*; however, in the late 1920s and 1930s they were ancillary to the main focus of Australian commemoration. Increasingly the emphasis on Anzac Day was on the comradeship of the men who served and their links with the fallen, which excluded other memories of the war.

The active role of individuals in the construction of memory also explains why remembrance was not just a tool which was manipulated by the elites. In Great Britain in the 1920s and 1930s the memory of the war was pervaded by a deeply felt individual desire to remember and mourn the dead. The presence of thousands of pilgrims in mourning at the temporary Cenotaph in 1919 and at the unveiling of the permanent Cenotaph and the burial of the Unknown Warrior in 1920 altered the attempts by the organisers of these events to provide a symbolic close to the war. As a consequence commemoration in Great Britain was increasingly dominated by the memory of the dead and the loss felt by the bereaved. Throughout this period the bereaved remained an important feature of organised pilgrimages to the battlefields, in both Great Britain and Canada, particularly during the 1928 Legion pilgrimage and the 1936 Vimy pilgrimage.

Finally, pilgrimages were also a public ritual, and in this context played a role in the formulation of national identity. In Great Britain the sacrifice of the dead and their achievements merged with descriptions of British identity. The planning for the British Legion pilgrimage was influenced by the organisers' belief that understatement and respect for the dead were fundamental features of the national character. The stress on the dead in Great Britain implied that their sacrifice was worthwhile, which was an important theme in discussions about the meaning of the war. In the late 1920s and the 1930s it was widely accepted that the sacrifice of the dead would not be in vain if it taught the lesson that the Great War should be the war to end all wars.

In Australia and Canada pilgrimages reflected a very different formulation of national identity. The war was perceived as a rite of passage to nationhood in both countries. Pilgrimages recreated the journey of the servicemen to the war, which had begun the process leading to the new status of the nation. The pilgrimage and the unveiling ceremony for the Vimy Ridge Memorial combined a strong attachment to the British Empire with a growing sense of a separate Canadian identity. It concluded in London, where the pilgrims paid homage to the wartime achievements of the Empire and renewed their attachment to it. By contrast Edward VIII unveiled the Vimy Memorial as King of Canada, and the use of 'O Canada', and the decision to include a Canadian band, Guard of Honour and broadcaster ensured that it was a distinctively Canadian event. The memorial itself remembered Canada's missing and the achievements of Canadian servicemen, as well as standing as an example of the artistic achievements of the Dominion.

In Australia national identity was fused by the Anzac tradition with a strong attachment to the British Empire. The nationalist emphasis of the Anzac tradition was linked almost exclusively with the men themselves, and had little to say about the independent identity of the nation. Thus the pilgrimage of the Coronation contingent took it for granted that when the Australians excelled in the war they did so while fighting on behalf of the Empire. This also helps to explain why the Australian Government agreed to a British architect, Edwin Lutyens, designing the national memorial at Villers Bretonneux, and why they did not attempt to make the unveiling ceremony of the memorial a distinctively Australian event, but concentrated on the achievements of Australian servicemen.

In 1939 the outbreak of the Second World War effectively brought an end to this remarkable period of travel. There was a brief interlude in the first months of 1940 as a new group of travellers visited the war cemeteries and memorials on the Western Front. Fabian Ware noted that 'in place of the peacetime pilgrims to the cemeteries came the soldiers of the new BEF who saw engraved upon the massed multitude of visible memorials the story of the stupendous sacrifice made by the British Commonwealth in the first phase of its struggle for liberty and existence'.[2] These men must have felt a mixture of emotions when they saw the evidence of the 'War to end all Wars'. One soldier wrote a poem as he stood in a war cemetery in which he prayed that the deaths of men in the last war for their country would not be in vain and hoping that he might be 'a worthy follower of these my comrades'.[3] Another serviceman, Anthony Rhodes, travelled over many of the old Western Front battlefields when his unit crossed to France in 1939. In his poem about the cemeteries he found the images they evoked more sinister:

> The shadowed turf and the mouldering granite cross
> The wind on the wold, and the smarting sense of a loss
> That breaks into perpetual step with the regular dawn:
> So, confirmed in my mind by such things, incredulity shorn
> of its questioning, wondering damnable doubt –
> Will I too be snuffed out?[4]

2. IWGC, *Annual Report* (1939–1940), p. 2.

3. A Soldier in France, 'I Thought', *Iron Duke*, XVI (June 1940), p. 98.

4. A. Rhodes, 'Repetition (First War Graves at Ypres)', in M. Stephen (ed.), *Never Such Innocence: A New Anthology of Great War Verse* (London, 1988), pp. 324–5. Rhodes survived the fighting in France in 1940 and the remainder of the war, being invalided out of the Army in 1947.

Bibliography

Unpublished Primary Sources

Australia:

Canberra

(i) Australian Archives

A461/1 - E337-1-9 Part 1.
A663 - 0100/1/102 Attachment C.
A663 - 0100/1/102 Attachment E.
A664 - 462/401/253.
A1608/1 - F27/1/7 part 1.
A5954 - 1552/7.
A6006 - 1924/05/02.
A 6006 - 1936/11/13.

(ii) Australian National Library

R.S.L. Papers
MS 6609, Series B Box 28 file 2535.
MS 6609, Series B Box 32, file 3476.
MS 6609, Series B Box 64 file 8180.

(iii) Australian War Memorial

A.W.M. 27 - 623 [17].
Newspaper Cuttings – Anzac Day 1990, Boxes 1-2.
Newspaper Cuttings – Australian War Memorial.
Newspaper Cuttings – Coronation Pilgrimage 1936-1938.
Newspaper Cuttings – Pilgrimages – Gallipoli; Europe.
Newspaper Cuttings – Pilgrimages – British Legion, Miscellaneous anniversaries.

(iv) Revd Colin Holden

Letter from William Grant to his family, 12 November 1919.

Canada:

Ottawa

(i) National Gallery of Canada

War Memorials file.

(ii) National Archives of Canada

MG 28 I 298 vol. 8.
RG 24 Vol. 6298.
RG 25 A-2 Vol. 330.
RG 25 G1 Vol. 1778.
RG 38 Vols. 346-351.

France:

Clermont-Ferrand

(i) Michelin

'Ce que Michelin a fait pour le Tourisme'

United Kingdom:

Leeds

(i) Peter Liddle Collection (Edward Boyle Library, Leeds University)

Leeds 'Pals' 1928 Battlefield Tour.
YMCA, 'Visitation of Graves in France and Flanders'.

London

(i) British Legion

Comité International Permanent des Anciens Combattants, Résumé of Work Accomplished, n.p.,1939.
FIDAC
General Secretary's Monthly Circulars.
Resolutions of the Annual Conference of the British Legion, 1937.
Special Circulars.

(ii) British Library - Manuscripts

Bruce Bairnsfather, 'Old Bill M.P.', LCP 1922/10.
C. Watson Mill, 'The Eternal Flame', LCP 1928/43.

(iii) The Imperial War Museum

Papers of J. W. Gamble, P.P. MCR 82.
Papers of P. E. Goodliffe VAD.
Papers of W. W. Johnson, P.P. MCR 47.
Miscellaneous Papers, Misc. 100 Item 1556.
Miscellaneous Papers, Misc. 1964, item 1964.
Papers of J. M. Ross MM, 92/19/1.
Imperial War Museum Information Sheet, No. 25.

(iv) Lambeth Palace Library

Davidson Papers, Vol. 202.

(v) The Oriental and India Office Collections

Curzon Papers
MSS Eur F112/316.
MSS Eur F112/318.

(vi) The Public Record Office

Cabinet Papers
CAB 23 - 11.
CAB 23 - 22.
CAB 23 - 46.
CAB 23 - 48(23).
CAB 23 - 49(23).

Foreign Office Papers
FO 371 - 11346.
FO 371 - 11557.
FO 371 - 12333.
FO371 - 12621.
FO 371 - 13346.

Home Office Papers
HO 45 - 11557.

Metropolitan Police Papers
Mepo 2 - 1957.
Mepo 2 - 3144.

Office of Public Works Papers
Work 16 - 26(8).
Work 20 - 1/3.
Work 20 - 139.
Work 20 - 205.
Work 20 - 226.
Work 21 - 74.

War Office Papers
WO 32 - 3000.
WO 32 - 3134.
WO 32 - 3135.
WO 32 - 5569.
WO 32 - 5853.
WO 32 - 5879.

(vii) Thomas Cook Archive

'How to See Paris and the Battlefields: Automobile Tours', 1922.
'How to See Paris and its Environs and the Battlefields', *c.*1925.

(viii) Westminster Abbey Library

Miscellaneous Correspondence
Unknown Warrior File
Westminster Abbey Guide, London, 1924

Published Primary Sources

(i) Newspapers and Journals 1914–1946:

Australia

Age, Argus, B.P. Magazine, Duckboard, Herald, Listening Post, Reveille, Sydney Morning Herald.

Canada

Beaver, Le Devoir, Globe, Halifax Chronicle, Legionary, Ottawa Citizen, Veteran.

British Isles

All the World, Birmingham Post, British-Australasian, British Legion Journal, Cambridge Daily News, Catholic Herald, Catholic Times and Catholic Opinion, Church Army Review, Church Times, Comrades Journal, Cook's Excursionist and Home Foreign Tourist Advertiser, Country Life, Daily Chronicle, Daily Express, Daily Graphic, Daily Herald, Daily Mail, Daily News and Westminster Gazette, Daily Sketch, Daily Telegraph, DSS Bulletin, Eastern Daily Press, Evening News, Evening Standard, Ex-Service Man, Field, Glasgow Herald, Illustrated London News, Irish Independent, Irish Times, Iron Duke, Lady, Lancashire Daily Post, Leeds Mercury, Manchester Guardian, Morning Post, Nation, Observer, Our Empire, Outlook, Pall Mall Gazette, Pilgrim's Scrip, Punch or the London Charivari, Radio Times, Railway and Travel Monthly, Red Triangle, Review of Reviews, Reynolds Illustrated News, Rifle Brigade Chronicle, Sheffield Daily Independent, Spectator, Sphere, Sunday Dispatch, Sunday Express, Sunday Herald, Sunday Times, Tablet, The Times, Times Literary Supplement, Toc H Journal, Travel Log, Traveller's Gazette, War Cry, War Illustrated, Western Mail, World Travel Gazette, Yorkshire Herald, Yorkshire Post, Ypres Times.

France

L'Illustration, Le Temps.

(ii) Transcripts of Parliamentary Debates

Hansard: House of Commons Debates.
Hansard: House of Lords Debates.
Dominion of Canada: House of Commons Debates.

Secondary Sources – Published Prior to 1939

(i) Books

Allen, F., *A Wayfarer in Belgium*. London, 1934.
Allen, T., *The Tracks They Trod: Salonika and the Balkans, Gallipoli, Egypt and Palestine Revisited*. London, 1932.
Anzac Day Celebration Committee, *Anzac Day 1937*. n.p., *c.*1937.

Armistice Ceremonial Committee, *Armistice Ceremonial*. Toronto, 1928.

Bagnold, E., *The Happy Foreigner*. London, 1920.

Bairnsfather, B., *Wide Canvas: An Autobiography*. London, 1939.

Barman, T. G., and De Geynst, J., *Guide to Belgium and Luxembourg*. London, 1938.

Bart, J. R., *Pilgrim Scrip: More Random Reminiscences*. London, 1927.

B. B., *Over There: A Little Guide for Pilgrims to Ypres; The Salient and Talbot House, Poperinghe*. London, 1935.

Bean, C. E. W. (ed.), *The Anzac Book: Written and Collected in Gallipoli by the Men of Anzac*. London, 1916.

——, *The Official History of Australia in the War of 1914–1918*, Vol. 1. *The Story of Anzac*. St Lucia, 1981, first published 1921.

Bentley, E. C., *Peace Year in the City: 1918–1919*. n.p., 1920.

Bird, W. R., *Thirteen Years After: The Story of the Old Front Revisited*. Toronto, 1932.

Blomfield, R., *Memoirs of an Architect*. London, 1932.

Blunden E., *The Poems of Edmund Blunden*. London, 1930.

Blunden, E. and Norman, S., *We'll Shift Our Ground* or *Two on a Tour*. London, 1933.

Bolitho, H., *Alfred Mond: First Lord Melchett*. London, 1933.

Brice, B., *The Battle Book of Ypres*. London, 1927.

——, *Ypres – Outpost of the Channel Ports: A Concise Historical Guide to the Salient of Ypres*. London, 1929.

The British Legion Pilgrimage Handbook. n.p., 1928.

Brittain, H. E., *To Verdun From the Somme: An Anglo-American Glimpse of the Great Advance*. London, 1917.

Brittain, V., *Testament of Youth: An Autobiographical Study of the Years 1900–1925*. London, 1933.

——, *Honourable Estate: A Novel of Transition*. London, 1936.

Brooke, R., *The Collected Poems of Rupert Brooke*. London, 1918.

Brown, A. J., *A Joyous Entry into Brighter Belgium*. London, 1923.

Buchan, J., *Nelson's History of the Great War*, Vols. I–XXIV. London, 1915–19.

Cairns, D. S., *The Army and Religion*. London, 1919.

Callwell, C. E., *Field Marshal Sir Henry Wilson, His Life and Diaries*, Vol. 2. London, 1927.

Canadian Battlefields Memorials Commission, *Canadian Battlefield Memorials*. Ottawa, 1929.
Church Army, *Annual Reports*. 1919-1939.
Churchill, W. S., *The World Crisis 1911–1918*, abridged edition. London, 1931.
Clark, S. A., *France on £10*. London, 1934.
Coop, J. O., *A Short Guide to the Battlefields: Where to Go and How to See Them*. Liverpool, n.d.
Cooper, C. S., *The Outdoor Monuments of London: Statues, Memorial Buildings, Tablets and War Memorials*. London, 1928.
Dafoe, J. W., *Over the Canadian Battlefields: Notes of a Little Journey in France in March. 1919*, Toronto, 1919.
Dark, S., *The Anglo-Catholic Pilgrimage: A Diary of the Great Adventure*. London, 1924.
Dean and Dawson Ltd., *British Memorials of the Great War 1914–1918*. n.p., n.d.
Dodd, A. B., *Up the Seine to the Battlefields*. New York and London, 1920.
Doyle, A. Conan, *A Visit to Three Fronts, Glimpses of the British, French and Italian Lines*. London, 1916.
Earle, L., *Turn Over the Page*. London, 1935.
Ellis, W. T., *Bible Lands To-day*. New York and London, 1927.
Elston, R., *The Traveller's Handbook to Belgium*. London, 1929.
Fielding, R., *War Letters to a Wife, France and Flanders 1915–1919*. London, 1929.
Fitzgerald, F. Scott, *Tender is the Night*. London, 1934.
Fleming, A. T., *How to See the Battlefields*. London, 1919.
Fox, F., *The King's Pilgrimage*. London, 1922.
French, G. (ed.), *Some War Diaries, Addresses and Correspondence of Field Marshal the Right Honourable The Earl of Ypres KP, GCB, OM, GCVO, KCMG*. London, 1937.
Gavin, L. J. D. and Harter, J. (eds), *The Story of an Epic Pilgrimage: A Souvenir of the Battlefield Pilgrimage*. n.p., 1928.
Geoffrey Franklin. London, 1933.
Gibbons, J., *Roll On, Next War! The Common Man's Guide to Army Life*. London, 1935.
——, *I Wanted to Travel*. London, 1938.
Gillespie, A. D., *Letters From Flanders*, 3rd edn. London, 1916.
Glyn, E., *Six Days*. London, 1924.

B. F. Goodrich Co., Ltd., *Guide to the War Regions of France and Belgium*. London, n.d.

Gosling, H., *Up and Down Stream*. London, 1927.

Graham, S., *Europe – Whither Bound? (Quo Vadis Europa?): Being Letters of Travel from the Capitals of Europe in the Year 1921*. London, 1921.

——, *The Challenge of the Dead*. London, 1921.

Graves, R., *Goodbye to All That: An Autobiography*. London, 1929.

Guide Book of the Pilgrimage to Vimy and the Battlefields. Ottawa, 1936.

Haggard, H. Rider, *A Winter Pilgrimage: Being an Account of Travels Through Palestine, Italy and the Island of Cyprus, Accomplished in the Year 1900*. London, 1901.

Hammerton, J. A., *The Wrack of War*. London, 1918.

—— (ed.), *Wonderful Britain: Its Highways, Byways and Historic Places*, Vol. III. London, 1928/9.

Hay, I., *The Ship of Remembrance*. London, *c*.1926.

——, *Their Name Liveth: The Book of the Scottish National War Memorial*. London, 1931.

Herbert, A. P., *Half-Hours at Helles*. Oxford, 1916.

Holmes, J., *A Pilgrimage to Gallipoli*. London, *c*.1926.

Hope, W. E. Stanton, *Gallipoli Revisited: An Account of the Duchess of Richmond Pilgrimage Cruise*. London, *c*.1934.

Housman, L., *War Letters of Fallen Englishmen*. London, 1930.

Hutchison, G., *Life Without End*. London, 1932.

——, *Pilgrimage*. London, 1935.

Imperial War Graves Commission, *Report*. 1918.

——, *Annual Reports*. 1921–40.

Imperial War Museum, *Annual Reports*. 1921–1939.

Kenyon, F., *War Graves, How the Cemeteries Abroad will be Designed*. London, 1918.

Lee, S., *King Edward VII: A Biography*, Vol. II. *The Reign*. London, 1927.

Lowe, T. A., *The Western Battlefields: A Guide to the British Line, Short Account of the Fighting, the Trenches and Positions*. London, 1920.

Lunn, H. S., *Nearing Harbour: The Log of Sir Henry S. Lunn*. London, 1934.

McNair, W., *Blood and Iron: Impressions From the Front in France & Flanders*. London, 1916.

Masefield, J., *The Old Front Line: Or the Beginning of the Battle of the Somme*. London, 1917.
Maskell, H. P., *The Soul of Picardy*. London, 1930.
Michelin & Cie., *The Marne Battlefields 1914: An Illustrated History and Guide*. Clermont-Ferrand, 1917.
——, *Rheims and the Battles for its Possession*. Clermont-Ferrand, 1919.
——, *Ypres and the Battles of Ypres*. Clermont-Ferrand, 1919.
Michelin Tyre Co. Ltd, *Amiens: Before and During the Great War*. London, 1919.
——, *Lille: Before and During the Great War*. London, 1919.
Morton, H. V., *The Heart of London*. London, 1925.
——, *The Spell of London*. London, 1926.
——, *In Search of London*. London, 1951.
Mottram, R. H., *The Spanish Farm Trilogy*. London, 1927.
——, *Through the Menin Gate*. London, 1932.
——, *Journey to the Western Front: Twenty Years After*. London, 1936.
Muirhead, F., *Belgium and the Western Front, British and American*. London, 1920.
——, *Belgium*. London, 1924.
——, *Belgium and Luxembourg*. London, 1929.
Murray, W., *The Epic of Vimy*. Ottawa, 1936.
Newman, B., *In the Trail of the Three Musketeers*. London, 1934.
——, *Cycling in France (Northern)*. London, 1936.
Newman, E. M., *Seeing France*. New York and London, 1930.
Nichols, B., *Cry Havoc!* London, 1933.
Norval, A. J., *The Tourist Industry: A National and International Survey*. London, 1936.
Ogilvie, F. W., *The Tourist Movement: An Economic Survey*. London, 1933.
Oxenham, J., *High Altars: The Battlefields of France and Flanders as I Saw Them*. London, 1918.
Pemberton, T. J., *Gallipoli Today*. London, 1926.
Pimlott, J. A. R., *Toynbee Hall: Fifty Years of Social Progress: 1880–1934*. London, 1935.
Pollard, H. B. C., *The Story of Ypres*. London, 1917.
Prist, P., *Ypres*. Brussels, n.d.
Pulteney, W. and Brice, B., *The Immortal Salient: An Historical Record and Complete Guide for Pilgrims to Ypres*. London, 1925.

Rae, W. Fraser, *The Business of Travel: A Fifty Years Record of Progress*. London, 1891.
Rathbone, I., *They Call It Peace*. London, 1936.
Richardson, E. M., *Remembrance Wakes*. London, 1934.
Rimington, F. C., *Motor Rambles Through France: Some Descriptions and Reflections*. London, 1925.
St Barnabas Society, *Ypres/The Somme*. London, *c*.1923.
——, *Empire Pilgrimage, Scottish Pilgrimage*. London, *c*.1924.
——, *Croydon Pilgrimage, The Second Scottish Pilgrimage, Italian Pilgrimage, The Smaller Pilgrimages*. London, *c*.1925.
——, *Gallipoli and Salonika*. London, *c*.1926.
——, *The Menin Gate Pilgrimage*. London, *c*.1927.
Salmond, J. B., *The Old Stalker and Other Verses*. Edinburgh and London, 1936.
Singleton, J., *The Battlefields of Natal Revisited*. Durban, n.d.
Southern Railway, *The Battlefields and War Graves of France and Flanders and How to Visit Them*. n.p., 1924.
The Story of the Canadian Corps. Toronto, 1934.
Story, S., *Present Day Paris and the Battlefields: The Visitors Handbook with the Chief Excursions to the Battlefields*. New York and London, 1920.
Swinton, E. (ed.), *Twenty Years After: The Battlefields of 1914–18, Then and Now*, Vols. 1–2 and Supplementary Volume, London, 1936–7.
Talbot House, *The Pilgrim's Guide to the Ypres Salient*. London, 1920.
Taylor, F. Irving, *The Cathedral Pilgrimage*. London, 1934.
Taylor, H. A., *Good-bye to the Battlefields: To-day and Yesterday on the Western Front*. London, 1928.
Thomas Cook, *Cook's Traveller's Handbook – Belgium and the Ardennes*. London, 1913.
——, *The Traveller's Handbook for Constantinople, Gallipoli and Asia Minor*. London, 1923.
Thurlow, E. G. L., *The Pill-boxes of Flanders*. London, 1933.
Tomlinson, H. M., *All Our Yesterdays*. London, 1930.
Townroe, B. S., *A Pilgrim in Picardy*. London, 1927.
Ward, M. A., *Fields of Victory*. London, 1919.
Ward Lock & Co. Ltd, *Handbook to Belgium and the Battlefields*, 8th edn. London, 1924.
War Graves of the Empire. London, 1928.

Williams, G. Valentine, *With Our Army in France and Flanders*. London, 1915.
Williamson, C. N. and Williamson, A. M., *Crucifix Corner: A Story of Everyman's Land*. London, 1918.
Williamson, H., *The Wet Flanders Plain*. London, 1929.
Willson, B., *Ypres: The Holy Ground of British Arms*. Bruges, 1920.
——, *From Quebec to Picadilly and Other Places: Some Anglo-Canadian Memories*. London, 1929.
Wood, E. M., *The Polytechnic and its Founder Quintin Hogg*. London, 1932.
Workers' Travel Association, *1928 Holidays*. n.p., n.d.
Yeats Brown, F., *Dogs of War!* London, 1934.

(ii) Articles

Allerton, A. R., 'Hesdin', *Artists' Rifles Journal*, IV (1921), 80–1.
Allinson, H. W., 'August Pilgrimage to Ypres', *Ypres Times*, 3 (1926), 104–5.
A Soldier in France, 'I Thought', *Iron Duke*, XVI (1940), 98.
B. B., 'The Pilgrim's Way', *Toc H Journal*, V (1927), 339–48.
Bennett, J. B. Sterndale, 'The Return to Passchendaele', *The Nation and Athenaeum,* XLVII (1930), 345–6.
Bird., W. R., 'From the Things That Are to the Things That Were', *Veteran*, 11 (1934), 7–9, 15.
Blunden, E., 'We Went to Ypres', in Blunden, E., *The Mind's Eye*. London, 1934, 44–9.
Bolitho, H. (ed.), 'A Victorian Woman in the Crimea', *English Review*, LIX (1934), 459–69.
Brittain, V., 'Somme Battlefield, 1933', *Weekend Review*, VIII (1933), 156–7.
——, 'Illusion on the Somme', in Berry, P. (ed.), *Testament of a Generation: The Journalism of Vera Brittain and Winifred Holtby*, pp. 213–16. London, 1985.
Butler, P. R., 'Farmsteads and Inn-Names of Picardy and Artois', *English Review*, LIX (1934), 209–17.
——, 'Twenty-One Years After', *Blackwood's Magazine*, CCXXXVIII (1935), 832–9.
Channing-Renton, E. M., 'The Somme Battlefields and War Cemeteries, Summer 1926', *Ypres Times* 3 (1927), 88–93.

Cook, E. Thornton, 'Gallipoli: Twenty Years After', *Cornhill Magazine*, 151 (1935), 257-63.

Cooke, G., 'Cry Not Farewell', *The Comrades Journal*, II (1920), 9.

Dr Dearmer, 'Ypres', *Cornhill Magazine*, 40 (1916), p. 712-16.

De Trafford, G. E., 'Lest We Forget', *A Journal of Remembrance*, 1 (1931), 78-9.

Ewart, W., 'A Pilgrimage', *National Review*, LXXIV (1919), 514-23.

——, 'After Four Years: The Old Road to Ypres', *Cornhill Magazine*, XLIX (1920), 734-41.

——, 'Ghosts of Arras', *The Nineteenth Century and After*, LXXXVIII (1920), 1099-1106.

——, 'Auburs Revisited', *Household Brigade Magazine*, (1921), 14-15.

——, 'Vimy Heights to Auburs Ridge', *Ypres Times*, 1 (1922), 94-5.

Exham, R. K., 'A Battlefield Tour', *Iron Duke*, XV (1939), 51-4.

'"For ever England": The Graves in France and Flanders', *Country Life*, XIV (1928), 654-61.

Forshaw, W. T., 'A Battlefield Unchanged', *British Legion Journal*, 10 (1930), 34, 36.

Gibbs, P., 'The Cemeteries in the Salient', *Ypres Times*, 1 (1923), 198-9.

Gilmore, D., 'Belgium in 1919', *Cyclists Touring Club Gazette*, XXXIX (1919), 20-1.

Gosse, E., 'The Battlefields of the Ourcq', *Cornhill Magazine*, XLII (1917), 24-33.

Gwynne, S., 'France of the Battle-Zone', *The Nineteenth Century and After*, LXXXIX (1921), 162-74.

H., 'The Old Road', *New Statesman*, XVIII (1921), 74.

Hearne, R. P., 'The Battle Museum on Zeebrugge Mole', *Sphere*, XCIX (1924), xiv.

Hickman, A., 'The Pilgrims to France', *Red Triangle*, V (1921), 15-16.

Hill, A. W., 'Our Soldiers' Graves', *Journal of the Royal Horticultural Society*, XLV (1919), 1-13.

Hitchcox, K. M., 'A British Cemetery', *English Review*, XLIV (1927), 462.

Hunter-Weston, A., 'War and Peace at the Dardanelles: An Impression', *Army Quarterly*, III (1921), 70-6.

Hyde, V., 'The Greatest No More War Advertisement', *British Legion Journal*, 16 (1937), 293-4.
Johnson, G. H., 'An Ex-prisoner Returns', *Ypres Times*, 5 (1931), 168-70.
Johnston, C. H., 'Mons 1914-1934', *Spectator*, 5539 (1934), 249-50.
Katin, L., 'The Flowering Graves of Palestine', *British Legion Journal*, 13 (1933), 210.
Kipling, R., 'The Gardener', *Debits and Credits*, pp. 399-414. London, 1926.
Lewis, J. C., 'A View of France and Flanders in 1928', *Household Brigade Magazine*, (1928/9), 18-20.
Lineton, F. J., 'Kamarad', *Ypres Times*, 6 (1932), 19-21.
Lutyens, E., 'The Story of the Cenotaph', *A Journal of Remembrance*, 1 (1931), 5-6.
McMoran, G., 'A Visit to Vimy', *Legionary*, XIII (1937), 44.
Markham, V. R., 'In a Devastated Area', *Fortnightly Review*, DCXXX (1919), 937-48.
Moore, M. M., 'Our Buried Caesar's', *United Empire*, XII (1921), 735-7.
Robb, L. A., 'Gone the Debris, Gone the Death', *Reveille*, 7 (1934), 16-17, 31.
Sheppard, A. T., 'Northern France Revisited', *Spectator*, 5185 (1927), 808-9.
Sillar, F. C., 'Stones of Remembrance', *Empire Review*, XLVIII (1928), 398-404.
Thompson, E. H., 'A Reminiscence of a Recent Visit to France and Flanders', *King's Royal Rifle Corps Chronicle* (1939), 72-4.
Tuohy, F., 'Shall the B.E.F. March in Flanders Fields Again?', *Sphere*, CX (1927), 449.
——, 'The Return to Flanders Fields', *Sphere*, CXIV (1928), 298.
Urquhart, J., 'Via Dolorosa: The Battlefields of Belgium and France', *B.P. Magazine* (1929), 19-21, 91.
'The Visit to Ypres', *City of London Rifles and Quarterly Journal*, 1 (1931), 12-13.
Ware, F., 'War Graves and the British Commonwealth', *The Nineteenth Century and After*, DCIX (1927), 631-41.
——, 'The Price of Peace', *Listener*, II (1929), 636-7.
——, 'The Empire's Homage: Memorials of a Million Dead', *Listener*, VIII (1932), 651-2.

'War Graves in Flanders', *Round Table*, XVI (1926) 310–17.
Whibley, C., 'Belgium in 1919', *Blackwood's Magazine*, CCVI (1919), 528–37.
Williams, E. F., 'Ypres Calling', *Ypres Times*, 3 (1927), 151–4.
H. Williamson, '7000 Miles to a Grave: Battlefield Quest of Poor Parents', in *The Weekly Dispatch: Articles Contributed by Henry Williamson in the Years 1920–21*. n.p., 1983, 52.
Woods, R., 'War Graves Visitation in France', *Officer's Review*, VII (1938), 495–9.
WRNS, 'In the Peace Procession: From a Wren to its Mother', *Englishwoman*, XLVIII (1919), 202–6.
Yapp, A. K., 'The Western Front Revisited', *Red Triangle*, III (1920), 213–16.

Secondary Sources – Published Since 1939

(i) Books

Adey, L., *Class and Idol in the English Hymn*. Vancouver, 1988.
Anderson, B., *Imagined Communities: Reflections on the Origin and Spread of Nationalism*. London, 1983.
Assouline, P., *Lourdes: Histoires D'eau*. Paris, 1980.
Audoin-Rouzeau, S., *Men at War 1914–1918: National Sentiment and Trench Journalism in France*, trans. H. McPhail. Providence and Oxford, 1992.
Bassett, J., *Guns and Brooches: Australian Army Nursing from the Boer War to the Gulf War*. Melbourne, 1992.
Bean, C. E. W., *Gallipoli Mission*. Canberra, 1948.
Beatty, D. P. (ed.), *The Vimy Pilgrimage, July 1936 from the Diary of Florence Murdock, Amhurst Nova Scotia*. n.p., 1987.
Becker, A., *La Guerre et La Foi: De la Mort à la Mémoire*. Paris, 1994.
Behrend, A., *As From Kemmel Hill: An Adjutant in France and Flanders 1917 and 1918*. London, 1963.
Berton, P., *Vimy*. Toronto, 1986.
Birdwood, W., *Khaki and Gown: An Autobiography*. London, 1941.
Blackbourn, D., *The Marpingen Visions: Rationalism, Religion and the Rise of Modern Germany*. Hammersmith, 1995, originally published 1993.
Blythe, R., *The Age of Illusion: England in the Twenties and*

Thirties 1919–1940. London, 1963.
Bogarde, D., *A Postillion Struck By Lightning*. London, 1977.
Bothwell R. *et al.*, *Canada, 1900–1945*. Toronto, 1987.
Bourke, J., *Dismembering the Male: Men's Bodies, Britain and the Great War*. London, 1996.
Bracco, R., *Merchants of Hope: British Middlebrow Writers and the First World War*. Oxford and Providence, 1993.
Branson, N., *Britain in the Nineteen Twenties*. London, 1975.
Brendon, P., *Thomas Cook: 150 Years of Popular Tourism*. London, 1991.
Brittain, V., *Testament of Friendship: The Story of Winifred Holtby*. London, 1940.
Brunner, E., *Holiday Making and the Holiday Trades*. London, 1945.
Burkart, A. J. and Medlik, S., *Tourism: Past, Present and Future*. London, 1974.
Buzard, J., *The Beaten Track: European Tourism, Literature and the Ways to 'Culture' 1800–1918*. Oxford, 1993.
Cohen, B., *Count Your Blessings*. London, 1956.
Cox, J., *The English Churches in a Secular Society: Lambeth. 1870–1930*, New York, 1982.
Cranston, R., *The Mystery of Lourdes*. London, 1956.
Curl, J. S., *The Victorian Celebration of Death*. Newton Abbott, 1972.
Davies, J. G., *Pilgrimage Yesterday and Today Why? Where? How?* London, 1988.
De Groot, G. J., *Blighty: British Society in the Era of the Great War*. London and New York, 1996.
Eksteins, M., *Rites of Spring: The Great War and the Birth of the Modern Age*. London, 1989.
Feifer, M., *Going Places: The Ways of the Tourist from Imperial Rome to the Present Day*. London, 1985.
Fuller, J., *Troop Morale and Popular Culture in the British and Dominion Armies 1914–1918*. Oxford, 1990.
Fussell, P., *The Great War and Modern Memory*. London and New York, 1975.
——, *Abroad: British Literary Travelling Between the Wars*. Oxford, 1980.
Garton, S., *The Cost of War: Australians Return*. Oxford and Melbourne, 1996.
Gill, R., *The Myth of the Empty Church*. London, 1993.

Graham, S., *Part of the Wonderful Scene: An Autobiography*. London, 1964.

Grainger, J. H., *Patriotisms: Britain 1900–1939*. London, 1986.

Graves, R. and Hodge, A., *The Long Weekend: A Social History of Great Britain 1918–1939*. London, 1940.

Gregory, A., *The Silence of Memory: Armistice Day 1919–1946*. Oxford and Providence, 1994.

Hannington, W., *Unemployed Struggles 1919–1936: My Life and Struggles Amongst the Unemployed*. East Ardsley, 1973, facsimile of 1936 publication.

Harrison, T. and Madge, C., *Britain By Mass-Observation*. London, 1986, first published 1939.

Hibberd, D. and Onions, J. (eds), *Poetry of the Great War: An Anthology*. Basingstoke, 1986.

Hussey, C., *The Life of Sir Edwin Lutyens*. London, 1950.

Hynes, S., *The Auden Generation: Literature and Politics in England in the 1930s*. London, 1976.

——, *A War Imagined: The First World War and English Culture*. London, 1990.

Index to the Correspondence of the Foreign Office for the Year 1927. Part 1, Nendeln/Lichtenstein, 1969.

Jalland, P., *Death in the Victorian Family*. Oxford, 1996.

Kahn, E. L., *The Neglected Majority "Les Camoufleurs", Art History and World War I*. Lanham, 1984.

Kennedy, D., *Over Here: The First World War and American Society*. Oxford, 1980.

Kristianson, G. L., *The Politics of Patriotism: The Pressure Group Activities of the Returned Servicemen's League*. Canberra, 1966.

Leed, E., *No Man's Land: Combat and Identity in the First World War*. Cambridge, 1979.

——, *The Mind of the Traveller: From Gilgamesh to Global Tourism*. New York, 1991.

Lever, T., *Clayton of Toc H*. London, 1971.

Lewis, C. Day, *The Buried Day*. London, 1960.

Lickorish, L. J. and Kershaw, A. G., *The Travel Trade*. London, 1958.

Lloyd, R., *The Church of England in the Twentieth Century*, Vol. II. London, 1950.

Longford, E., *Wellington: Pillar of State*. London, 1972.

Longworth, P., *The Unending Vigil: A History of the Common-*

wealth War Graves Commission 1917–1967. London, 1967.
Lowenthal, D., *The Past is a Foreign Country*. Cambridge, 1985.
Mace, R., *Trafalgar Square: Emblem of Empire*. London, 1976.
Macfarlane, D., *The Danger Tree: War, Memory, and the Search for a Family's Past*. Toronto, 1992.
McKernan, M., *Here is Their Spirit: A History of the Australian War Memorial 1917–1990*. St Lucia, 1991.
McLachlan, N., *Waiting for the Revolution: A History of Australian Nationalism*. Melbourne, 1989.
Manley, D. (ed.), *The Nile: A Traveller's Anthology*. London, 1991.
Marnham, P., *Lourdes: A Modern Pilgrimage*. London, 1980.
Moorhouse, G., *Hell's Foundations: A Town, its Myths and Gallipoli*. London, 1992.
Morgan, K., *Consensus and Disunity, The Lloyd George Coalition Government 1918–1922*. Oxford, 1979.
Morton, D., *Canada and War: A Military and Political History*. Toronto, 1981.
Morton, D., and Granatstein, J. L., *Marching to Armageddon: Canadians and the Great War 1914–1918*. Toronto, 1989.
Morton, D. and Wright, G., *Winning the Second Battle: Canadian Veterans and the Return to Civilian Life 1915–1930*. Toronto, 1987.
Mosse, G., *Fallen Soldiers: Reshaping the Memory of the World Wars*. New York, 1990.
Moynihan, M. (ed.), *God on Our Side: The British Padre's in World War One*. London, 1983.
Nicolson, H., *King George the Fifth: His Life and Reign*. London 1952.
North, J., *Gallipoli: The Fading Vision*. London, 1966, first published 1936.
Onions, J., *English Fiction and Drama of the Great War, 1918–39*. Basingstoke, 1990.
Orel, H., *Popular Fiction in England 1914–1918*. Hemel Hempstead, 1992.
Ousby, I., *The Englishman's England: Taste, Travel and the Rise of Tourism*. Cambridge, 1990.
Pemble, J., *The Mediterranean Passion: Victorians and Edwardians in the South*. Oxford, 1988.
Pimlott, J. A. R., *The Englishman's Holiday: A Social History*. Hassocks, 1976, first published 1947.

Place, J. A., *The Non-Western Films of John Ford*. Secaucus, 1979.

Pocock, T., *Horatio Nelson*. London, 1987.

Reader, I. and Walter, T. (eds), *Pilgrimage in Popular Culture*. Houndsmills, 1993.

Reilly, C. W., *Scars Upon My Heart: Women's Poetry and Verse of the First World War*. London, 1981.

Robin, R., *Enclaves of America: The Rhetoric of American Political Architecture Abroad, 1900–1965*. Princeton, 1992.

Sassoon, S., *Collected Poems*. London, 1947.

Shipley, R., *To Mark Our Place: A History of Canadian War Memorials*. Toronto, 1982.

Sidgwick, C., *The Feast of the Locusts: Being a Soldier's Retrospect in Time of War, of a Europe Known in Peace*. London, n.d.

Stephen, M. (ed.), *Never Such Innocence: A New Anthology of Great War Verse*. London, 1988.

Stevenson, F., *Lloyd George: A Diary*, ed. A. J. P. Taylor. London, 1971.

Stevenson, J., *British Society, 1914–45*. Harmondsworth, 1984.

Studd, R. G., *The Holiday Story*. London, 1950.

Swinglehurst, E., *The Romantic Journey: The Story of Thomas Cook and Victorian Travel*. London, 1974.

Thomson, A., *Anzac Memories: Living with the Legend*. Melbourne, 1994.

Thompson, P., *The Edwardians: The Remaking of British Society*. London and New York, 1992.

Thorpe, A., *Britain in the 1930s*. Oxford, 1992.

Tippett, M., *Art at the Service of War: Canada, Art and the Great War*. Toronto, 1984.

Turner, V. and Turner, E., *Image and Pilgrimage in Christian Culture: Anthropological Perspectives*. Oxford and New York, 1978.

Tylee, C. M., *The Great War and Women's Consciousness: Images of Militarism and Womanhood in Women's Writings, 1914–64*. Houndsmills and London, 1990.

Urry, J., *The Tourist Gaze: Leisure and Travel in Contemporary Societies*. London, 1990.

Wall, R. and Winter, J. M. (eds), *The Upheaval of War: Family, Work and Welfare in Europe, 1914–1918*. Cambridge, 1988.

Wallace, S., *War and the Image of Germany: British Academics 1914–1918*. Edinburgh, 1988.

Walton, J., *The English Seaside Resort: A Social History 1750–1914*. New York, 1983.
Walvin, J., *Beside the Seaside*. London, 1978.
Walvin, J., *Leisure and Society 1830–1950*. London and New York, 1978.
Weintraub, S., *Victoria: Biography of a Queen*. London, 1987.
Whalen, R., *Bitter Wounds: German Victims of the Great War*. Ithaca, 1984.
White, R., *Inventing Australia: Images and Identity 1688–1980*. Sydney, 1981.
Wilder, A., *Armageddon Revisited: A World War I Journal*. New Haven and London, 1994.
Wilkinson, A., *The Church of England and the First World War*. London, 1978.
Williamson, H., *The Sun in the Sands*. London, 1945.
Winter, J. M., *The Great War and the British People*. London, 1986.
——, *Sites of Memory, Sites of Mourning: The Great War in European Cultural History*. Cambridge, 1995.
The Wipers Times: A Complete Facsimile of the Famous World War One Trench Newspaper. London, 1973.
Wootton, G., *The Official History of the British Legion*. London, 1956.

(ii) Articles

Bartov, O., 'Trauma and Absence: France and Germany, 1914–1945', in Addison, P., and Calder, A. (eds), *Time to Kill: The Soldier's Experience of War in the West 1939–1945*, pp. 347–58. London, 1997.
Beaumont, J., 'The Politics of a Divided Society', in J. Beaumont, *Australia's War 1914–18*, pp. 35–63. St Leonards, 1995.
——, 'The Anzac Legend', in J. Beaumont, *Australia's War 1914–18*, pp. 149–80. St Leonards, 1995.
Becker, A., 'From Death to Memory: The National Ossuaries in France after the Great War', *History and Memory* 5 (1993), 32–49.
Bogacz, T., '"A Tyranny of Words": Language, Poetry, and Anti-modernism in England in the First World War', *Journal of Modern History*, 58 (1986), 643–68.

Brandt, S., 'Le Voyage Aux Champs de Bataille', *Vingtième Siècle Revue d'histoire*, 41 (1994), 18–22.

Bushaway, B., 'Name Upon Name: The Great War and Remembrance', in Porter, R., (ed.), *The Myths of the English*, pp. 136–67. Cambridge, 1992.

Cannadine, D., 'War and Death, Grief and Mortality in Modern Britain', in Whaley, J., (ed.), *Mirrors of Mortality: Studies in the Social History of Death*, pp. 187–242. London, 1981.

Cooper, A., 'Textual Territories: Gendered Cultural Politics and Australian Representations of the War of 1914–1918', *Australian Historical Studies*, 25 (1993), 403-21.

Dahlberg, A., 'The Body as a Principle of Holism: Three Pilgrimages to Lourdes', in Eade, J. and Sallnow, M. J. (eds), *Contesting the Sacred: The Anthropology of Christian Pilgrimage*, pp. 30–50. London, 1991.

Gilbert, S. M., 'Soldier's Heart: Literary Men, Literary Women and the Great War', in Higonnet, M. R. *et al.* (eds), *Behind the Lines, Gender and the Two World Wars*, pp. 197–226. New Haven and London.

Greenberg, A., 'Lutyens' Cenotaph', *Journal of the Society of Architectural Historians*, XLVIII (1989), 5–23.

Grey, A., 'Will Longstaff's *Menin Gate at Midnight*', *Journal of the Australian War Memorial*, 12 (1988), 47–9.

Homberger, E., 'The Story of the Cenotaph', *The Times Literary Supplement*, 896 (1976), 1429–30.

Hüppauf, B., 'War and Death: The Experience of the First World War', in Crouch, M. and Hüppauf, B. (eds), *Essays on Mortality*, pp. 65–86. Kensington, NSW, 1985.

K. S. Inglis, 'The Anzac Tradition', *Meanjin Quarterly*, XXIV (1965), 25–44.

——, 'Anzac and the Australian Military Tradition', *Revue Internationale d'Histoire Militaire*, 72 (1990) 1–24.

——, 'Monuments in the Modern City: The War Memorials of Melbourne and Sydney', in Fraser, D. (ed.), *Cities, Class and Communications: Essays in Honour of Asa Briggs*, pp. 81–102. London, 1990.

——, 'War Memorials: Ten Questions for Historians', *Guerres Mondiales et Conflit Contemporains*, 167 (1992), 5–21.

——, 'Entombing Unknown Soldiers: From London and Paris to Baghdad', *History and Memory*, 5 (1993), 7–31.

Inglis K. S., and Phillips, J., 'War Memorials in Australia and New

Zealand: A Comparative Survey', in Rickard, J. and P. Spearritt, P. (eds), *Packaging the Past? Public Histories*, pp. 179-91. Melbourne, 1991.

Lake M., 'Mission Impossible: How Men Gave Birth to the Australian Nation - Nationalism, Gender and Other Seminal Acts', *Gender & History*, 4 (1992) 305-22.

Laqueur, T. W., 'Memory and Naming in the Great War', in Gillis, J. R. (ed.), *Commemorations: The Politics of National Identity*, pp. 150-67. Princeton, 1994.

Longenbach, J., 'The Women and Men of 1914', in Cooper, H. M. *et al.* (eds), *Arms and the Woman: Gender and Literary Representation*, pp. 97-123. Chapel Hill and London, 1989.

Mendelson, E., 'Baedeker's Universe', *Yale Review*, 74 (Spring 1985), 386-403.

Moriarty, C., 'Christian Iconography and First World War Memorials', *Imperial War Museum Review*, 6 (1992), 63-75.

Mosse, G., 'National Cemeteries and National Revival: The Cult of the Fallen Soldier in Germany', *Journal of Contemporary History*, 14 (1979), 1-20.

Patterson, J. S., 'A Patriotic Landscape: Gettysburg, 1863-1913', *Prospects*, 7 (1982), 315-33.

Pfaffenberger, B., 'Serious Pilgrims and Frivolous Tourists: The Chimera of Tourism in the Pilgrimages of Sri Lanka', *Annals of Tourism Research*, 10 (1983), 57-74.

Piehler, G. K., 'The War Dead and the Gold Star: American Commemoration of the First World War', in Gillis J. R. (ed.), *Commemorations: The Politics of National Identity*, pp. 168-85. Princeton, 1994.

Pierce, J., 'Constructing Memory: The Vimy Memorial', *Canadian Military History*, 1 (1992), 5-14.

Prost, A., 'Les Monuments Aux Morts, Culte Républicain? Culte Civique? Culte Patriotique?', in Nora, P. (ed.), *Les Lieux de Mémoire*, Vol. I. *La République*, pp. 195-225. Paris, 1984.

——, 'Verdun', in Nora, P (ed.), *Les Lieux de Mémoire*, Vol. II. *La Nation*, pp. 111-41. Paris, 1984.

Samuel, R., 'Exciting to be English', in Samuel, R. (ed.), *Patriotism: The Making and Unmaking of British National Identity*, Vol. 1. *History and Politics*, pp. xviii-lx. London, 1989.

Shute, C., 'Heroines & Heroes: Sexual Mythology in Australia 1914-1918', *Hecate*, 1 (1975), 7-20.

Simmons, J., 'Railways, Hotels, and Tourism in Great Britain

1839-1914', *Journal of Contemporary History*, 19 (1984), 201-22.

Thomson, D., 'National Sorrow, National Pride: Commemoration of the Great War in Canada 1918-1945', *Journal of Canadian Studies* 30, (1995/6), 5-27,

Turner, V., 'Death and the Dead in the Pilgrimage Process', in V. Turner, *Process, Performance and Pilgrimage: A Study in Comparative Symbology*, pp. 121-42. New Delhi, 1979.

Walter, T., 'War Grave Pilgrimage', in Reader, I. and Walter, T. (eds), *Pilgrimage in Popular Culture*, pp. 63-91. Houndsmills, 1993.

White, R., 'The Soldier as Tourist: The Australian Experience of the Great War', in Rutherford, A. and Wieland, J. (eds), *War: Australia's Creative Response*, pp. 117-29. St Leonards, 1997.

Wilson, M., 'The Making of Melbourne's Anzac Day', *Australian Journal of Politics and History*, XX (1974), 197-209.

Young, A. R., '"We Throw the Torch": Canadian Memorials of the Great War and the Mythology of Heroic Sacrifice', *Journal of Canadian Studies*, 24 (1989/90), 5-28.

Unpublished Papers and Ph.D. Theses

Eksteins, M., 'Michelin, Pickfords and the Great War: Tourism on the Western Front 1919-1991', Paper presented at Histoire Culturelle Comparée du Premier Conflit Mondial: La Guerre et La Mémoire de la Guerre, Colloque, Péronne (1992). French translation in J. J. Becker *et al.*, *Guerre et Cultures*. Paris, 1994.

Inglis, K. S., 'Anzac Day in Australia and New Zealand', Paper presented at Histoire Culturelle Comparée du Premier Conflit Mondial: La Guerre et La Mémoire de la Guerre, Colloque, Péronne (1992). French translation in J. J. Becker *et al.*, *Guerre et Cultures*. Paris, 1994.

Kimball, C. C., 'The Ex-Service Movement in England and Wales, 1916-1930', Ph.D. thesis, Stanford University (1990).

King, A. M., 'The Politics of Meaning in the Commemoration of the First World War in Britain, 1914-1939', Ph.D. thesis, University College, London (1993).

Lerner, J. C., 'The Public and Private Management of Death in Britain 1890-1930', Ph.D. thesis, Columbia University (1981).

Mews, S. P., 'Religion and English Society in the First World War', Ph.D. thesis, Cambridge University (1973).

Stryker, L., 'Languages of Sacrifice and Suffering in England in the First World War', Ph.D. thesis, Cambridge University (1992).

Index